THE MESTIZO STATE

D1521736

THE MESTIZO STATE

Reading Race in Modern Mexico

Joshua Lund

 University of Minnesota Press

Minneapolis

London

An earlier version of chapter 1 was published in *PMLA* 123, no. 5 (2008): 1418–34; reprinted with permission from the Modern Language Association. Portions of chapter 2 were published in *Colorado Review of Hispanic Studies* 4 (2006): 45–58; reprinted with permission from the University of Colorado. An earlier version of chapter 4 was published in *MLN* 121 (2006): 391–416; reprinted with permission from the Johns Hopkins University Press.

Published by the University of Minnesota Press
111 Third Avenue South, Suite 290
Minneapolis, MN 55401-2520
http://www.upress.umn.edu

Library of Congress Cataloging-in-Publication Data

Lund, Joshua.
    The mestizo state : reading race in modern Mexico / Joshua Lund.
    Includes bibliographical references and index.
    ISBN 978-0-8166-5636-3 (hc : acid-free paper)
    ISBN 978-0-8166-5637-0 (pb : acid-free paper)
    1. Mexican literature—History and criticism.   2. Mestizaje in literature.
3. Mestizos—Mexico—History.   4. Literature and society—Mexico.
5. Mexico—Race relations—History.   I. Title.
    PQ7122.M47L86   2012
    860.9'9723529—dc23   2011044242

Printed in the United States of America on acid-free paper

The University of Minnesota is an equal-opportunity educator and employer.

19 18 17 16 15 14 13 12   10 9 8 7 6 5 4 3 2 1

For my grandmothers, Florence and Natalie

Contents

Introduction   The Mestizo State

EVERY NATION PRODUCES AN IDENTITY through which its natural history as a political formation is expressed. In European-derived societies, these national identities emerge through and in dialogue with racial discourse. Mexico is no exception to this rule; it is in fact an archetypal case. Yet the idea of race in its modern Mexican specificity has been insufficiently thought.

This borders on a paradox when we consider the fact that race in Mexico is blindingly present, central to the very stories that Mexico tells itself about itself. As New Spain became Mexico and the country slowly emerged from the detritus of centuries-long colonial rule, intellectuals, statesmen, and poets rallied around the figure of the mestizo—understood as an individual of mixed-race heritage, usually assumed to be of European and indigenous American ancestry—as the symbolic protagonist of a new project of state formation.[1] After all, the still young republic could not seek its modern national identity in the indigenous version of powerful, proto-bureaucratic states; these had been destroyed by Spain and now inhabited the intellectual imagination as a glorious but surpassed history. And it certainly could not draw unproblematically from an ambivalently despised enemy that Mexico itself had just defeated, thrice: first in gaining independence (1821), then in vanquishing the retrograde factions of Catholic conservatism (1861), and finally in repelling the invasion of a more progressive strain of European domination in the form of a French empire led by an Austrian emissary (1867). Benito Juárez, the sanctified hero whose presidency would yield a Mexican modernity complete with a liberal constitution, represented an enormous leap toward a nation whose racialization would properly articulate its own historical exceptionalism in his very person: an Indian *de pura raza* with a secular outlook, a uniquely Mexican visage with a rather severe European haircut, comfortably clothed in black frock suit, morning vest, and bow tie. A political generation later, Porfirio Díaz would finish the dialectic, integrating the politics of a fragmented state, just as the permeable borders of intercultural contact had integrated the nation's races. The great mestizo president would preside over a mestizo nation for thirty years, a record of success that would enable the sharpest social theorist of his time, the unsung Andrés Molina Enríquez, to put Mexico at the vanguard of a greater Latin American hybridology in attributing Díaz's magic to the very quality that the man himself incarnated: a talent for balancing antagonisms, for converting a war between races into the totalizing racial discourse of the state.[2]

If the nineteenth-century mestizo was the idealized citizen-subject who could capture Mexico's immediate national condition, its early-twentieth-century reinvention in the wake of the Revolution would sublimate that same racialized identity as a way of universalizing Mexico. A certain fanaticism around *mestizaje* arose, one that would be brought to its greatest intensity with the publication of José Vasconcelos's megalomaniacal thesis about the "cosmic race," which placed Mexico's mestizo identity at the leading edge of the emergence of a universal antiracial (or hyperracial) race to come. Although his book was published in exile in 1925 and did not circulate in Mexico until much later, Vasconcelos had nevertheless already made his mark by giving the country a certain language of race. Its impact can be felt from the slogan trumpeting the racial spirit of Mexico's (and possibly Latin America's) most important university—*por mi raza hablará el espíritu*—to prominent murals allegorizing the rise of the mestizo and then on to its export appeal, which would stretch all the way to U.S. civil rights struggles (e.g., the National Council of La Raza).

With this national history in mind, it is surprising to learn that philosophical and analytical reflection on the topic is so remarkably narrow. Since Vasconcelos brought the logic of mestizaje to its endpoint, scholarly work that has reflected on this already scholarly project of constructing Mexico's national race has been limited to a few basic, albeit crucial, themes. We can readily identify three general, and very much related, trends in modern intellectual work, each with its signature text and corresponding genealogy. First are the studies that contemplate the relation between the rise of mestizo identity and the role of indigenous communities in the construction of this historical narrative. This kind of work is often summarized as dealing with the relations between mestizaje and *indigenismo*, which are in fact two strains of the same project. Scholarship around the history of this relation, then, yields a spectrum of analyses considering aspects of the indigenous soul of Mexican national identity (see, for example, Villoro 1950). Second is the more critical and denunciatory project of interrogating the limits of the alleged inclusivity of the cosmic race model of racialization, especially as it pertains to the nation-form. This kind of work deals with variations on the idea that the statist discourse of mestizaje is a way of emptying the national narrative of its living, semiautonomous, indigenous traditions, which are at once reduced to a past grandeur and sublimated to the higher order of something greater, more national (see, for example, Bonfil Batalla 1987). Third, and until very recently at the margins of these two more prominent projects, are the efforts around uncovering the usually veiled history of the African presence in the formation of modern Mexico (see, for example, Aguirre Beltrán 1946).

Although this scholarship tells us much about the history of racial identity formation and practical race relations in Mexico, its diversity shares the common premise of taking its basic category, race, as self-evident. That is, all of it in some way reduces race to an affirmative reflection of reality that can effectively apprehend already existing human groups in ethnological terms. What is missing from this panorama, then, is work that takes race itself—as a philosophical and political category that impinges on social relations—as its object of critical reflection. This book aims to shed light on the history of the material specificity of race as it unfolds within the cultural production of modern Mexico. The objective, then, is to think race beyond its function as theme or symbol, beyond its operations as something that transparently illuminates the social world. Instead I seek to address race as a cultural-political problematic. I am interested in getting beyond the idea of race as something that unproblematically attaches itself to the nation-form or to capitalist accumulation or to the processes of territorialization that accompany the rise of modernity. Rather than let race dangle, off to the side, as a marginal player in these phenomena, floating around somewhere in the superstructure of aesthetic forms, I want to consider race as integral to the very production of this national history. I propose that race is the category that stands as the central pillar for the very conceptualization of these social-historical dynamics out of which emerges modern Mexico. It is through race that we think this cultural history.

———

Years ago, while working on a different book project, I came across a pro-vocative thesis. *Mexico, Biography of Power* (1997) is Enrique Krauze's entertaining history of modern Mexico. Its approach is charmingly old-fashioned and revolves around the history of great men—namely, presi-dents and some of the heroes of the Revolution—who constitute the political pantheon of the country. The book traces a trajectory from the Revolution through the age of the North American Free Trade Agreement, and in order to get to his starting point Krauze embarks on a forced march through the nineteenth century. The culminating transition to the Revolu-tion is centered on Porfirio Díaz in a chapter called, no less, "The Triumph of the Mestizo." Therein Krauze proposes a historical thesis to explain the rural unrest and outright rebellion that were abundant during the tur-bulent nineteenth century. Agrarian strife, of course, was a sign of those times, for modes of production within the nation-space were still some-what segmented and differentiated, and thus the process of nationalization can also be understood as the penetration of capitalist accumulation into all areas of rural life. As is well known, the story is not free of violence, written "in the annals of mankind in letters of blood and fire," as Karl Marx (1867, 715) or, for that matter, Gaspar Ilóm, puts it. It is a transi-tional chapter, and Krauze is moving quickly, expressing himself through a large dose of truisms. I was not surprised to find him invoking mestizaje as a metaphor for the process of state formation. We've seen all of this before, and although it is ideological, it is the kind of thing that, at this point, does not really warrant comment.

What amazed me about Krauze's own handling of the dialectic was his literal, somehow both scientific and ecstatic, racialization of differently cate-gorized national spaces. Krauze's proposal was that these restive, and ulti-mately dangerous, spaces within Mexico's nineteenth-century terrain—what Raymond Craib eloquently calls "fugitive landscapes"—were those that had experienced the processes of mestizaje only superficially. Simply put, the most rebellious and intractable regions, those most resistant to effective nationalization, were the least racially and culturally mixed. And this, of course, leads to the obverse thesis: the most successfully national, the most Mexican, spaces of the country called Mexico were the most mixed. Moving beyond the generic affirmation of a mestizo nation, Krauze was proposing a heterogeneous map of distinctly racialized spaces. He was inverting the generic move of nationalist mestizaje, making it more suggestive while maintaining its discursive rigor: rather than impose an ideologically homogeneous "mestizo identity" on a materially diverse national society, Krauze was proposing a materially diverse society whose territorialized fragments recognized their Mexicanness to a greater or lesser degree. The measuring stick of *mexicanidad*, now within Mexico, was mestizaje.

As a historical or sociological thesis, Krauze's idea is empirically baseless. It rests on the implicit question of how to identify this or that degree of mestizaje. Generations of Mexican anthropologists can speak to the shipwrecks that await all attempts to measure levels of cultural purity and admixture. And yet Krauze's thesis has a strangely seductive quality that speaks to the truth effects of the discursive formation in which it resides. It can thus stand as something like conventional wisdom. It is not hard to imagine its outlines: a history of little race wars in which enraged Indians rise up and descend on their Creole oppressors, only to be suppressed by the federal army or local militia, eventually relenting to the inexorable tide of nationalization, that is, mestizaje. Moreover, and of special importance for my own thinking on the topic, it immediately ties race to space, with areas of weak mestizaje framed as spaces of exception. It is a historical lie inhabited by a kernel of truth.

Krauze's narrative stuck in my head as I embarked on my own forced march, this one through the history of Mexico's national literature that I would be assigned to teach to graduate and undergraduate students at an American university with a prominent Latin American studies profile. It is important, too, that my formation as a literary critic happened when it did, in the wake of a revolution in literary studies that turned away from aesthetics and toward what we could broadly call, using a term that I learned from John Mowitt, "sociocriticism." This turn was especially important in Latin American literary studies, where a wide generation of scholars such as Roberto Schwarz, Hernán Vidal, Jean Franco, Gerald Martin, Mabel Moraña, John Beverley, and Doris Sommer would mobilize literary studies as a way of fleshing out the paradoxes of ideological formations, the nation-form, gender normalization, political economy, and human rights in Latin America. Before them, scholars such as Gilberto Freyre, Antonio Candido, and Angel Rama had already theorized the interpenetration of borders between literary production, cultural practices, scientific research, and statecraft in the history of Latin America's republics. In many ways, Krauze's thesis is symptomatic of this sui generis interdisciplinarity that

propels contemporary Latin Americanism: it is at once a historical conclusion and a literary postulate. Krauze was ultimately engaged in writing
Mexico, in making a narrative that can offer a plausible explanation for the
nature of national identity that cleanly articulates to a longer trajectory of
affirming race in Mexico. If, at some level, Krauze was producing literature,
how can we read race more systematically, more materially, in and across
the Mexican literary tradition? How can we interrogate Krauze's thesis at
its strongest point?

My working assumptions are reducible to three basic ones. First, race is
a theory of the organization of human difference that, even with the best
of intentions, hides (or reveals) within itself a structure of hierarchy. Second, race is dependent on an aesthetic vision of the human species; it is tied
to beauty, form, representation, and narrative. Third, race is productive of
group identity. That is, it can pull people together and form networks of
solidarity. But because it is ultimately governed by a hierarchical impulse,
race always returns to segregation.[3]

Read in the light of these premises, the Mexican literary tradition represents a wealth of analytical possibilities. Race, and its conversion into discourse, is everywhere, from Lizardi's *El Periquillo Sarniento* (1816; 1831)
onward. This is another way of saying that race is being produced in major
work after major work. And yet there is no critical reflection on this fact
that moves beyond the mestizaje paradigm. Either with or against Vasconcelos, scholars have spent decades taking up the problem of race as a question of blood, community, or spirit and the critical possibilities and limits
of this national process of racialization. What we should have spent more
time looking at, with or without Krauze, is the problem of race as a question of space or, more specifically, land.

My contention is that race becomes meaningful in the real word only as
it operates at the historical division of material resources and the institutional vigilance over that division. Given that literary discourse is a product
of and participates in the reality of political life, an analysis of its production of race should attend to these determinations. After all, this history of
the production and naturalization of inequality is ultimately the central
political stake of the modern state and its accompanying nation-form. In
this book, then, I seek out and focus on writers that problematize race at its
most basic, as the philosophical ground for a social category that articulates immediately to—indeed, enables—the modern politics of space and
its human occupation. I examine writing as a means for mobilizing race in

a way that complicates this essentially political concern. This is to say that I read writers whose aesthetics of race impinge directly upon the politics of space.

The mestizaje paradigm and its critique correctly locate the aesthetic dimensions of race. But so far it has stopped there. That is, it is limited to the symbols of national identity and hovers at the level of the aesthetic without ever reaching the ground. This book represents an attempt to reread race as the concept around which the actual political battle over land resources comes to light and is rendered narrative. Racialization is the aesthetic mode for the representation of this battle. The project is to bring this battle back to earth.

The "mestizo state," as the expression that gives this book its title, has three dimensions that resonate simultaneously, and its invocation throughout the project always expresses all three. First, it is meant structurally as a reference to Mexico's institutions of sovereignty. This hegemonic state formation has been explicitly conceptualized in a way that resonates racially, at least since the appearance of Molina Enríquez's 1909 masterpiece, as a mestizo state. Díaz himself was heralded as the mestizo man who could balance Mexico's difficult and antagonistic contradictions. Even when he became the enemy against whom the war of Revolution was waged, the cultural expression of mestizaje surrounding projects of state has never dwindled, with the long rule of the Partido Revolucionario Institucional taking up many of the Porfiriato's rhetorical tropes and making them its own. Second, the mestizo state resonates symbolically as a way of indicating a "state of being" that can define a national subjectivity and a national family, specifically, in Justo Sierra's influential terms, a *familia mestiza* that would rise and stand as Mexico's fictive ethnicity, its national race. Finally, and most urgently, the mestizo state resonates materially as a historical-political process of state formation and capitalist penetration that explains itself to itself, indeed sustains itself, by drawing on a discourse of race. At once structural, symbolic, and material, the mestizo state is nothing less than the name for the historical consequences of the confluence of race and nation in modern Mexico.

Although this project is an attempt to systematically "read race" through a set of literary works, the method should not be confused with an interest in "reading for racism." Racism has a history, and any book that attempts to trace race transhistorically needs to come face to face with its own anachronism. On the one hand, expressions such as "progressive for its time" always feel like a cop-out; on the other hand, positions, statements, and attitudes that seem self-evident today may have their own history and moment of social radicalism, to the point that real individuals risked or lost their lives for the sake of articulating and defending them. Confronted with the delicacy of this challenge, the only reasonable analytical posture to take in a field as subjective as literary criticism is to maintain a certain level of sympathy with the object of study. Like all modern nation-states, Mexico is a racist society. Its cultural producers often reflect, but also miraculously transcend, this fact. One can find racism where one wants; the point is to pursue how it works, its conceptual bases, its governing categories, how it changes, and how it does not. The fight against racism is one of the great social struggles of our time; if reading race can make some small contribution to that fight, so much the better. Issues of social justice certainly come up throughout the book, but discovering racism as a social practice, and denouncing it, is not my central concern here. The workings of race, the idea, are infinitely mysterious and arise in strange places, often with surprisingly critical results. The purpose of this book is to pursue, consider, and problematize them.

This book does not have the scope or the ambition to realize a historically comprehensive study of the idea of race and its relations to literary discourse in modern Mexico. My objective here is to make a contribution to this larger critical project by analyzing major works of four writers, divided into two generalizable historical scenes. The first pair—the editorialist Luis Alva and the polymath Ignacio Altamirano—pertain to what we might call the high Porfiriato, the middle years of the Díaz administration's political rule, roughly the 1880s and 1890s. The second pair are two titans of mid-twentieth-century literary production, Rosario Castellanos and Elena Garro, who flourished during a period of hegemony associated with the dominant position of the Partido Revolucionario Institucional (PRI). The principal works of these two pairs that I examine are masterpiece novels published in the early 1960s. I was interested in the work of these four figures as writers before I started to more systematically engage with their contexts, but I believe that there is a certain historical logic that links them, one that somehow spoke to me unconsciously before I began to make the connections.

The historical scenes of both pairs of writers are deceptive periods of extended peace in a country punctuated by long stretches of intense social unrest. I say deceptive because, of course, "peace" is simply the sublimation of a social-political condition that can adequately represent itself as stability; peace can be understood as, in Alva's terms, merely a word for quietism or, in Michel Foucault's terms, the name for a war that the state never stops waging. In her fascinating study on PRI-era land activism, Tanalís Padilla sums it up nicely when she writes, "Hailed for its political stability and rapid economic growth, the period between 1940 and 1968 actually witnessed a steady progression of social unrest . . . [that] demonstrates the extent to which state terror undergirded Mexico's 'perfect dictatorship'" (2008, 7). The same could be said—indeed, is often said—of the Porfiriato. Nevertheless, the illusion—or "myth" in Padilla's account—is ideologically effective, insofar as it corresponds to a certain sense of reality. The Porfiriato and the PRI hegemony are something like the opposite of the shooting wars that define the social instability of the first two-thirds of the nineteenth century, the Revolution and its aftermath, and the war between the state and drug gangs that ravages Mexican society today. Their long middle periods represent eras of institution-building and intellectual projects whose own spectacular social crises do not quite erupt into widespread civil war. For intellectuals, they are moments of reflection and, in this, it makes sense that they represent the two richest periods of literary production in the history of modern Mexico. They are productive of state, and this implies not only state intellectuals (an astoundingly important category in Mexican cultural history, from Justo Sierra to Carlos Fuentes) but also the often more interesting creative thinkers who exist at the margins of these institutional formations.

As I have said, this book takes up the writings of four of these figures.[4] The protagonist of chapter 1 is the essayist Luis Alva, unstudied and almost completely unknown in contemporary Mexican scholarship. Through a brief citation in Charles Hale's classic history of Mexican liberalism, I was led to Alva's remarkable 1882 essays on "la raza indígena," published serially in a Mexico City newspaper. In the essays Alva takes up the intersecting problem of race (reified as indigenous Mexicans) and space (thematized as state policies of rural development) and, in doing so, sounds out the limits of the liberal critique of racism. In a political culture dominated by the official sanction of a certain liberalism, Alva gives form to the outlines of the mestizo state, the specificity of its racialization, and the contradictions that it cannot resolve. Alva's own commitment to liberal political economy provides the ground for a rather devastating critique of state racism in which he highlights the ways in which state policy and social norms fail to respect the liberal promise of cultural tolerance within the overarching category of citizenship. But his daring critical position collided with its own aporia, as his case for racially neutral citizenship proves brittle against a form of social life that his liberalism simply cannot tolerate. In terms of the articulation between discrete communities and their relationship to material resources, the liberal nation-state must be grounded in homogenization and the totalizing commitment to a single social relation: capitalism.

The normalization and universalization of capitalist accumulation, the contradictory center of liberalism's commitment to freedom of cultural practice, requires enforcement, and this was a major task of Porfirian Mexico. The work of Ignacio Altamirano, specifically around his great bandit novel *El Zarco* (finished in 1888; published in 1901), is the era's most complex and enlightening treatment of this historical process, especially insofar as it rests on and becomes entangled with racial discourse. Chapter 2 examines how Altamirano's work, in a very immediate and even personal way, deals with the militarization of space in the formation of the mestizo state. During the Porfiriato, the figure of the mestizo would rise up and become the stable symbol that could articulate the urban to the rural and state to nation. Ultimately, the mestizo would come to symbolize the resolution of the central political problem of the time, the negotiation of sovereignty and hegemony, the formation of a state that could not only represent but also somehow reflect its nation. Critical examination of this problematic becomes especially interesting when we consider it in the light of the fact that its most sophisticated thinker, Altamirano himself, was racially marked "Indian." Thus a personal (and symbolically collective) history of identity becomes entangled with the political history of the nation-form and its relation to, on the one hand, territory and, on the other hand, sovereignty.

Chapters 3 and 4 bring us to the postrevolutionary period and open up new dimensions of the relations among race, space, and violence that frame the first half of the book. In terms of the conditions of literary production, the career of Rosario Castellanos, the principal subject of chapter 3, operates within a new set of conditions when considered alongside those of Alva and Altamirano. Mexico is now a mature, and convincingly stable, developing nation, and the more thorough institutionalization of intellectual work, including literary production, provided Castellanos with resources and collaborative opportunities not available in Porfirian Mexico. As a woman writer in a *machista* society, and yet one who participated actively in political culture as both a public intellectual and an employee of the state, Castellanos offers something of an oblique view of dominant cultural politics. Moreover, she spent much of her childhood in the state of Chiapas, remote from national politics and culture. Like Altamirano, she cultivates the identity of a marginal player at the center. In terms of the political dimensions of her work on race, they invite an immediate question: how is it that the quintessentially pessimistic literary exploration of racism in Mexican society emerged out of the fundamentally optimistic project of midcentury state-sponsored anthropology? Castellanos's literary writing, and her own professional biography, run alongside the rise of anthropology and its role in nation-building, from the influential ideas of Manuel Gamio to the salad days of anthropological practice realized in the Instituto Nacional Indigenista, charged during the 1950s with advancing the cultural bases of economic development throughout the country. In short, her generation was inspired to think about the durability of the articulation of race and violence in rural Mexico as a way of defeating it. Through their work a new geography of race was drawn up, with the "mestizo town" as its problematic center and a progressively holistic approach to race relations as its basic theory. A participant in the practical application of this work, Castellanos would use her literary talents to demonstrate the density of history that weighed against the project. Mexico, she concluded, had not yet, and would not anytime soon, break free of the violence that anchors the idea of race to the spaces of savage material inequality. State policy would be theorized and young optimists would be sent forth, with unbridled enthusiasm, to realize its execution. And there the old forces of colonial domination would rise up and mobilize racial discourse with the refinement that comes with generations of practice, exposing the ugly compromises that nourish the mestizo state. All of this is staged and contemplated in her epic 1962 novel, *Oficio de tinieblas,* and my chapter 3 revolves around a reconsideration of this text and the racial narrative with which it confronts us.

While Rosarios Castellanos was engaged with a state project of development in Chiapas, the protagonist of chapter 4, Elena Garro, was finding herself affiliated with a much more idiosyncratic form of activism. Interpellated by a group of peasant dissidents, during the 1950s Garro became something of an accidental agitator, staging protests, trying to arrange meetings with the president, making her peers nervous. She invested much of this critical energy in her signature novel, *Los recuerdos del porvenir,* published in 1963. Of all the great novels of mid-twentieth-century Mexico, none can rival Garro's work for its sophisticated problematization of the race–nation relation. If Castellanos remains somewhat aloof, detached from the fight between *ciudad y campo* that she narrates in her prose fiction, Garro's position is the most visceral, self-reflective, and devastatingly critical treatment of the failures of her own social class. At the center of this critique is the inability of the Mexican bourgeoisie—for Garro, mestizo Mexico—to realize the promise of its own rhetoric and find common cause with its national other, the indigenous peasants who feel most intensely the violence of material inequality. Garro confronts us with the utopia of a Revolution that cannot accommodate both Madero and Zapata, political rights and economic rights, a commitment to democracy and an equal commitment to justice, and the internalized logic of race that repetitively frustrates its realization.

If Krauze's racialized map of the nation is productive, its usefulness is to be found in its coherence as an expression of ideology: it outlines the geography of a mestizo state that explains its national disarticulation through the language of race. Each of the four writers whose work constitutes this study engage and resist this ideological formation in different ways. The common quality that unites the four is the immediacy with which their prose articulates race to space. By resisting the cosmic race thesis that animates the mestizaje paradigm of race in modern Mexico, they engage the mestizo state at its ideological core and at its most political. Race saturates the land and divides its material bounty accordingly. By seizing this process and confronting its historical contradictions head on, Alva, Altamirano, Castellanos, and Garro think race anew, speak to its social violence, and perhaps offer clues to the possibilities of its material—not cosmic—end.

Chapter 1 — Colonization and Indianization in Liberal Mexico
The Case of Luis Alva

MEXICO HOLDS A CENTRAL PLACE in our postmulticulturalist moment of contemplating the theories, practices, and legacies of race, where hybrid identities (and their critique) reign. José Vasconcelos's 1925 *La raza cósmica*, still widely cited as a pioneering attempt at thinking beyond race, is only the most spectacular example. An important synthesis, Vasconcelos's stylized mestizaje—which promised the end of race via universal race mixing—along with Mexico's postrevolutionary turn to a discourse (if not always a practice) of indigenous rights, helped to consolidate the vocabulary of a delicate conversation around race that is still playing out, often in pantomime form, on Mexico's national stage. As recently as 2003, in an address delivered to the nation's indigenous communities, then-president Vicente Fox refers not to his fellow citizens but rather to his "indigenous brothers." And Mexico's most charismatic spokesman for indigenous rights, the former urban intellectual now internationally known as Subcomandante Marcos, is regularly attacked from across the political spectrum as suspiciously nonindigenous.

This racialized morass, in which white presidents hail their indigenous siblings and activists for indigenous rights are subjected to a kind of genetic testing in the blogosphere, hardens into a frustratingly impenetrable landscape at the site of a discursive formation that produces two well-known and contradictory truths. On the one hand, Mexico's indigenous inhabitants are the authentic source of a cultural patrimony that has coalesced into the nation; on the other hand, that same nation is founded on their abandonment. These are the outlines of the discourse that resides at the heart of the "mestizo state" and nourishes the national culture that corresponds to it. Operating from it, President Fox's famously brash promise (in 2000) to end the six-year-old Zapatista rebellion in a matter of hours collapsed in a matter of days. Even now, while Mexico's bicentennial celebrations have been dampened by a drug-crazed insurgency that throws into question the near-term future of the country as a viable state-formation, the quiet stalemate in the far south, Chiapas, grinds on.

But Vasconcelos's cosmic idea was, even in 1925, already derivative, and its roots were firmly embedded in the very historical milieu that it sought to forget. Indeed, the cornerstone identities of Mexican racial politics—*mestizo e indio*—were well worked out at the theoretical level during the last quarter of the nineteenth century.[1] This period is often summarized as Porfirian Mexico (or el Porfiriato, 1876–1910) after the president, Porfirio Díaz, antagonist to the 1910 Revolution that would, at least in theory, change everything.[2]

A widespread commitment to a certain "liberalism"—what Charles Hale (1989) usefully summarizes as Mexico's "liberal consensus"—is the red thread of Mexican political history, formalized with the Constitution of 1857, consolidated under the Porfiriato, surviving the Revolution in a sometimes more progressive form, and maintaining its hegemony today.[3] Under the rubric of this liberal state, a perennial challenge has had to do with race relations: addressing the place of indigenous communities in Mexico's heterogeneous cultural landscape. Thus the history of racialization in Mexico is particularly useful for thinking about the limits of the liberal critique of race and racism in a general sense. These limits, I maintain, arise at the very formulation of liberalism's assumptions and are reached at the basic articulation that converts the idea of race into racist practice: the joint-point that binds economic and social relations, what Karl Marx called "modes of production." Liberalism, as an ideology of freedom and equality, cannot deliver what it teaches us to demand when confronted with the chauvinism of its own economic ground, that is, its commitment to a singular hegemonic mode of production: capitalism.[4] And modes of production, in the modern world, have a "racialized" analogue.

In this chapter I explore the limits of the liberal critique of racism as it first plays out in Mexico by focusing on the dynamic interactions among race, space, and modes of production. My context is a national-historical moment when the confluence of these themes was being debated with intensity: Mexico's 1880s project of colonization *(colonización)*. Enabling my analysis is a critical reading—the first ever, to my knowledge—of a daring argument set forth by an advocate of the colonization policy, the newspaper editor and political activist Luis Alva. Beyond the historical interest of the case of Alva, I think that these nineteenth-century essays can shed light on a process that is still unfolding. Although there is much to be distinguished between the neoliberal state, hegemonic since at least 1994, and the simply "liberal" state of the nineteenth century, there is an essential tie that binds the Porfiriato to contemporary Mexico: if liberalism, whether neo- or classical, relates to space, it does so through its tenacious drive to make space productive, in the capitalist sense, enlisting the state (the government and its armed forces) in this task. People, of course, usually get in the way. This is Alva's concern, and it is a problem that has not diminished in the intervening century. As we will see, his striking essays are at once exemplary of the ideological parameters of his moment and also exceptional, insofar as he presses against those same parameters, reaching their limit and going well beyond his contemporaries. Indeed, Alva's unusual consideration of the Indian within the terms of production leads us right into today's familiar territory: the daily fight between maintaining locally plural ways of life and expanding a globally singular mode of production. At stake in this book, then, is an aspect of the history of this struggle: the race–space relation and its articulation to liberal ideology.

After decades of conflict and open warfare between liberals and conservatives, the second half of Mexico's nineteenth century—despite significant bumps along the road, including the brief installation of an Austrian emperor on behalf of French imperial expansion—was largely defined by the effective national sovereignty of an explicitly liberal state.[5] With conservatives settling in as a tamed opposition after 1867, the liberals turned their attention to the task of national consolidation. This project inspired a new and tenacious line of conflict: the border marking the liberals' desire to forge an articulate nation-state and the resistance to these efforts on the part of communities and political formations constitutive of vast sectors of the rural hinterlands.[6] And even within a broadly construed liberalism, the installation of what would be the most durable political force of Mexico's bloody nineteenth century emerged out of a fight, what was known as the Tuxtepec rebellion. Its battle lines were drawn between a metropolitan civilian elite (itself divided among the competing factions of Sebastián Lerdo de Tejada and José María Iglesias) and a peripheral military reaction, eventually ushering Porfirio Díaz into the presidency. Fitting neatly into Domingo F. Sarmiento's Argentine nightmare from three decades before, Mexico's political consolidation into a modern state was realized when the military strongman arrived at the seat of government. Now at the national center, Díaz found himself in the middle of a disarticulate nation-state with more than one restive faction to bring under control and into the project of national development.

Out of this problem the old idea of "colonization" returned as a strategy for social and political consolidation, becoming a substantial topic of debate, especially during Díaz's long presidency. Not to be confused with the overseas expansion of imperial sovereignty that constitutes traditional colonialism, *colonización* exerts its force domestically as a rigorously national project.[7] Indeed, a major impetus for its promotion was the consolidation of the northern territories against the possibility of further annexation by the United States. But as much as they concerned the protection of territory, Mexico's colonization plans were also dedicated to the developmental question of productivity. The idea driving the colonization campaign was that rural Mexico represented a mass of bottled-up capital waiting to be liberated in the name of national progress. Colonization, then, referred to the recruitment of immigrants and nationals for settlement in and development of unoccupied lands, either purchased by the government or appropriated after being declared *terrenos baldíos*.[8] *Baldío* is a Spanish legal term connoting land that is untilled or fallow but also vacant. A major impediment to the colonization plan was that much of the land on which it had designs was not, in fact, unoccupied or even untilled but often represented the homes of existent rural communities.[9] These communities were understood to be indigenous, in the ethnocultural sense.[10]

The colonization program named a conflict that, although not reducible to race, was premised on a number of assumptions whose truth emerged from (and sometimes against) the influential racial discourses of the day. This is because colonization efforts became explicitly entangled with the articulation of a national conundrum that, by the end of the century, would have a generic name and a number of illustrious commentators: *el problema del indio*.[11] If we see the not-so-unoccupied lands as the currently occupied—if not always traditional—lands of indigenous civilizations, *colonización* stands unveiled as a developmental scheme raggedly draped over a project of conquest, a state-sponsored version of what, around the same time, Marx would call "primitive accumulation."[12] But the concern over the "problem," placed within its historical context, was sincere and not reducible to cynicism: from the perspective of an urban, liberal elite seeking desperately to anchor itself within capitalist modernity, the rural, communalist "Indian" could be seen only as a problem to be solved (or a menace to be dealt with), whether by more or less terrifying means. In turn, it is no surprise that many indigenous communities would understand the modernization imposed through the terms of colonization, no matter how friendly the rhetoric, as something to be mistrusted, as historical experience had taught them.

This conflictive dynamic, which traced the tension between capitalist expansion and popular sovereignty, created moral and philosophical dilemmas for the liberals, some of whom were attentive to the historical suffering of indigenous communities at the hands of various state formations (both colonial and national): Guillermo Prieto gingerly begins this sympathy campaign in 1857, and in 1864, in the first modern study of Mexico's prominent indigenous groups, Francisco Pimentel makes much of their abuse at the hands of Spanish colonialism.[13] By the late Porfiriato (c. 1900–1910), the Indian-as-victim-of-history thesis is conventional. Thus emerges a second rhetorical device that stood alongside the pacification discourse attached to colonization, often in conflict with it but also at times buttressing its claims. I call this reaction Indianization. With *Indianization* I attempt to put a finer point on traditional *indigenismo*. Broadly put, *indigenismo* indicates the various intellectual movements, government programs, and aesthetic projects that take as their primary goal the advocacy for the social and cultural condition of the Indian; it begins to coalesce as a discourse in the mid-1910s, reaching something of an ideological heyday in Mexico during the 1950s and 1960s.[14] By *Indianization,* in turn, I mean to capture the promotion of the idea that the indigenous communities represented not an irritating margin but rather the very center of Mexican national identity, a thesis that may or may not pertain to any particular *indigenista* work. So when in the 1880s the Mexican state erected a prominent monument to the Aztec warrior Cuauhtémoc in the name of national heritage, as a source of Mexico's nationhood, this would be a clear example of Indianization.[15] Or when Luis Villoro, in 1950, favorably cites Manuel Gamio's conclusion that a history of mestizaje has resulted in Mexico's "growing indigenization" (Villoro 1950, 207), he is invoking a variation of the term exactly as I mean it, with all of its rhetorical qualities intact. For how do we empirically measure indigenization?

These relations among colonization, Indianization, and the "Indian problem" can be identified and analyzed in a multitude of editorial debates, political documents, and literary texts from Porfirian Mexico. Nobody, however, treats the problem with the verve of Luis Alva and his surprising essays. Moreover, his essays are a unique example of the rigorous treatment of the *problema del indio* in its political immediacy: the relations between race and space, between ethnological and geographical discourse.

Largely forgotten today, Alva was a curious figure on the Porfirian intellectual scene. Blessed with a certain eloquence, he never found himself quite at the center of things. His writing life begins in 1881 at *El Monitor Republicano*, a venerable Mexico City newspaper associated with an ardently constitutionalist strain of liberal politics. His stay there as a *boletinista* (what we would today call a columnist) was a short one. The topics that he took up dealt with aspects of national development, and we can already perceive in these early essays two qualities that resonate throughout Alva's writings.

First, his philosophical liberalism (prioritization of private property, freedom of expression, and especially, equal protection within the framework of a strong constitution) is couched in a broad commitment to the laws of political economy. If positivism, especially in Latin America, is the conversion of political economy into a kind of progressive religion, then Alva's writings often represent a return to an earlier moment in theorizing the relations between society and the state. Generally hostile to Herbert Spencer and his appropriation by the Mexican political elite—in 1893 he dismissed Spencer as "de moda" (*El Monitor Republicano*, August 19)—Alva exhibits ideological parameters more in line with a figure like Benjamin Constant, whom he admired and cited with regularity.[16] In the terms of Hale's useful typology of the Porfirian intellectual scene, he was a throwback, one of the constitutionalists who found themselves striving against the current of a more statist turn to positivism within the liberal consensus that ruled the day. And yet Hale overstates the case when he calls him a "doctrinaire" constitutionalist (1989, 115), for Alva often tempers his dedication to individual rights and demonstrates a pragmatic outlook in prioritizing the state's role in economic expansion. Ultimately, the consistency of Alva's twin interests in a rights-oriented liberalism and a prototechnocratic perspective on the relations between society and the state lend his views a refreshingly off-center perspective rarely found in the political debates of Porfirian Mexico City.

The second quality of Alva's writings that immediately becomes apparent is his polemical tendency, which can be described only as fearless.

Wasting no time, his first 1881 essay, "Economías," was a frontal attack on bureaucratic inefficiency in the current (and famously corrupt) González administration. Intelligently framed within a discussion of "economy" that distances the concept from its popular reduction to saving money (think "economical") and resuscitates its etymological root as the "law of the household" *(ley de la casa),* Alva asserts that efficient bureaucracy is a question not of how much but rather of *how* the state spends. In short, as in a well-managed home, good national spending practices can produce good results (*El Monitor Republicano,* February 24, 1881). Regardless of topic, Alva was consistent with this kind of appreciation for positive law. In this, he is ideologically more consistent than the mainline positivists that he increasingly criticizes, who, drawing at once on Spencer and Comte, embrace a naturalistic biologism (Spencer) within their tendency toward statism (Comte). And in what will become commonplace with Alva, his very first essay elicits a sharp and intellectually less evolved response, here from the *Diario Oficial.* Never afraid of a fight, he happily replies in a subsequent editorial. Within two months he will be departing the *Monitor,* under uncertain circumstances.

This sequence of events would become routine for Alva as he bounced around the active newspaper scene of Porfirian Mexico. His stints at some of the key metropolitan periodicals of the day—*La Patria* (under the auspices of Ireneo Paz, grandfather of Octavio), *La Voz de España,* and *El Monitor,* at which he took two turns—are invariably brief, sometimes ending with a terse announcement in the back pages to the effect that "Luis Alva doesn't work here anymore." He had a tendency to say too much—this during a time when saying too much carried potential consequences that went beyond simple employment. With the 1890s revision of the Constitution's Article 7, the Porfiriato began to actively harass opposition writers. When he returned to *El Monitor* in 1893, just as the persecution of the free press was becoming especially intense, Alva was a clear voice of protest and, indeed, an exception in the pages of the mainstream periodicals.

He seems to have had ambitions to run his own show. These attempts ended in failure, however; two publication projects—one called *La Policía,* dedicated to the "defense and instruction of the gendarmerie" (*La Patria,* May 31, 1881), another called *El Museo de la Casa,* on home economics (*El Siglo Diez y Nueve,* November 19, 1883)—never got off the ground.[17] Yet one senses a general affection for Alva among the capital's fraternity of statesmen-intellectuals: when he suddenly died of an illness in early

December 1893, *El Monitor* canceled its annual New Year's ball in recognition (*El Monitor Republicano*, December 30, 1894).

The timing of his death was unfortunate, coming at a historical moment when the Porfiriato was beginning to feel the first significant tremors of popular dissatisfaction with the regime. Alva relished the role of gadfly within this societal transformation, and he had finally hit his stride as a writer and social polemicist in his return to *El Monitor Republicano* as a *boletinista*. Beginning in May 1893, Alva was prolific, producing a *boletín*, or editorial column, up to four times per week. His last column appeared on November 23, little more than a week before his death. This final episode in Alva's trajectory carries suggestive symbolism, marking something of a turning point in Mexican intellectual culture. As Hale explains, 1893 was the last hurrah for the constitutionalists and their forum, *El Monitor*, which never recovered from losing a debate against the *porfiristas* over judicial appointments (by 1896, *El Monitor* is defunct). Alva's death, then, is simultaneous with the defeat of what Hale calls "doctrinaire liberalism" (1989, 121), whose spokesmen were either converted or forced underground by the more state-centered liberal establishment associated with the Díaz regime. And, as often happens, just as the so-called doctrinaire position becomes theoretically less palatable in its privileging of popular sovereignty and the right to dissent, so does it become historically more urgent. Indeed, the year of Alva's death, 1893, is also the year that Heriberto Frías's account of military atrocities in the hinterlands—*Tomochic*—begins to circulate serially in *El Demócrata*.[18]

Several themes attract Alva's attention during this most intense period of his writing life. With support from his brother, Ramón L. Alva, who occasionally contributed a column of his own, he offered a resolutely minority opinion against an intellectual clique just coming to be known as the Científicos, led by a powerful Justo Sierra. This small but influential group of scholars, editors, and statesmen is often credited with much of the ideological work that underwrote the Porfiriato but is also known as the most important internal critic of Porfirian policies. The political distinction of the Científicos, as Hale teaches us, rests on their effective transformation of liberalism from a program of combat to one of consensus. That is, they did the ideological work of aligning revolutionary liberalism with the consolidation of state power, in this case under the auspices of the Díaz presidency. This entailed the renovation of a host of liberal premises, but if we were to reduce their project to a single theme, it would revolve around the thorny problem of popular sovereignty. In short, if a liberal society must be based on democratic principles in which the citizens transfer their sovereignty to a state authority through explicit consent, how can one justify the blunt fact that in Mexico this authority radiates from a largely autocratic government effectively in power (by 1893) for seventeen years and counting? Well aware of the contradiction, the Científicos were not unperturbed by the issue.[19] But their response was to be expected, and, in a society still emerging from decades of internecine conflict, they subsumed the question within what they understood as a larger struggle for institutional stability. That is, in constructing the basic apology for Porfirian autocracy, they helped to consolidate a refrain that has become a notorious convention throughout Latin America's modern history: the Mexican people, in effect, were not ready for democracy; the Porfiriato would institutionalize the proper conditions; we just need to wait a little longer; and so on.

Alva's 1893 writings rail against this thesis as he takes up the great political controversies of the day: the increasing persecution of opposition journalists; the conflict over an unpopular governor in Guerrero; the failures of national economic development, made especially visible by the global collapse of silver prices; the *ley fuga*, or "law of flight," which effectively provided a legal loophole for extrajudicial executions; and, most extensively, a constitutional debate over the mechanism for appointing federal magistrates. In a tone that becomes sharper and louder through the year, all of these themes collapse into a tenacious denunciation of the Díaz regime. Rarely mentioning the president by name, Alva simply refers to "Tuxtepec," the provincial region that produced Díaz, his allies, and their political platform (the famous Plan de Tuxtepec). He perceives the Tuxtepec rebellion and subsequent hegemony as an affront to Mexico's progressively liberal Constitution, an illegal power grab promising national regeneration that has instead provoked nothing but decay, institutionalizing a dangerous politics of "personalismo" and the tyranny of favoritism that accompanies all dictatorships (*El Monitor Republicano*, June 2 and 15, 1893). In 1893, then, Alva's Mexico, then, is a nation in decline, failing to realize its potential, and on the brink of renewed civil war, an apocalyptic vision that he never tires of promoting. It has abused its own political progressivism, ignoring its constitutional legitimacy: "Mexico has a Constitution, but it is not constituted" (May 25). He makes much of the thuggery and fraud that mars general elections and issues repeated calls for the end of the Tuxtepec cabal through the invocation of constitutional term limits (e.g., June 20).

These dominant themes of Alva's writing are prescient and put him at the leading edge of a political critique that will gain strength over the coming decades, eventually culminating in the very slogan that would propel the opening shots of the Mexican Revolution.[20]

If *sufragio efectivo, no reelección* stands as the rather technical, constitutionalist slogan of the land-owning bourgeoisie that would take up arms against the Porfiriato in 1910, a more visceral note associated with the peasant activism of Zapata's south was struck by its complementary slogan: *tierra y libertad.* In its simple elegance, land and liberty is the modest demand that liberalism realize its own populist promises: equal access to justice before the law, recognition of the legitimacy of good-faith contracts (especially those that protect the powerless from the powerful), and the basic right to economic sovereignty over one's property. Moreover, and more important for this study, it also marks the point at which the Mexican politics of race hit home most directly. For the land rights that concern *tierra y libertad* are those of the peasant, the communal farmer, and the small proprietor, ultimately a social category that takes on a racialized connotation. In short, the plight of the peasant is coterminous with the *problema del indio.* To take up the banner of *tierra y libertad,* then, is to confront the political at its most immediate: the profoundly unequal distribution of resources. That this fundamental inequality affects some racialized subjects in ways more drastic than others situates the political struggle over land and liberty as the point at which race and space most dramatically intersect in Mexican political history.

Alva was a creature of his time, so it is not surprising to learn that he turned to race throughout his writings. His 1893 essays provide the outlines of his thinking on and mobilization of the idea. First, in the most general sense, his understanding of race can be described as contextualist. This is to say that he does not cling to any biologically driven essentialist position on human difference; better, he understands phenotypical differences between human groups as the products of prolonged contextual forces. This is not to say that Alva's understanding is particularly radical at the conceptual level, even if it lent his views a progressive luster in 1890s Mexico. What the contextualist position represents is the logical outcome of the softer mode of thinking about race in the West, one that ties human difference to space, owing its first scientific elaboration to Immanuel Kant and its development to the culturalism of Franz Boas (whose ideas had an important emissary in postrevolutionary Mexico in the figure of Manuel Gamio; see chapter 3) and running right up through today's hegemonic view of race, which is often described as "multiculturalist." In short, Alva sees all men as corresponding to a single human family whose obvious physical and cultural variations can be explained by the vicissitudes of environment and history. Here is his most concise and explicit statement on human difference: "Humanity is one regardless of location; but the climate, food, customs and traditions of each distinct group form the races; the races acquire type and character, special habits and needs, which differentiate them among each other within the species, and imprint upon them a particular physiognomy and organic constitution" (*El Monitor Republicano*, November 11, 1893).

For Alva, this contextualism has juridical implications. He argues that law should flow from, not be imposed on, the local population to which it applies.[21] Given the historical conditions of America's entry into global modernity, Alva proposes as self-evident the premise that America is no place for monarchy or, by extension, tyranny: America is fundamentally democratic (ibid.). But this historical regeneration of humankind, sealed by the great revolutions from 1776 on, has been stunted by a countervailing truth: the fact that the epochal contact between European and American civilizations led to the triumph of conquest over collaboration. Proposing that Columbus had brought "immense good" to "our species and to civilization," Alva ultimately laments that world-historical moment as an opportunity missed: "If our country hadn't been conquered, but rather merely placed in contact with the peoples [*pueblos*] of the Old World, by means of international relations and commercial traffic, perhaps we would be happier; and we would be, beyond a shadow of doubt, more advanced" (*El Monitor Republicano*, September 16, 1893). The consequences of this epochal violence are especially grave for Mexico, where roughly half of the population has had to live with the stigma of being on the losing side of the equation. The failure to seriously grapple with and rectify this historical crime is Mexico's great tragedy (ibid.).

This, in broad strokes, is Alva's remarkably consistent take on race, and one that, I argue, marks the limits of the liberal critique of racism. It represents a clear move away from the orthodox discourses of inferiority and degeneracy, a fact reflected even in Alva's earliest work. So when in a lyrical 1881 essay he offers a definition of *barbarism*, he refrains from indulging in a discourse on the so-called lower races. Rather, he understands barbarism as the basic force that negates the creative freedoms associated with popular sovereignty, writing that the "barbarous man is the most terrible of ferocious animals, because his strength and intelligence make him capable of imposing himself over all else" (*La Patria*, May 1, 1881). The barbarian is a universal Facundo, without a trace of race. With barbarism capable of appearing anywhere, without regard to any racial typology, the fundamental question of race relations must not be idealist, for example, how do we rid ourselves of our barbarian enemies? Rather, his race relations puzzle is materialist: how do we protect against the emergence of barbarism within and among us? As Michel Foucault explains in his 1976 lectures, there are many possible responses to this question, some profoundly menacing. For Alva, with race standing as a product of context, the management of material transformations in that context will hold the key to national progress. Race, for Alva, will not be reducible to biology; it is something that can be dealt with only through the wise application of liberal policy.[22] His colonization essays are a case study in this regard.

The motivating force behind Alva's 1882 turn to the colonization question is unknown. Whatever the precise provocation, his contribution was significant, even visionary, and the topic consolidated a number of themes that Alva sees as fundamental to Mexico's progress as a nation. As early as 1881, he had clearly articulated the relation between population and development, proposing that what was happening in the northern hinterlands was a competition between colonization projects. In this context, his enemies are not the indigenous communities but rather the encroaching U.S. settlers. In short, northern Mexico is at risk of annexation; Mexico finds itself in a contest of population: "Eventually," Alva argues, without appropriate action, "our Mexican population will come to form an insignificant minority among the foreign population" (*El Monitor Republicano*, March 10, 1881).[23]

The colonization essays are dedicated to working out these interlocking problems of economy, development, territory, population, and race relations. The essays appeared during the summer of 1882 in *La Libertad*. The newspaper was founded and led by Sierra, and it had quickly become a dynamic forum for the nascent articulation of the positivist-guided "conservative liberalism" eventually associated with the "scientific politics" of the Díaz administration (against which Alva would later write).[24] For its short and intense life (1878–84), it was required reading for the political elite of the day. Alva's eloquently combative set of essays came out under the title "La colonización extranjera y la raza indígena" (Foreign colonization and the indigenous race, 1881). The forthright tone of the essays,

framed by the context of legislative debates over formal policies of colonization (see González Navarro 1960; Powell 1968, 21; Hale 1989, 238),
went well beyond the apprehensiveness of the capital's intelligentsia on
these themes, especially with regard to the essays' sympathetic portrait of
indigenous Mexicans. For example, in the years prior to Alva's articles, *La
Libertad* had published a number of frightening essays linking the indigenous "threat" to the threat of socialism.[25] And a year after Alva wrote his
1882 essays, three titans of the liberal intelligentsia—Sierra himself, along
with Ignacio Altamirano and Francisco Cosmes—would have a monthlong
debate in the same pages, arguing over whether or not the Indian could and
should be educated *at all*, a self-evident point of departure for Alva. Indeed,
the 1883 debate crystallizes the conventional wisdom on the Indian in
an intellectual climate dominated by idiosyncratic applications of liberalism, positivism, and progressive evolutionism: the Indian might exhibit a
civilizational deficit, but this is merely the function of historical and envi-
ronmental accidents; modernization will transform the Indian into a productive citizen; and good state planning can help achieve this goal.[26] These
assumptions would survive the Revolution well into the twentieth century,
largely intact, even in the guises of socialist idealism or militant indigenism.
But in 1882, nearly three decades before the inauguration of the short-lived
Sociedad Indianista de México, which in 1910 took as its task the "social
redemption" of the abused Indian, Alva had already arrived at the horizon
of this trajectory of race thinking.

The contemporary canon of research on race in Porfirian Mexico revolves
around the attitudes exhibited toward indigenous peoples by the intellectual elite (see Villoro 1950; Stabb 1959; Powell 1968; Hale 1989, 205–44;
Knight 1990). This is a reasonable reflection of the epoch itself, dominated,
as it was, by abstract and unfounded discussions about whether or not the
Indian could be educated, that is, occidentalized. Ultimately, however, these
conversations yield more about the prejudices of the historical participants
in question than about any theoretical or empirical innovation. Alva goes in
a different direction and succeeds in getting right to the heart of the problem that confronted the state. First, in Humboldtian fashion, he grounds his
concerns in geography (the science of the relations between man and land),
political economy (the science of economic progress), and their intersection
at demography; this will allow him to make his case for the Indian in terms
of economic development in an immediate way, eschewing the metaphysics
of the educational debate. Second, and drawing rhetorical strength from

Las Casas himself, he ferociously invokes juridical rights, which enable him to make a legal and moral case for the redemption of the Indian as a responsibility of the state. It is here, as we will see, that Alva's brand of Indianization comes off as visionary. For his Indian-as-Mexican is not a monument but a historical actor, one endowed with all human faculties, including the capacity for organized violence in the face of exploitation; his Indianization thus makes a striking move from the rhetorical to the real. Armed with his popular liberalism, rather than flee from the threat of socialism embodied in indigenous rebellion, he appropriates its historical and moral force.[27] And yet, ardent liberal that he was, he leaves his ideology's ground untouched, leading him to the limit of its critical possibilities. In thus framing his argument for colonization, he not only resituates the problem of the Indian's place in the national culture but also speaks to the thorny relations between liberalism and race in ways that point toward an indigenism to come.[28] Between the precociousness and the forum of the essays, Alva's is a notable intervention in the Mexican genealogy of indigenism that is worth reconsideration.

The concepts of colonization and what I call Indianization stand at the center of Alva's larger argument. In "La colonización extranjera y la raza indígena," Alva's concern, far beyond that of foreign immigration, is the question of indigenous communities and their place within the nation. How does he frame this place? Surprisingly, given the Eurocentrism often bluntly (and perhaps too blandly) ascribed to Porfirian Mexico, Alva situates the Indian at the very heart of the nation, as a key historical actor standing as nothing less than the steward of the national spirit. Now, the modern reading strategies categorized under the rubric of postcolonial criticism will always, and very quickly, expose the political limits of this move. Nevertheless, it is important to recognize how Alva makes a case for an inclusive national culture that went beyond those made by his contemporaries in important ways.

In the first of thirteen essays of varying length on the topic, three broad points emerge that will define Alva's consideration of the problem of "foreign colonization and the indigenous race": (1) why immigrants should be recruited and what kind should be recruited, (2) why the carefully managed program of colonization is key for building a national race, and (3) why the Indian should be thought of in terms of a colonizing participant. The first point is quickly resolved and, given the very title of the essays, receives far less attention than one might expect: immigrants should be recruited in order to develop sparsely populated regions, and they should be of a culture that is disposed to absorption within the specifically Mexican project of nation. The Irish, he concludes, make the best candidates, for reasons of religious commonality (June 17, 1882), their political motivations to emigrate (June 7), and a supposed proclivity to miscegenate (July 13).[29] But it is the second and third points that define the heart of his argument and that will receive my attention here. Let us begin with the question of a potentially national race.

Understanding the coherence of nations in terms of racial commonality was almost universal in the nineteenth century, although it should be emphasized that the nature of the relations between race and nation was nowhere near settled.[30] In general, however, it is fair to say that there was a certain conventional wisdom attached to the idea that at least a relative racial commonality, or a feeling of racefulness, was a necessary pillar for the stability of the nation-form. The racial heterogeneity of Mexico was therefore an object of considerable concern to intellectuals in and around the consolidation efforts of the liberal state.[31] Drawing upon European philosophers and their own local realities, the liberal intelligentsia had begun to promote a theory of race mixing, mestizaje, as Mexico's particular route to an articulate race–nation couplet. Invoked by the early positivists as a metaphor for historical progress (Barreda 1867, 78), by the time of Alva's writings, an increasingly optimistic rhetoric of mestizaje had begun to point toward the possibility of an active protoeugenic social program.[32] And if mestizaje sought to pacify racially marked social resistance by synthesizing the races and thus, in theory, diluting empirical cultural difference and lubricating its attendant social friction, the object of its ideological force was the indigenous communities. Or, more precisely, as we see in the very title of Alva's essay, the object was the "indigenous race." Through biological and cultural mixing, as the story went, the Indians could be drawn into the national project and objectively "improved." For the leading positivist of the day, Justo Sierra, the "properly Mexican family, that is, the mixed family" (1885, 301), was understood as the "dynamic" engine of Mexican national identity and consolidation (299).[33] Thus it was clear that the Indian, for his own benefit, must be brought into the mix and "transformed" (297). The way to go about this would be through the inevitable cultural osmosis that would occur through state-sponsored colonization (313). Vicente Riva Palacio, the prominent historian, military officer, and minister of development, concurred, naming "la astucia mestiza" as the key ingredient in the birth of the nation. And even though he went as far as to place the Indian ahead of the European on a purely evolutionary scale, he was careful to distinguish physiological evolution from cultural civilization, an area in which he declared that the Indian was deficient (1889, 480).

Already ahead of both of his far more prominent contemporaries, Alva took a provocative rhetorical turn with these ideas on how to manage the problem of producing an integral nation vis-à-vis the uncomfortably autonomous indigenous race, a significant social force that constituted a majority in some regions.[34] He frames his case as the redemption of a race that had been unjustly discredited (June 21, 1882), and his opening move is to temper the grim conclusions of race as biological essence in favor of his commitment to contextualism. If the Indian today appears degenerate, it is not due to any intrinsic factors: "The Indian suffers from some defects in his manners, an effect of the poor treatment that he has received, and of the abjection in which he has been maintained" (June 7). The Indian, in short, has been historically abused, and his condition must be attributed to this fact. Alva continued: "But, at the same time, [the Indian] has congenital virtues that cannot be ignored" (ibid.). Essentially, that is, "congenitally," the Indian is hardworking, faithful to tradition, a "lover of the principle of association" (social in his decision making, implying a promoter of the public good) (ibid.). The essence of race stays on as a potentially positive force, whereas context is put forth as a promoter of decadence. The trick, then, is to change the context. So far, even while looking ahead toward the culturalism of Boas (e.g., 1894), and already arriving at the same model that would provide the basis for Manuel Gamio's influential postrevolutionary indigenismo (1916, 23), Alva's half-turn away from biological essence in order to allow for the power of contextual contingency remains conventional, within the purview of his contemporaries such as Sierra, Altmirano, and, perhaps most prominently, the Jacobin liberal Ignacio Ramírez (1872, 199–211).

Alva's gambit, we see, is not to abandon race with a radical appropriation of culture; discursive formations are not so easily dissolved. Rather, he precisely *reasserts race* and, in the same gesture, apparently undermines the hierarchy that enables its violence.[35] He posits that in America's mestizo race it is the Indian's spirit that triumphs. Reversing Hegel's dialectic, which could make only a "vanishing feeble race" (1830) of the indigenous American, Alva argues that "the American race is younger and stronger than the European race. . . . The Indian pertains to a newer, and thus more vigorous, race, stronger and more disposed to learn" (June 7, 1882). *Mejorar la raza*, then, is to Indianize the white, or whitish, man. Now, this gesture, on its own, is unimpressive. Hemmed in by the degradation of social relations that always accompanies discourses of race, Alva's revindication of the Indian itself emerges from a set of racist banalities: the Indian's vigor is demonstrated by his "prolonged youth" versus that of the European; the Indian's value as a sidekick for nation-building stems from his assumed docility, reticence, tractability, and so on. Nevertheless, Alva's construction of the Indian as the essence of the nation's racial spirit is significant. It is significant because his Indian is in fact not merely "the Indian" of the standard Porfirista rhetoric: a set of myths foundational to a national prehistory, a now-eclipsed grandeur, accessible only through ruins and monuments. Rather, Alva's Indian is the real, living, active indigenous community. If he invokes a historical Indian to make his contemporary case, he does this not in the name of mythmaking but in the name of, precisely, history: a history of violent appropriation and abject racism that has ostensibly left the indigenous communities scraping by at the margins of national society.[36] Not something to be harkened from the past, Alva's Indian is something to be included as a participant now.

Alva's idea of colonization, and its relevance for the indigenous race, is thus propped up by considerations both practical and moral. Practically, in keeping with the expressed opinions of his liberal contemporaries, Alva really believed that Mexico could "improve the race"—not necessarily the indigenous race but the national race, the Mexican race.[37] The colonization project, involving both Indians and immigrants, if well managed, will be central here. On this point he is explicit, and, in his opening turn from the colonizing immigrant to the native Indian he notes the need to find "peoples" that "will produce a new race," one with "more virtues and fewer vices" (June 7, 1882). Later he concludes:

> With the conditions of the Mexican [by which he meant the Indian, as is clarified in a later essay] colonist and foreign colonist being equal, good friendship will develop between them. The sons of the one will marry with the daughters of the other, and, before half a century, we will have a better race, since it is known that all races improve by crossing, *as long as this happens under good conditions.* (Ibid., my emphasis)

Improving the race is a question of management; programs of colonization are the context for that management, and the Indian has to be included in this project.

This inclusive process is a moral imperative. In the seventh essay, adopting a more fervent tone, Alva invokes for the first time a real fear that occasionally raised alarm among the metropolitan bourgeoisie: fear of indigenous insurrection. But rather than take the well-worn path of emphasizing mestizaje as a mode of diluting the frightening social rage often attributed to racial difference, Alva instead provokes his urban audience by speaking directly to the justice inherent to the indigenous cause.[38] At once stating the obvious and the unsayable, he asserts that the indigenous communities, were they to take up arms (which, in fact, they did, and with some frequency throughout the second half of the nineteenth century), would be justified in their violence: not only on the grounds of self-defense and indemnification but even on the grounds of simple vengeance.[39] He concludes that effective indigenous uprising in this world would only hasten what is sure to come in the next, where "people of reason, [who] have never really had any, [and] don't have it now," will be called before "Divine Justice" for their "crimes of race" (July 1, 1882). By the eighth essay, which Alva frames as a response to the Colombian evangelist Federico Aguilar's call for "the destruction of the indigenous race," Alva's "crimes of race" morph into accusations of what we would today call genocide: "We do not want to see claimed against us the crime of *lesa civilización* [crime against humanity], which today already confronts us, if we further tolerate the indigenous race in their contemporary, shocking state of abjection and servitude" (July 5).[40] He concludes: "We come requesting on their behalf not grace, but rather justice; not mercy, but equity" (ibid.).

How, then, does a national elite effectively atone for its crimes of race and promote "equity" for a marginalized sector of society? This brings us to Alva's primary concern, which has to do with why the Indian must not be excluded as the object of colonization but rather included, as a colonizing participant. His case revolves around two answers, the one in tension with the other. First, the Mexican elite widely assumed that the indigenous communities would need to take on certain cultural norms alien to their traditions in order to modernize along with the nation as a whole. As we will see, Alva subscribes to this central tenet of liberal conventional wisdom. But he will also take a radical step and do much more. His argument works like this. The Indian, he contends, is a stalwart of "tradition," and not simply of his own eccentric cultural practices but also of the kind of autochthonous local customs that provide the material substrate of Mexicanness: "He loves everything that defines the country" (June 21, 1882). In this sense, "the Indian exceeds us," Alva writes, by "us" meaning the *criollos* and mestizos who suffer from "genomanía" *[sic]*, or "love of the foreign" (ibid.). With the "xenomaniac" mestizo elite corrupting the national culture all the way down to the most basic level of language (ibid.), it is the Indian who can become the bulwark of Mexican civilization and national singularity against potential cultural corruption on the part of (economically necessary) new immigrants. In short, way before the anarchist and communist *indigenistas* of the Andes would execute the same move— Mariátegui, even González Prada—the liberal Alva points out that Eurocentric Mexico would need its Indians in order to recognize its own national singularity: the Indian would "conserve the living, national spirit, institutions and customs, which are like the physiognomy that distinguishes the peoples [orig.: *pueblos*] that constitute what is called the *patria*" (14 June). The Indian is the authentic Mexican; and this authentic Mexican has been abused to the point of legitimate rebellion; this couplet went well beyond what mainstream, urban, literate Mexico was willing to hear.[41]

But even if the Indian stands as the resentful guardian of national culture, a second line of argumentation for the inclusion of the Indian emerges, not easily squared with the first. This argument is legal in theory, economic in practice, and stems from the rights granted to all Mexicans through the liberal republican Constitution of 1857. Alva's argument traces a historical trajectory that unfolds from the following assumption: with the 1810 movement toward independence, the Indian actually became worse off. Given that Alva has just spent ample rhetorical energy invoking the Spanish colonial project and damning it to hell, this is a strong accusation. Indeed, making an important theoretical point that still resonates, Alva maintains that with the rise of the modern state, the Indian is literally *abandoned*, in what today would be Giorgio Agamben's sense (1995), by the law. Alva writes: "The Indian, then, gained nothing with Independence; indeed, he lost the little that had been legally conceded to him by the colonial administration [orig.: *leyes de indios*]. . . . After Independence, he was stripped of his privileges; he was made a *citizen* through ridicule" (July 8, 1882). With the law of the land in hand, he continues: "Is this not where the Constitution of 1857 should govern, stating expressly in one of its precepts that *nobody* is obligated to lend personal labor without FAIR COMPENSATION and *full consent?"* (ibid.). Abandoned by the Constitution itself, the Indian stands exposed as something like bare labor. The moral task is to apply the law and turn him into active labor, that is, to make good on the liberal promise and recognize the Indian as Mexican, a productive citizen with all of his rights and responsibilities in place. Alva goes on to argue that the *paz porfiriana*—the long period of political consensus, if not social stability, associated with the Díaz regime—is the necessary condition for the Indian's redemption as an active citizen. But this activity rests first and foremost on work and compensation. The Indian problem, then, is *social* in nature, *legal* in theory, but ultimately its solution will be an *economic* one. The solution to the problem of moving the Indian from bare labor to active labor will revolve around a transformation of the Indian's mode of production.[42] And it is there that apparent contradictions in Alva's case will transform into a productive aporia that marks the limits of critical possibilities around theories and practices of race in liberal Mexico.

The aporia is literal in the sense that Alva has arrived at a contradiction that affords no passage. But the aporia is also productive in the sense that it represents the stopping point upon which the race–nation articulation of Mexican, state-sponsored identity will rest well beyond Alva, perhaps right up until today. The terms of the contradiction are basic and can be summed up as the hoary problem that has inspired reams of cultural criticism and even textbook titles within the study of Latin American cultures and societies: the tension between *tradición* and *modernidad*.[43] In short, how can the Indian be preserved as a bastion of tradition and yet simultaneously be transformed into a "productive citizen," that is, a modern subject articulated to a capitalist mode of production and thereby effectively inscribed within the nation-form? The short answer is that this formula is bunk, at least in terms of its potential realization: to become a modern citizen in Alva's terms is precisely to leave behind the tendency toward the traditional.[44] But, as Roberto Schwarz's theory of "misplaced ideas" makes clear, contradictions are usually in themselves productive and, taken seriously, can offer insight into some of the most profound and suggestive cultural problems of a given epoch.[45] This is the case here. Alva's contradiction points to a logic surrounding the liberals' Indian problem deeper than anything directly revealed by the superficial dream of a happy mestizo state, deftly mediating cultural osmosis through its programs of colonization. We can begin to get at this logic, and at the limits of the liberal critique of racism, by paying special attention to the play of modes of production in Alva's argument.

At the heart of Alva's vision for the formation of an articulate and productive nation, a modern Mexico, is what he calls "mixed agricultural colonies," a state-sponsored community formation to which he returns again and again (see especially the essay of June 14). The tag itself says a great deal about the product that Alva is trying to sell. (And there is an element of salesmanship here; many of his rhetorical turns are addressed explicitly to the Secretaría de Fomento under the direction of its ambitious minister, Carlos Pacheco.) As "colonies" these communities are to be the direct result of a state project of appropriation, accumulation, redistribution, and (re)settlement. We have seen that they will be "mixed" insofar as they are to be populated by relocated Indians and new immigrants. And perhaps the blandest is in fact the crucial term "agricultural." These communities are to be agricultural in that they are expressly proposed as nodes of national expansion and development, key to the consolidation of an export economy sustained by capitalist agriculture. The plan, then, is driven by a preoccupation, common throughout so much of the nineteenth-century Americas, with populating (or, better, repopulating) national territory. And this project of population revolves around the nation's potential as an agricultural producer: the mix between Indians and immigrants, while participating in the production of a national race, will also feed the nation's bottom line (June 7 and 28; July 13). Biopolitically, Mexico finds itself at a propitious place and time: "A territory capable of supporting, comfortably, one hundred million inhabitants . . . [and one that] has the natural talent, today dormant, of its inhabitants that must be awakened to the progressive fiber of our century" (June 28).[46] The Indian, a "natural" agriculturalist (June 14), is an untapped resource in this regard. Therefore, redeeming the Indian—"perhaps the best element of our population" (June 7)—and developing the nation are the same project.

But what does it mean to redeem the Indian? And who is the Indian, anyway? Answering these questions confronts us with the centrality of modes of production within Alva's vision of a modern Mexico. The Indian, inscribed within a logic of race (the indigenous race), is reduced to a series of not necessarily commensurable social relations. The basis for this division is, indeed, the mode of production. In the fourth essay Alva proposes three kinds of Indians-as-producers: agriculturalist-slaves, peddlers ("industriales"), and agriculturalist-proprietors (June 17, 1882). Clearly, the first is the most abject, dispossessed of his land and forced to work through a cruel and illegal system of debt bondage. The second category is not much better off, permanently itinerant and a victim of spirit-killing taxes and outright extortion. Together these categories represent "the shameful fate of the most active and hard-working race that populates our territory" (ibid.). Reduced to bare labor, both types find themselves abandoned before the law.

The dynamic category is the third. This "Indian, [as] proprietor or renter of a parcel of land" (ibid.), is at once stable and productive, consuming what he needs and selling the rest, a protocapitalist ready to be modernized. But we wouldn't know it to look at him. This is because he hides his success, blending in with other, less productive Indians for fear of exploitation by the nonindigenous capitalist elite (June 28). This condition represents a massive failure for Mexico, an opportunity missed that plagues the country: the Indian-as-miser gums up the wheels of capitalism, slowing down the circulation of capital and, with it, the development of the nation. Thus for Alva the redemption of the Indian is not merely a question of empowering a potential producer or modernizing a pool of labor and thereby maximizing the productivity of natural resources, that is, land. The redemption of the Indian is also the conversion of the indigenous communities themselves, "liberating" them from a tradition of alleged communal isolationism and articulating them to the national project as not simply citizens but, more important, consumers. Alva writes: "The Indian must be made to understand that nothing is forbidden to him that is not forbidden to white people, as long as the means for acquiring it are licit and honest. Thus will consumption increase and public wealth grow" (June 17).

Here we have the core of the contradiction. The Indian, as we have seen, is acquitted of any charges of racial (essential, biological, genetic) inferiority and made instead into a victim of history. And yet even within that degrading context, his natural tendencies to preserve local tradition have stood firm, leading Alva to frame the indigenous communities as an asset to the consolidation of an authentic national identity. But now, in reessentializing the Indian as a particular kind of producer and consumer, the most basic and defining element of indigenous communities—their particular noncapitalist or eccentrically capitalist modes of production—find themselves explicitly under attack by Alva. Alva's tradition stands as an empty category: a set of vague references to a dubious patriotism, a love for "everything that defines the country." For the concrete cultural practices that constitute living traditions emerge from a worldview, a mode of production, that must be abandoned.

"Abandonment" *(abandono)* is a key term for Alva, and it cuts in two directions, marking the spot where his discourse of Indianization folds into a politics of *de-Indianization.* The first kind of abandonment arises alongside his calls for redemption, via which Alva indicates that his project should be understood as a *regeneration* of the Indian. Speaking to the importance of learning indigenous languages for Mexico's educated classes, he notes that such a reaching out "would be the prologue to the regeneration of the Indians" (June 21, 1882). This reference to regeneration, a favored political metaphor of the day, resonates with all of the biopolitical implications of the term. To give new life to the Indian means to convert him into a productive citizen. This, in turn, will make the indigenous communities into a productive resource: once the Indian becomes a citizen "hermano," the secrets of the "once prosperous and rich settlers [orig.: *pobladores*] of the New World" will be forthcoming, readily convertible into patents (ibid.). Moreover, the essential virtues of the Indian will be made exploitable, including his artistic talents, his gift for imitation, his moderation of his passions, his patience, graciousness, work ethic, silence, and sweetness of character (ibid.). Do not abandon the Indian: "How can we leave in this condition, abandoned, the most important element of our population?" (ibid.).

But a second-order abandonment will now emerge alongside the first. The simultaneous appearance of "regeneration" and "abandonment" in Alva's text is significant. María del Pilar Melgarejo has analyzed how these two terms play off of and through each other in a perverse logic of productive contradiction. She argues that in the nineteenth-century political discourse of Latin America, "the enthusiasm for regenerating the population . . . exhibits its true force through a gesture of abandonment," calling this relationship "the basic structure of the force of [political] language in the nineteenth century" (2006, 189).[47] What Melgarejo seems to suggest is that if the tendency of regeneration was to draw margins into the center, it was not so that the marginals could adopt the social norms that would "make them well" politically, allowing them to become active citizens in the Arendtian sense and thereby occupy the polis shoulder to shoulder with the elites. Regeneration was an inclusion in the name of exclusion, a mechanism necessary to make legal the expendability (or abandonment) of social actors whose agency could in any way threaten the stability of the state.

What we have seen so far is Alva's sharp, if partial, recognition and critique of the Indian's abandonment before the law. Alva thereby identifies a scandal that is nothing less than a "crime of race" and is something that must be redressed: abandoned by the executors of the law of the land— the Constitution itself—the Indian must now be "regenerated," incorporated into the national community. But for the project of regeneration to take hold, mutual action will be required on the part of the Indian. Rather than simply apply the justice of reparation to the Indian's "morbid" condition, Alva instead argues that the Indian's (and Mexico's) regeneration will require a second-order abandonment. That is, the Indian must learn to abandon himself: there is a need for "regulations that should be invoked in order to lift up the Indian, beginning with obliging him to abandon his habitual, miserable nudity, making him more productive, less vicious, and a greater master over himself" (July 5). The Indian, in short, must become less Indian; the Indianization of Mexico slyly shifts into the de-Indianization of the Indian.

If the Indian must be *redeemed* as a citizen whose commitment to tradition is an asset to Mexican identity, yet must also be converted into a new kind of producer, the object of redemption is not the indigenous communities per se, but the indigenous communities insofar as they constitute a mass of bare labor that can be made into something else. How will this happen, or what is the mechanism of this transformation? The "colonias mixtas agrícolas," while providing a necessary context, will not, Alva suggests, be enough. Enforcement of cultural mediation between foreign immigrant and local Indian will be required, and this will happen in the form of institutions: the school and the police. The task of provoking the transformation of the Indian into an active consumer "will have to be carried out through education," he says, invoking the pillar of liberal discourse. And this will require regulation: "Thus the need for schools throughout the land; and thus the need for assiduous vigilance on the part of the authorities" (June 17, 1882).

More than anything, for Alva, this vigilance on the part of the authorities seems to focus on one particular problem: the Indian is naked. Clearly, nudity itself here stands in for something else: the cultural difference, grounded on the differential mode of production, that separates the indigenous communities from the state's vision of the nation at large. The Indian's symbolic nudity becomes symptomatic of this chasm, a metaphor for his condition as bare labor. Wrapping up his argument in the penultimate essay, Alva plays the two problems—bare life and bare labor—off of each other as he proposes something like a dialectic of "tyranny" (his term, July 16) as a means for ushering in a new era of effectively universal citizenship, democracy, and the free exchange of goods. Alongside the problem of the Indian's nudity is the fact that the Indian is exploited by the hacienda *(latifundia)*. (It is significant that, at this decisive moment in Alva's argument, the question of "mixed agricultural colonies" disappears before the perhaps more concrete problem of *latifundista* exploitation.) Both problems must be confronted at once: "[We should] oblige the Indians to clothe themselves, and the proprietors of outdated [orig.: *rústicas*] farms to increase their salaries" (July 16).

Both solutions will require a meager sacrifice when compared with the potential gains. Once law forces the Indian to clothe (and shoe) himself, law will eventually become *custom*, through which, tautologically, "custom will later acquire the force of law" (ibid.). A similar logic holds for obliging the latifundias to increase pay and improve conditions. Once this happens, the Indian will become a consumer, and any expense lost in better conditions will be recouped as an investment when the Indian starts buying stuff. Indeed, as Alva's argument intensifies at these final points, the idea of the Indian as consumer comes to the fore, conflating the redemption and citizenship of the Indian with his desire to buy: "When the Indian has needs, he will become a consumer; and his consumption will increase the yields of capital investment and industry. . . in turn increasing the public wealth . . . and thus contributing to the greatness of his *patria*, to national prosperity, and to the redemption of his noble race" (ibid.). Law, as Alva here emphasizes, is not merely juridical; it must be thought at once in terms of both the social and the economic. Again he reasserts that the Indian is abandoned, "without rights and without pleasure," a "stranger in his own land and not the citizen that the Constitution wanted to form" (ibid.). He calls his solution a kind of tyranny, but a necessary one, better understood as a "correction" (ibid.). And he concludes by reminding us that the redemption of the indigenous race, and the attendant regeneration of the national economy, will rest on the success of the indigenous communities in abandoning themselves in order to become what they are not: "Hacemos consumidor al indio, ciudadano y hombre libre" (ibid.).[48]

Alva's case, a polemical plea for the redemption of the Indian, demonstrates the limits of the liberal critique of racism, limits that are not limited to the nineteenth-century Mexican scene. For race in the West has always been a way of speaking about economic exploitation. It rises alongside and within projects of colonial expansion, the enslavement of human beings, and the consolidation of the hegemony of bourgeois industrialism with the emergence of the modern nation-form. Liberalism, a name for the fundamental worldview that arose from the same Enlightenment tradition that spawned the modern idea of race, runs into its own aporia when attempting, like Alva, to attack the material effects of racial discourse. In its drive to mobilize the tolerance of universal freedom as a weapon against racism, the liberal critique of race reveals the end of its own tolerance. Although liberal ideals are centered on preserving the security of property and the diversity of opinion, creed, and innocuous cultural practices within its basic communal form—the nation—they screech to a halt before the diversity of production. This is the point at which the guiding ideology of industrial capitalism, Walter Benjamin's "modern economy," becomes "a beast that goes berserk as soon as its tamer turns his back" (1921, 246).

Alva's generation of liberal statesmen, residing in a country where modes of production were still to some extent differentiated, stumbled against the aporia at its origin. Indeed, questions of production were at the very center of the indigenous and peasant uprisings that they sought to contain: these "rebellions" consistently articulated their demands in the terms of economic justice; they were, and still are, calls for freedom against productive coercion.[49] The subjects of rural rebellions were implicit, and sometimes explicit (through manifestos, editorials, petitions, etc.), in the defense of their basic right to be the authors of their own existence, to be citizens precisely in the very act of making this case for freedom.[50] Alva's plan of *colonización* and his politics of *indianización*, however sincere, creative, or even progressive they might be, simply cannot be reconciled with the demands of its objects, the traditional communities whose modernization he sought. His colonization, while liberating the flow of capital, precisely recolonizes the indigenous communities by formally obliging them to abandon the right to practice modes of production that do not articulate the liberal assumptions of capitalist development. And his Indianization, while pressing the case for the Indian's formal equality, ends with a de facto call for de-Indianization. His indigenous communities, then as today, are expected to recognize their citizenship by inscribing themselves within a new order of governance, transferring their sovereignty to that of a mestizo state that assumes their obsolescence.

Chapter 2

Altamirano's Burden

If the previous speaker says: "*la salud pública* is an empty expression," for me it is not. I am convinced that the revolution will founder in the constitutional rut. Moderatism insists that Congress is limited to serving as a funeral procession for the victims of the reactionaries. My rule will always be: "*La salud del pueblo* is the supreme law."

—IGNACIO MANUEL ALTAMIRANO, 1861

The quietism that reigns below, when arbitrariness prevails above, is not peace; it is war in its dormant state.

—LUIS ALVA, 1893

LUIS ALVA'S IDEAS ABOUT RACE and national development remain intact until his death, eleven years after his essays on colonization appeared. In 1893, his most prolific year as a *boletinista*, he would recapitulate his 1882 discourse of Indianization within the confines of his regular column for *El Monitor Republicano*. But time and what he perceives as the proliferating crises of Mexican society (from unpopular governors in the provinces to unregulated street food in the capital) have distilled his old theses to their essence and pushed them in a more focused direction. With all of the best "qualities" of the Indian having been "sterilized" by the "dominating race," the state risks being forced to reap the "fruits of its neglect and its criminal abandonment": a disarticulate nation with a premodern economy. The middle and productive path, away from both social rebellion and economic stagnation, is agricultural development. Immigration, however, is no longer a key term, and he more bluntly turns to the obvious: agrarian reform, that is, the redistribution of the land. "Subdividing" fallow lands and transferring them to "indigenous families" will represent a twin victory: "to redeem a race of slaves and to expand national wealth" (*El Monitor Republicano*, July 23, 1893).

Develop the land, redeem the race, just as in 1882. But now, turning to agrarian reform, with its emphasis on redistribution, Alva engages more critically and directly the great social issue of his time: capitalist penetration and its relationship to the liberal project of the nation-state. What he faces up to in 1893 is the way in which the readily perceptible "failures" of liberal political economy reside in the paradoxes of its own enforcement. Recall that in 1882 he had emphasized the role of the police in the effective establishment of an acculturalist colonization program. A decade later, he finds himself confronted with the excesses of state policing. The mechanics of agrarian reform, then, cede to this larger emergency and end up reading as something of an afterthought. Thus 1893 will become a year of resistance, of sustained and tireless critique for Alva, weighed down by a decade and a half of Pax Porfiriana, an exhausting year that will end in his sudden illness and death. His target is explicit: the regime itself. Constitutionalist liberalism will still be a major part of Alva's discourse, but at this point the race-nation preoccupation is overwhelmed by a less metaphysical concern: the violence that seems to be holding Mexican society together. Or, perhaps, tearing it apart. Alva's is an incessant critique of the "paz" that is everywhere announced, ostentatiously and not without menace, as the great triumph of the Díaz presidency.

Alva identifies this peace that underwrites Porfirian stability as another name for state violence, even civil war. He writes: "Peace is nothing, it means nothing, when limited to the cease-fire in the state of war, and not to the calming of passions, the meeting of the collective will and the harmony of social forces" (September 5). Porfirian peace is the temporary stalemate between warring camps. The social triumph of the Díaz regime, then, is not the end of the state of war but its sublimation to, precisely, peace. The state of war, under Díaz, is rendered "latent." Open conflict has been replaced by "quietism," political confrontation by a generalized cowardice. Alva's liberalism depends on a robust civil society realized through the free exchange of ideas. His attack on the Díaz regime, then, is launched against what he understands to be the opposite of this ideal: militarism.

A number of legal outrages attract Alva's attention in his documentation of Mexico's frustrated exit from autocracy. Of immediate, even personal, concern is the suspension of jury trials in cases of libel, a mechanism aimed directly at suppressing the freedom of the press (e.g., June 1). But he saves his most denunciatory columns for a quasilegal police practice of no particular threat to the metropolitan intelligentsia. The *ley fuga*, or "law of flight," allowed for extrajudicial executions by authorizing police to shoot suspects actively attempting to flee arrest. It is another, perhaps the supreme, example of the confusion between state of exception and rule of law, the most devastating symptom of the "permanent state of latent warfare" in which Mexico dwells, and, as Alva writes, it "impedes the development of public wealth and binds and chains all social forces" (September 5). Alva concedes that the ley fuga, originally a wartime decree, was perhaps once a necessary tool in the fight against bandits and insurrectionist conservatives, but its legitimate use is now long past. In short, it has since become a scandal: "Civilization is horrified by such procedures; Humanity is in mourning before these evils." The ley fuga places Mexico outside the "great society of nations [orig.: *pueblos*]" (ibid.). Especially sick is that the ley fuga, as opposed to simple murder, is authorized by the state and therefore often enforced by soldiers, now degraded to little more than rank "sicarios." He concludes a September *boletín* dedicated to the topic by offering the shocking example of a young boy summarily executed for warning his father of the imminent approach of a state-sponsored death squad (ibid.).

Two points of criticism flow from Alva's recurrent denunciations of the ley fuga. The first revolves around liberal political philosophy and its prioritization of the life of the individual. Like all liberal constitutions, Mexico's founding document enshrines this ideal. Therefore, the "extraordinary faculties" through which the executive invokes the ley fuga are always problematic. Alva writes of these faculties: "The suspension of individual freedoms [orig.: *garantías*] was important, but nevertheless, the limitation established by the aforementioned Article 29, which makes an exception for guarantees that ensure life [orig.: *vida del hombre*], has been killed, killed outside of the proper legal order by this damned ley fuga" (June 20). As a tool of the state, Mexico's ley fuga transcends even the barbarism of the "Lynch law": "It is more offensive and horrible than the Lynch law in the United States; because in Mexico the ley fuga is applied by the authorities and in the United States the Lynch law is applied by the people [orig.: *pueblo*] or through corruption as in the case of the governor of Carolina" (ibid.). The ley fuga denies life, and the removal of the protection of life places the legitimacy of Mexican liberalism in question.

If this first point of criticism revolves around the philosophical bases of liberal ideology, the second cuts more deeply toward the practical contradictions of the liberal project within Mexican political history and the social implications of these contradictions. The ley fuga is the law of the periphery, the world of bandits and strongmen, the ragged edges that capitalist development has yet to fully smooth over. Díaz, with a dreaded, if not especially competent, paramilitary force—the Guardia Rural—at his disposal, represents the liberal contradiction at its extreme crisis point. But for Alva, Díaz merely represents the culmination of an entire tradition. For the "extraordinary faculties" that first opened the door to the ley fuga were invoked under the sacred hero of liberalism, Benito Juárez, and left intact by its first great institution builder, Sebastián Lerdo de Tejada. Alva's major pronouncements on the evils of the ley fuga are explicit on this point: in his *boletín* of June 20 he accuses Juárez and Lerdo of "violating" the "virgin" Constitution of 1857, and on September 5 he reminds his readers that the origins of the ley fuga, and the "society of *sicarios*" that it has wrought, are traceable to Ignacio Mejía, the minister of war under Juárez. Finally, after six months of relentless opposition to the Porfiriato, Alva's final published words are issued not against Díaz but against Mexico's last, failed hope: Lerdo.[1]

Homing in on the problem of the ley fuga and its state authorization, Alva points toward, without explicitly stating, the great conundrum for liberals everywhere: the tension between the individual rights guaranteed by law and the totalitarian expansion of liberalism's ideological ground, the capitalist mode of production. By the 1880s, this state–society problematic is felt with greatest intensity in the countryside.[2] This spacialization of the nation-state articulation is thus also, to a large extent, the racialization of a political process. For in Alva's world, the *ciudad–campo* distinction registers racially. Francisco Cosmes, writing on the difficulties of obligatory education in an 1883 essay for *La Libertad,* describes the national demography like this: "The white race and relative civilization predominate in the Federal District. . . . But in the rest of the Republic it's another question. An immense indigenous population resistant to all civilization" (February 16). Attentive to the racialized nation-space, to what extent is the violence of nation-building that Alva attacks a project of race? On the one hand, a polemicist by nature, Alva is very effective at denunciation—what Foucault would call "counterhistory"—and at creating a generalized ambience of a victimized "us" oppressed by a diabolical "them." On the other hand, Alva's Mexico, as we have seen in his essays on "la raza indígena," is racialized in a more conventional sense, that is, it rests on an ethnological ground of categorized human difference. And while Alva is more than happy to mobilize this social relation, he does little in the way of confronting the contradictions of nation-state consolidation in the context of radical social heterogeneity and its difficulty. His essays are denunciations, and he gives no autobiographical suggestion of being anything but a man of the city. In short, he does what he can with press reports. But for a deeper analysis and more harrowing confrontation with the liberalization of the nation-form, we need to look elsewhere.

The ley fuga stands as Alva's symbol of everything that is wrong with liberal Mexico and represents an affront to liberalism's guarantees of due process and the protection of life. Executed in the countryside, far from displacing Mexico's dominant politics of race, the ley fuga reinforces those politics, churning up all kinds of problems for any idealistic vision of the national project. Ignacio Manuel Altamirano, more than any other public intellectual of his time, wrestled with the paradoxes and contradictions of national consolidation. A soldier and officer in the war against French occupation and a statesman who held elected and appointed posts under both the Juárez and the Díaz administrations, Altamirano had a front-row seat at the central debates of the three most intense decades of Mexican political history. He wrote constantly, in multiple genres. A man of the countryside from the restive state of Guerrero, Altamirano perceived Mexico's negotiation of its national identity into the formation of the mestizo state as a topic of special urgency. Add to this the fact that his biographical itinerary took him to all corners of Mexico—as a soldier, politician, jurist, journalist, and amateur geographer—and one begins to understand that he was uniquely positioned to think through the crises and contradictions of the epoch-making social transformations that would act as levers for the rise of the mestizo state. It is to his work that we now turn.

Ignacio Homobono Serapio "Manuel" Altamirano is arguably Mexico's most intriguing—and, in many ways, illustrative—public intellectual when it comes to thinking about the politics of race in the nineteenth century. A certain narrative stability around his biography has been canonized through various critical and interpretive readings of his life's work. Taking his own declaration that he was born "in the cabin of a family of Indians" (1880, *Obras completas*, 19:69) as a starting point, Mexicans generally remember him as having grown up in poverty, an illiterate monolingual speaker of

Nahua. His own intellect, luck, and a moment of progressive politics resulted in his winning a scholarship to an elite secondary school, the Instituto Literario de Toluca. There he studied under the Jacobin rabble-rouser
Ignacio Ramírez, eventually becoming Ignacio Manuel Altamirano, articulate statesman and decisive modernizer of Mexican literature.[3] Alongside
Benito Juárez, he is often called, in the words of María Rosa Palazón Mayoral
and Columba Galván Gaytán, one of the nineteenth century's two "paradigmatic figures of the indigenous individual" that overcame their humble
social origins (1997, 99; see also Conway 2007, 8).[4] His student and con-
fidant, Luis González Obregón, recalls that "up until fourteen years of age
he was one of those children of our *indígenas* that has nothing more than a
milpa and a couple of asses, a hut and a little work ethic. Altamirano lived
like that, humble, almost savage, without even knowing the Spanish language" (cited in Monsiváis 1999, 9).

A formidable orator and public figure from his early twenties onward,
Altamirano strategically cultivated this life story, invoking it in prominent
places. In an 1889 homage to Ramírez, he refers to arriving at Toluca
"barely understanding the Spanish language, and nearly mute due to my
rustic and semi-savage bashfulness" (*Obras completas*, 13:105). He had
won a scholarship that "not only favored me, but also many other young
indígenas from the State of Mexico" (ibid.). In a piece for *El Federalista* in
1871, he describes himself as "having been born in the cradle of the poorest [orig.: *infelices*] classes and having had a childhood full of misery" and
again asserts, "I hardly speak Spanish" (18:12). Most famously, in his
1870 address "La educación popular," a vigorous plea for universal education, he declares: "I too am a son of charity, I too, born in the most humble and impoverished class, the indigenous class" (1:211). Twenty years
later, in Paris before the Eighth Americanist Congress, he would introduce
himself to a large audience as "le premier indien demi-civilisé qui vient en
France" (cited in Segre 2000, 276). And although Altamirano rarely put
it in terms so dramatic as the Paris speech, scholars routinely describe him
as an "indio," a point not uncommonly made emphatic with a colorful tag
such as "de pura raza" or "de pura sangre." All of this is a little far-fetched,
and it greatly simplifies Altamirano's life and his social context.

The first problem is that Altamirano was not really an Indian, certainly
not of "pure race." To begin with, there is the immediate complication of
race in the traditional sense, as genetic descent. In the fascinating and icono-
clastic biography by Herminio Chávez Guerrero, we learn that Altamirano's

mother, Juana Gertrudis Basilio, was "of mestizo caste" (1985, 22). Now, "mestizo caste" is indeed a fluid category that can imply a spectrum of genealogical factors, social relations, and cultural contexts. But if nothing else, it is worth noting the testimony of the descendants of Altamirano's hometown who serve as Chávez Guerrero's sources. Several indicate the wide range of physiognomy and pigmentation of Altamirano's natural siblings and their descendants, making it likely that Basilio was what we might call a visible mestiza, that is, phenotypically identifiable as nonindigenous (23). Iconic photographs of Altamirano himself, however, show that he had undoubtedly inherited strong indigenous features, so it is easy to discount the technicality of his maternal bloodline.

But then there are the more analytically relevant questions of discourse and historical context. On these counts, too, Altamirano's indigenous identity is fluid. In nineteenth-century Mexico, "indio," like "mestizo," is a social category that casts a wide net. In general, however, it is possible to define *indios* negatively as subjects or communities that have not experienced a thorough penetration of Eurocentric cultural norms and practices, above all, modern capitalism. In nineteenth-century Mexico, in other words, *indio* is Alva's *raza indígena:* individuals pertaining to peasant communities on the periphery of capitalism, tangential to the rhythms of national life, often speaking Spanish as a second language, if at all.

This does not describe Altamirano's life story. He was born in 1834 in Tixtla, Guerrero, a village with robust indigenous, creole (Spanish-descended), and mestizo populations.[5] The dominant language of the indigenous section of town would have been Nahua (aka Nahuatl). Although the village was informally segregated at the domestic level, interactions between the populations were the fabric of everyday life. Bilingualism was common. Altamirano's father was Francisco Altamirano, identified as "el indio" in order to distinguish him from his adoptive godfather, Don Francisco Altamirano. A wealthy creole celibate, Don Francisco had amassed his fortune through inheritance. This came by virtue of his relationship with another bachelor, the Spaniard Sebastián de Viguri, whom Chávez Guerrero describes as "immensely rich for the time" (1985, 16). Without legitimate heirs, he left much of his fortune to the poor, but bequeathed the bulk to the executor of his will, Don Francisco. It was sometime during the 1810s that, from the tumult of the wars of independence, a young indigenous boy "appeared down from the mountains . . . terrified and hungry, begging in his native language" (Chávez Guerrero 1985, 21). His birth name lost to history, this child would become Francisco Altamirano, el indio, the adopted godson of Don Francisco and, in 1834, father of Ignacio Homobono Serapio Altamirano.[6]

So besides the Spanish surname, there is also a Spanish fortune lurking in Altamirano's family history.[7] It seems quite clear, however, that neither he nor his father saw any of it, at least not in terms of direct inheritance. But what is important here is the fact that this social context throws considerable doubt on the conventional narrative—what Chávez Guerrero calls "the legends" (1985, 33)—attached to Altamirano's unlikely rise to El Maestro, as he would be called, teacher to a generation of Mexican literary nation builders.[8] As the godson of a prominent creole, it is highly unlikely that Francisco Altamirano, el indio, would have remained a monolingual Nahua speaker. Moreover, he almost certainly would have attained at least rudimentary literacy at the local school for indigenous children (Chávez Guerrero 1985, 22). His adult life suggests as much. He held the municipal post of alcalde de indios, a position of minor authority but one that would have put him in regular contact with both indigenous and nonindigenous populations and suggests a certain level of bilingualism and literacy. At the time of his son's birth he was a petty merchant with a small store near the zocalo. It would be strange if he did not encourage the acquisition of these increasingly basic skills of modern life for his son (see Chávez Guerrero 1985, 22, 35).

The Altamiranos, while not rich, were not indigent, and indeed were something of a successful family in the small world of Tixtla. Altamirano's claim to having been "born in the cabin of a family of Indians" could mean many things but probably not what we imagine it to mean today, unless by "cabin" [*cabaña*] the image that appears before the reader is that of a solidly constructed home near the center of town, one that still stands (see Chávez Guerrero 1985, 22–27). Given these circumstances and the fact that Altamirano attended primary school, the idea that he was either monolingual or illiterate when he arrived at Toluca at age fourteen (see, among others, Sommer 1991, 223; Monsiváis 1999, 9; Segre 2000, 267; Christ 2007, 40) is pretty much preposterous; indeed, as Chávez Guerrero points out, the Instituto presented a program of *cursos superiores*, not of remedial learning (1985, 36).[9] The picture of the illiterate, monolingual, barefoot Indian rising to the pinnacle of Mexico's cultural and political intelligentsia is an image ready-made for the movies.

And yet. Tixtla was an unimpressive village in the middle of a marginal and often chaotic sector of the still new republic associated with social unrest and indigenous activism. Girón notes that Altamirano "came from the district of Chilapa, repeatedly beset by serious indigenous uprisings precisely provoked by land confiscation and other abuses" (1993, 109) and that as a young boy he would have been witness to the uprisings of the 1840s remembered alternatively as the caste war or the revolution of Chilapa (110).[10] Girón also presents a document that sheds a certain light on the wider reputation of the region. Responding to a letter from the rector at Toluca suggesting that the young student had arrived broke, and from a dangerous "país" no less, the "cabildo de Tixtla," in charge of administering Altamirano's scholarship, describes Chilapa, by way of rejoinder, like this: "Its villages and roads are not infested with thieves, wild animals, or anything of the sort, nor are its inhabitants savages or cannibals, although they do live in misery" (59–60). The semantic battle is worth noting— indigenous resistance to exploitation becomes suggestive of thieves, wild animals, and cannibalism—and surely left its mark on Altamirano, who would have seen the "caste wars" firsthand, as the result of rural inequality and the struggle over resources.

Moreover, Altamirano's physical appearance certainly registers with many observers as "Indian." In the circles of the metropolitan elite, both his provenance and his visage made him something of an exotic. He was famously unattractive in his youth (he aged well, growing into his harsh features), a fact often conflated—irritatingly enough, even today—with his alleged Indianness: "indio feo" is a description one finds frequently attached to his person.[11] He thematizes the social consequences of these qualities in his fiction and had internalized the experience of discrimination to great rhetorical effect. For example, Christopher Conway unearths an 1873 account of a meeting with a Spanish journalist in which Altamirano declares that "he was proud of possessing the 'splendid ugliness' of the Aztec race" (2007, 20), suggesting a self-confident haughtiness that one can sense through his many photographic portraits. Ronald Christ, although indulging too enthusiastically in the Indian-identity thesis, sums up the issue nicely when he writes: "Altamirano took pride in referring to himself as ugly, an ugly Indian; but a glance at photographs of him shows an arms-folded, settled determination matched by an open seriousness, if not sternness. By 'ugly' he meant 'dedidedly' [sic], 'resolutely'—a self-respecting Indian" (2007, 43). Monsiváis refers to Altamirano's frequent references to the topic as a kind of "vanity" (1999, 14).

Then there are the stories. The most famous, about Altamirano and his father being asked to leave the reception room at Toluca "because this isn't a place that pertains to Indians" (Girón 1993, 57), seems likely to be apocryphal.[12] But it speaks to a larger truth, the fact that Altamirano, as a scholarship recipient who walked several days to his elite boarding school, was not the typical student at the Instituto. This exceptionalism extends back to his primary education. School in 1840s Tixtla was segregated, a legacy of the Spanish system of *castas*, and the dark-skinned Altamirano was originally placed with the indigenous group of children. This was not an educationally propitious context—Chávez Guerrero notes that the education of the indigenous focused largely on prayer—so Altamirano's father pulled strings with the school to have his son transferred to the group of "niños de razón," that is, "children with [or capable of] reason." A minor classroom protest arose, one that the teacher quickly crushed, almost by way of a magical incantation of identity transformation, by declaring: "From this day forward, this child 'shall be with reason'!" (Chávez Guerrero 1985, 39).

Add to this series of formative biographical moments the fact that he regularly expressed anything from sympathy to solidarity with Mexico's indigenous communities, and the race question around the figure of Altamirano becomes especially intense. In order to untangle its most significant threads, we must recall the specificity of his cultural context and historical moment. First, we need to recognize that to problematize the nature of Altamirano's Indianness is not comparable to, say, questioning the blackness of a major historical figure like W. E. B. Du Bois. Even if it could be argued that Du Bois's life story—the Harvard doctorate, the studies in Germany, a certain elitism—make him atypical of the African American experience of the early 1900s, he nevertheless resides in a social milieu defined by a hard segregationist impulse genetically vulgarized as the "one-drop rule." In short, the American experience, without a robust category of racial in-betweenness, blackens Du Bois.

No such logic of race governs the Mexican experience that defines the life of Altamirano. His rise to intellectual prominence, which traces precisely the rise of liberalism, comes at a watershed in the history of Mexican identity politics. Altamirano is witness to—moreover, an active participant in—the consolidation of the mestizo state, of the new fictive ethnicity that will now define Mexico's race–nation articulation. This does not mean that literal "people of mixed race" have now stormed the barricades and are running the national government or that the social advantages that attach themselves to visible whiteness suddenly disappear. What it means is that through the rise of the liberal republic, Mexican intellectuals reinvented national identity, and this process involved the imagination of a newly racialized protagonist of national progress: the mestizo. Rooted in the bloodline obsessions of Spanish *casticismo* and beset by all of the same hobgoblins of race politics everywhere, Mexican mestizaje has a much more explicitly enacted culturalist logic than the hard segregationism attributed to the U.S. context.[13] Given that the mestizo subject is essentially "of mixed race" and that this mixing is not subject to empirical quantification (there is no one-drop, or for that matter any-drop, standard), behaviors, practices, and social status come to the fore in modern Mexico's race politics. We saw this with Alva: the problem with the "raza indígena" is not the race but rather the mode of production. This is not to say that the mestizo state renders race neutral, overcomes racism, or dethrones pigmentocracy. Far from it: Altamirano himself was the target of racist attacks by his critics.[14] But what it does do is convert race into a cultural, and thus perhaps much thornier, category. Mestizaje is race made culture, or, conversely, culture made biological: the biopoliticization of cultural practices. The intellectuals at the leading edge of Mexico's republican transformation invested this newly robust fictive ethnicity into a general ideology of progressivist meritocracy with its attendant faith in the relations between education and economic development. Far from oppressed by this ideological shift, Altamirano becomes its spokesman, "paradigmatic" of the possibilities of progressivist liberalism where genetic descent cedes to merit. Far from being the "indio de pura raza" who succeeds in spite of everything, Altamirano is precisely the exemplary protagonist of the mestizo state: the de-Indianized Indian or the mestizo subject. Although he often highlights his multicultural biography, which distinguished him from most of the urban intelligentsia, nowhere does Altamirano speak of double consciousness or anything like it. It would not have occurred to him. *De pura raza:* Altamirano, unapologetically, is Alva's "raza indígena" to come, already consummated, the impure Indian rendered pure mestizo.

Altamirano, in this sense, is living proof of the liberal individualism to which he subscribes. If, like all births, the specificity of his entry into the world was a cosmic accident, the historical line of his family tree precisely traces the kind of progressive narrative that he—and, indeed, the intellectual consensus—saw as essential to national consolidation. The indigenous father, down from the mountains, moves from Nahua-speaking

Indian to bilingual citizen of the local economic, political, and cultural world of a stable Mexican village. The mestizo son, mobilizing his intellectual talents through the institutional mediation of the school, moves from bilingual villager to monolingual participant in national life. This is basically the outline of de-Indianization sketched by Alva, and it is the trajectory affirmed by Altamirano in his many writings on national development and public education. For example, it is well known that Altamirano promoted the study of indigenous languages for reasons of both cultural patrimony and pedagogical efficiency. But beyond the project of reconstructing a precolonial past through the recovery of indigenous esoterica, his case for bilingual education would coalesce as a means toward the end of national homogenization. So when in an 1883 debate he makes a case for the "introduction of the study of Aztec or Mexican in the normal schools," he proposes this as a means to the explicit end of "the generalization of Spanish," on which "depends, in large part, the culture of our indigenous people [orig.: *pueblo*]" (*Obras completas*, 15:266). Public education should represent a kind of national evangelization, and the secular missionaries should learn from an earlier epoch, when the "Catholics of the seventeenth century" took it upon themselves to learn "the language of all of the tribes, regardless of how insignificant, and thanks to their evangelical zeal, Christianity was extended everywhere" (267). In other words, bilingual education was about the Hispanization of indigenous communities, not the maintenance of parallel sets of cultural practices: Spanish is the national language of modernity, one that puts Mexico in touch with European civilization. Though Altamirano was less harshly ethnocidal than Justo Sierra, his steadfast ally in this debate, the implication is nonetheless clear: while some indigenous languages may exhibit a conceptual complexity comparable to that of European languages, they still represent an outmoded past, not the national future.[15]

Beyond the traditional expression of Altamirano's stylized indigenous family history, scholars have generally ignored the politics of race in his work or, at best, treated the topic lightly. Clementina Díaz de Ovando's 1954 judgment that the most important social function of his prose fiction is "that inspired message about the Indian and the mestizo, which had always been left to one side by the creole" (cited in Sol 2000, 41) captures the extent of the early analysis. But this has begun to change as race has come to the forefront as a significant theme of literary and cultural studies. In research on Altamirano, this new attention to race emerges in the form of greater scrutiny of the representation of indigenous culture in his works. Two critical positions, relatively polarized between affirmative and negative, have coalesced.

On the affirmative side, scholars have emphasized the ambivalence of negotiating a complex identity in troubled times and pointed to the productivity, even if tentative, of Altamirano's writings in this regard. Largely relying on his *costumbrista* sketches, these readings identify a certain tension between chains of signifiers that place enlightened, liberal, metropolitan, and Mexican on one side against rustic, communal, rural (especially southern), and Indian on the other, tracing how Altamirano struggled to reconcile these seemingly exclusive categories. In this vein, Edward Wright-Rios argues that Altamirano promoted an "Indian-centered nationalism" (2004, 48) and saw in the indigenous rural village an "innate passion for independence [that] makes Mexico's Indians the necessary foundation of the nation-state" (64). Thus Altamirano was probing the tension between city and countryside, preparing the reading public for the eventual rise of a more radical indigenism (68). Conway focuses more explicitly on the ambivalent nature of this project, contrasting the interplay of "autobiographcial Indianism" and anthropological discourse (2006, 43) in Altamirano's intimate portraits of his hometown. He understands Altamirano's challenge as "the principled need to counter racial determinism on a conceptual level, the prejudices of his urban readership toward the Indian and the rural, and undoubtedly, the unmeasurable but visible effects of his own ambiguous position as a Liberal, *letrado* mediator of his own Indian ethnicity" (46). This results in "a set of fragments that his situation as a *letrado* could not consolidate as a direct challenge to the dominant, nationalist project" (ibid.). Ultimately he "embraced his identity as a Mexican over that of the Indian" (ibid). The upshot of these conundrums is probably best summed up by Erica Segre in her elegant postcolonial argument that Altamirano, speaking from what she calls a "bi-locational" cultural context, promoted a more inclusive national identity, one that went beyond the privileging of mestizo identity and positivist racism in order to make a case for the Indian as a source of real (not just symbolic) citizenship: "The problem was of how to be 'esencialmente mexicano' in Spanish, of how to be an Indian without costume" (271).

But these well-crafted efforts representing the affirmative position on race in Altamirano seem able to get no further than to suggest a certain ambivalence around the topic. Wright-Rios's "Indian-centered nationalism,"

Conway's "autobiographical Indianism," and Segre's "italicised ethnicity" all represent suggestive readings that are precisely limited to their suggestions. In terms of the impact of his individual biography and personal struggles with a society that surely discriminated against him, Altamirano simply does not give us enough to go on, as Conway confesses, noting "the scarcity of direct references to his indianness in his published writings" (2006, 38).

Indeed, in the widely publicized 1883 debate over the value and relevance of obligatory primary education in the indigenous communities, not once does Altamirano, in his defense of the universal education position, bring up his own life story. Even when he speaks to the success of the very scholarship program that sent him to Toluca—usually misremembered today as a program specifically for indigenous Mexicans—he mentions nothing of race or ethnic identity, noting the qualifications as "having excelled in primary studies, being very poor, and being twelve years of age" (246).[16]

More polemical, and more productive of interpretive pause, is the negative position on race in Altamirano's work. Writing from our postcolonial moment of contemporary literary studies, critics have duly attacked Altamirano for his attitude toward the place of indigenous communities in the modern nation-form. No doubt, revisiting the history of the normalization of ethnocidal politics and condemning it are crucial and ongoing tasks. As a prominent liberal thinker and writer actively involved with the erection of the mestizo state, Altamirano operated within the ideological conventions of de-Indianization. But this does not imply that his discourse should be exempt from critical reinterpretation today. The problem is that much of this negative reinterpretation, along with the affirmative critique, has failed to grasp the complexity of Altamirano's position. Moreover, its rather ham-handed execution has at times confused the challenges that Altamirano faced with the moral precepts that surround identitarian categories today. Especially as we move toward a reading of Altarmirano's most racially charged piece of fiction, *El Zarco* (written in 1888), it is worth considering this critique at length.

Take, as one example, Palazón and Galván's essay "El centro contra las periferias (el nacionalismo defensivo de Altamirano)," published in Manuel Sol and Alejandro Higashi's *Homenaje a Ignacio Manuel Altamirano (1834–1893)* (1997), a collection that brought together important new work by nearly all of the prominent contemporary scholars of Altamirano. In this rich and provocative essay, Palazón and Galván draw from Altamirano's writings on education and language studies in order to condemn his participation in what they call a politics of "ethnocide" and "genocide" (109).[17] While they are certainly not wrong to advance this line of analysis, their argument loses steam when they take up the idea of race and the politics of representation as they play out in Altamirano's more subtle literary work. Citing a couple of well-known passages from Altamirano's two major novels, *Clemencia* (1869) and *El Zarco,* they point to descriptions of indigenous characters that today resonate with certain offense.[18] From this, Palazón and Galván attack what they perceive as his mobilization of Eurocentric racist stereotypes. But this is to accuse Altamirano of what is precisely his critical point, although he operates in a less essentialist register than his modern critics. So, when Altamirano describes the protagonist of *Clemencia,* the tragic soldier Fernando Valle, as having a "repugnant aspect" (*Obras completas,* 3:164) and a sickly constitution, Palazón and Galván quickly call this a "self-deprecating projection" and criticize Altamirano for promoting the idea that "'Indians' are ugly, repugnant and unappealing [orig.: *antipáticos*]" (101), concluding their point with the declaration that "in opposition to Altarmirano, we are convinced that our [Mexico's] *pluri-ethnicity is not a racial matter,*" but rather has to do with the history of national formation (ibid., emphasis in original).

Setting aside the quick assumption that we should read both the author and his protagonist as self-evidently Indian, two major obstacles arise when Palazón and Galván seek to criticize Altamirano by replacing race with nation. First we need to recognize that this kind of critique will always prove futile in the face of the historical alliance between race and nation, that is, the fact that the rise of the nation-form is also the consolidation of the discourses that align races with spaces and end in the production of national races. The virtue of Palazón and Galván's "pluri-ethnic" approach is that, in its very instantiation, it recognizes the collapse of the race–nation articulation, including the failure of Altamirano's own attempts at cultural homogenization through language education. But in wielding this historical fact uncritically, they fail to see their position as a symptomatic moment in a long history, as a new wrinkle in and a new affirmation of the process of the very fight in which Altamirano himself was already engaged: both the author and his critics set out to attack race—but from different directions.

And this brings us to the second obstacle, which is how to understand the racial politics of Altamirano's project. In effectively asking Altamirano to erase race, Palazón and Galván exacerbate the problems with their omission of the fact that he is operating within the terms of a delicate critique of the race–nation articulation as it is being formed around the mestizo state. So when Altamirano endows the hero of *Clemencia* with the most "repugnant" exterior qualities, suggesting a certain Indianness around these traits, only an epidermal interpretation could propose this as an empirical judgment on the physical aesthetics and abilities of "the indigenous race." As Carlos Monsiváis demonstrates in a powerful interpretation of Altamirano's prose fiction, his project is much bigger than that. When, in *Clemencia*, Fernando (the "ugly" protagonist) turns out to have all of the virtues of the ideal patriot—integrity, courage, honor, intelligence—in contrast to the beautiful officer Enrique Flores (who betrays his nation in favor of the French occupiers), what Altamirano is asking us to accept is a world in which physiognomy is irrelevant. He attempts to defuse race by displacing it with character. And while, for Altamirano, there may be a certain biblical fatalism around character itself, the important point is that it is disconnected from exterior form, in other words, it is racially unmarked. In his novels, whiteness does not register as physically degenerate or morally depraved at any essential level; but—and this is crucial—neither does indigenousness. In Altamirano's liberalism, progressivism, and, ultimately, nationalism, the *patria* must move beyond its long colonial history of *casticismo*, with its paranoia around the distinguishing mark that might call the legitimacy of origin into question at any time. From this obsession with lineage and appearance, Mexico must advance toward an ideology of citizenship, unmarked and untrammeled by the tyranny of phenotype. Monsiváis writes: "The message is unequivocal: Altamirano combats, even without hope, the belief in 'presentation' (the faith in exteriority)" (1999, 13).[19]

The implications of the anachronism of race in reading Altamirano today emerge even more dramatically in another essay from the Sol and Higashi volume. Evodio Escalante's "Lectura ideológica de dos novelas de Altamirano" (1997) is a sharp and conceptually nuanced reading of *El Zarco* and *La Navidad en las montañas* (1871). Perhaps the first theoretically engaged political reading of *El Zarco*, it is a pioneering text to which I will return later in the chapter. At this point, it is worth reviewing its turn to race, which deepens some of the problems that I indicated regarding Palazón and Galván's critique of Altamirano.

Escalante offers an interpretation of what he calls the "symbolic economy" (1997, 194) of the two novels, and this approach brings him to some of the key social and political contradictions at stake therein. One of these has to do with the relations among race, the representation of indigenous culture, and the nation-form. Especially within the context of *El Zarco*, Escalante's concern is with how Altamirano situates the presence of indigenous cultures in the landscape of the novel. That is, he deals with the intersection of race and space. He does this by dwelling on the two poles of action that provide the setting for the novel. The first is the village Yautepec, a real town situated in Mexico's central valley, here described in idyllic terms as "original and picturesque" (1901, 96). Significantly, it is "a half-Oriental and half-American pueblo," qualities linked directly to its local economy: "Oriental because its woods are comprised of orange and lemon trees" (ibid.). Escalante notes this fact and reads the emphasis on *mitad* as a "valorization" of what he calls "cultural mestizaje" (1997, 195). Altamirano's symbolic economy of valorization thus slips into a valorization of race. Escalante interprets this move as "a reflection of the mentality of the epoch" that informs "a racist argument that can be subtle but that at the same time appears as inevitable" (196–97). On the one hand, Altamirano's Yautepec is "the center of numerous, small indigenous villages" (1901, 100); on the other hand—and with these lines, set off as a single paragraph, Altamirano closes the opening chapter—the Indians do not live there: "The entire population speaks Spanish, since it is made up of mestizo races. The pure Indians have disappeared completely" (101).

Escalante is correct to perceive the hegemony of the mestizo state governing the prose of *El Zarco*. Altamirano does indeed valorize, or at least narrates, an ideological process that associates national consolidation with mestizaje. But Escalante's critique withers in the face of the historical rigor of Altamirano's description, even if the novelist's ideological expression is romantic. Accurately situating Altamirano as an active architect of liberal ideology in Mexico, Escalante seems to forget that the true force of ideology does not reside in the propagandistic action that propels the expression of political positions. Ideas become ideology as they become implicit, that is, insofar as they naturalize history. So, when Altamirano narrates Yautepec as a kind of mestizo town and then suggests that this space is an important node within a larger project of national development, he is rather precisely describing the lay of the land in 1870s Mexico. For Altamirano's Yautepec was exactly the kind of regional crossroads where cultural heterogeneity and mixture exploded as the incipient historical process of depeasantization gained steam throughout the second half of the nineteenth century, emptying the countryside, in all of its cultural diversity, into the towns.

Whether or not *valorize* is the correct word, the fact that Altamirano describes this process with a note of optimism simply makes him a man of his time, a literary mouthpiece for Alva's *indianización.*

The problem, then, is not what Altamirano, the man, thinks about this historical transformation. The problem is the naturalization of its social, political, and ethical effects. Again the problem is not whether or not Altamirano puts the mestizo on a higher plane than the Indian; the problem is how easily this hierarchical "process" can be presented as the outcome of a historical inevitability. Let us consider the key passage again, this time in the original Spanish: "La población toda habla español pues se compone de razas mestizas. Los indios puros han desaparecido de allí completamente" (101). The first line is a blunt demographic description of the setting of the novel, one that may or may not resonate convincingly with the actual Yautepec, circa 1870.[20] The second line is the expression of ideology. The passive quality of the present perfect, aligned with the word choice, converts into a natural process what is in fact a centuries-long war: "have disappeared" could have been expressed with greater historical accuracy as "have been displaced"; "have been killed"; "have seen their civilizations destroyed." By focusing on Altamirano's alleged valorization of one race over another, Escalante seems to want individual racism, when what is at stake is a much more profound social transformation that at once rests on, erases, and reinforces race: indigenous communities "disappear"; mestizo towns appear. The mechanism of violence (primitive accumulation) that lies between the two is rendered invisible. The land is the space of racialization: it is changing hands, and this is not a happy process. Altamirano sees possibility in an epoch-making, transformational mode of production, in the industrialization of rural life, but he expresses no more than ambivalence regarding the "pueblecillos de indígenas" whose inhabitants surely make Yautepec their primary marketplace. It is Escalante who seems to want to force the issue when he, not Altamirano, writes: "Yautepec is not a (vulgar) Indian village" (1997, 197).[21]

The critique of Altamirano as racist becomes even more tendentious when Escalante turns to the other main site of action in *El Zarco*, the bandit hideout at Xochimancas. A number of things happen at this turn in Escalante's essay, not the least of which is an attentive reading that links banditry to indigenousness by tracing a series of references to serpents and lizards within the text.[22] Most important for the purposes of my own reading is Esclante's reaction to Altamirano's explicit turn to anthropological discourse. In *El Zarco* Xochimancas is described as an old hacienda, now ruined (259). As its name suggests, it was once a kind of Edenic flower garden cultivated by the Aztecs (261). Much attention is given to the possibilities of production represented by the place, now abandoned. This abandonment is triple, with each level resonating ideologically. The failed hacienda represents a failed mode of production. The indigenous community at Xochimancas is gone, like so many indigenous communities, which, the narrator notes (citing the great Mexican historian, geographer, and jurist Manuel Orozco y Berra), simply "disappear completely" (264). And of course, this abandoned setting has been occupied by bandits, rendered a zone of exception. The narrator makes some comments on the nature of the place within the larger Aztec empire, an academic exercise made explicit with extensive citations from impressive sources: Vicente Reyes (261), José Fernando Ramírez (ibid.), Fray Bernardino de Sahagún (261–62), Cecilio Robelo (262), Juan de Torquemeda (263), and Orozco y Berra (264), an authoritative list within the ethnographic canon on Aztec civilization.

This is where Escalante objects. After noting that the narrator approaches Xochimancas with "the greatest reservations" (1997, 201), especially in comparison to the cozy portrait of Yautepec, he points out that in order to "describe the place the narrator finds it necessary to resort to erudite testimonies, to historical and geographical studies" (ibid.). Now, recalling that we are in fact confronted here with a ruin, we might wonder how else Altamirano would have had access to this ethnographic knowledge.[23] Escalante offers one possible answer, at the root of his disappointment with Altamirano in general: "Distance. Alienation. The necessity to add documentary support toward the goal of closely discussing something that one would suppose would be familiar to him. But that, from what we have seen, is not" (ibid.). What is it that one wants to suppose would be familiar to Altamirano? Something that we might broadly construe as indigenous culture. More directly, in Escalante's words, "his people" (200).[24]

This transhistorical exchange between Altamirano and Escalante can tell us a lot about the transformations around the idea of race in the intervening century. Upwardly mobile from a bilingual childhood with intimate contacts in more than one cultural world, by the time that he writes *El Zarco* Altamirano sees himself as, and has lived the life of, a cosmopolitan man of letters. And yet his identity as *pura raza* is hard to shake. We want Altamirano to be an Indian, the indigenous writer, with the expected implications of *su etnia:* to have intimate knowledge of indigenous cultural practices, including lore, and to express his political and cultural solidarity with Mexico's indigenous communities. Escalante's words resonate this desire for race. Surprise: "necesidad de allegarse un apoyo documental." Hope: "tendría que serle familiar." Disillusion: "por lo visto, no lo es." The conclusion to be drawn from Escalante's critique—one implied as well by Palazón and Galván—is that Altamirano, given his purported race, should have somehow transcended his historical context, that, as the great indigenous writer, he should have thrown his lot in with the Indian.

This seems to be asking too much. First is the problem that, even if Altamirano were compelled to feel a special sense of duty to what we today perceive as "his race," there is no reason to believe that he could speak with any conviction on Xochimancas, a pre-Columbian ruin that stands at least a day's journey, over mountainous terrain, from Altamirano's native Tixtla and that, very likely, by the late nineteenth century had little to do with the indigenous communities prominent around his hometown. The much larger problem is that this kind of race consciousness that Escalante seems to want did not exist in the 1880s. "El indio," as Altamirano's own writings on the topic demonstrate, was a heterogeneous category, here used to denote "a race," there used to indicate a set of cultural practices, here mobilized to make a claim on cultural authenticity ("nuestros indios"), there invoked to denounce a cultural enemy ("indios bárbaros"), here an economic class ("indio pobre"), there a social condition ("indios infelices"). In everyday speech, it would almost invariably be invoked as an insult. In the 1883 debate on obligatory education, for example, Altamirano very much subscribes to Alva's model that we saw in chapter 1, drawing a clear distinction between productive indigenous communities and the frontier "nomads . . . in open war with the nation" and "the sad and miserable *lacandones,* who live humbly and abandoned in Chiapas" (*Obras completas,* 15:291). But this is not the norm for Mexico's indigenous communities: "The exception constituted by these remote peoples [orig.: *pueblos*] is of little importance and does not argue against the general rule" (ibid.). The "general rule" is captured in Segre's useful description of Altamirano's embrace of the very category "indígena" in his writings "to mean simultaneously 'Indian' and 'native' against the widespread usage which split 'Indian' from original inhabitant . . . to designate a generic racial physiology" (2000, 270).[25] As Segre's analysis indicates, Altamirano's semantics are significant. His politics, however, remain at the level of the national symbolic. In other words, indigenous identity had not yet been positively rearticulated and invested into a national political platform of subalternity; elites could speak of "el indio" or "lo indígena," but real indigenous communities had not yet formed effective bonds of solidarity that linked their far-flung communities together in a common struggle for rights within the context of the nation-state.[26] "Yo soy un indio como nadie feo," writes Altamirano in a famous line of poetry.[27] The "nadie" leaps from the page. It is easily misread as an affirmative statement of identity, but a more accurate reflection of Altamirano's life would be obliged to read it negatively, as a lament of alienation, of cultural distance, of racial solitude.

While Altamirano was often sympathetic to the poor and the marginalized in the face of the powerful, for him the fundamental political problem behind the Indian was not multiculturalist: he was not concerned with segmented racial solidarity and the formation of a community of differences.[28] For him the indigenous communities are problematic only insofar as they represent an oddly shaped piece for the central political puzzle of the time: the nation-state. Altamirano is ultimately concerned with how to articulate hegemony (the feeling of nationness) with sovereignty (the mediation of that feeling in the manifestation of the state) in the wake of decades of civil war and instability. The intellectual currents of his historical moment lead him to think about the nation in the terms of race, and it is *only* within this problematic that he contemplates the place of the Indian in national culture. To blame Altamirano for his lack of solidarity with, in Escalante's words, "su etnia," is reminiscent of the historical scapegoating associated with the Tlaxcaltecas in Mexican nationalism. There is only one way to claim the Tlaxcaltecas, the bitter and oppressed enemies of the Aztecs, as traitors to the national cause, to blame them for their decisive alliance with the Spanish conquistadors. The claim makes sense only if we understand their history from an anachronistic perspective that places Aztecs and Tlaxcaltecas in a single category called "race," then tie that category to the foundations of the modern nation, an ideological maneuver that would have been completely foreign to their pre-Mexican world. Altamirano describes what he would have known with convincing intimacy: Yautepec, a rural center not unlike Tixtla, Toluca, or Cuautla, the towns formative to his youth.[29] Xochimancas would have been as exotic to him as to any other member of the elite. And to demand more of him is, in turn, a kind of elitism. It is the refusal to allow the "indigenous" writer to be what in fact he authentically was: a statesman, a nationalist, an unabashed promoter of Eurocentric form, one who sometimes masqueraded as Indian to flesh out a national politics.

Of course, Altamirano's own elitism is certainly something to be considered critically in any reinterpretation of his work today. But the best way to do this is to read his work against the limits that mark the discursive parameters of his own historical moment. Claiming that Altamirano fails the test of indigenous solidarity seems to speak more directly to our contemporary concerns. The affirmative critique also overshoots, albeit in the opposite direction, making Altamirano a kind of secret agent for an ethnocentric indigenism to come but never explaining in a convincing manner his explicit calls for the nationalist Hispanization of indigenous communities. Both of these positions would have been inconsequential to the historical Altamirano, who was politically much closer to the national politics of a figure like Luis Alva than to any incipient indigenous politics of protest objectified in this or that local grievance. Paradoxically, in the wake of the poststructural revolution in literary criticism and all of the fluidity and ambivalence that it embraced, the critical tendency to Indianize Altamirano today seems to speak to a desire for essence, for race war, for clear ethnic lines and a political position to match.

Altamirano, however, was all about nuance. Having abandoned his famously rabid denunciation of amnesty from 1861, by the 1870s he had become one of the clearest examples of the Latin American *letrado* who turned to the mechanism of literature as a way of fomenting national reconciliation and solidarity. In reading him as a kind of indigenous writer who then betrays "su etnia," we are reading our idea of race back against his. This, in turn, detracts from our ability to adequately comprehend his deceptively complex literary narratives. In order to do so, I maintain that we should think about Altamirano's writings as he thought about them: as a political project where race is at stake, but implicit not central. This perspective, I think, makes the thematization of race in his literary narratives that much richer with interpretive possibility. *El Zarco*, the great Mexican novel of the nineteenth century, is a case in point. Much is made in contemporary criticism about the rivalry between the Indian blacksmith and the blue-eyed bandit, two of the central characters in the story, or about the complexions of their competing objects of affection, the blond Manuela and the dusky Pilar.[30] But the novel is ultimately not about that particular race war. The novel is about the state. That state is mestizo. And there is a mestizo figure who enables the novel's resolution. But even here, we are not confronting race in any conventional sense. Rather, the mestizo is a contradictory figure, at once the novel's hero and antihero, the wraith of justice and the materialization of the violence of national consolidation. It is the mestizo through whom a thinker of the depth and subtlety of Altamirano contemplates the promises and horrors of state formation, a history in which he participated and that he could not take lightly. Let us turn now to *El Zarco*.

After pollution, frogs, stinging gnats, mosquitoes, anthrax, boils, hail, locusts, and thick darkness, there descends the infamous tenth plague, the massacre of the first-born (Exodus 7:8–12:23). All are marked for death: the heir of the pharaoh, of the maidservant, of the captive, even of the cattle in the fields (11:4–5; 12:29). Only the Lord's chosen nation, the enslaved Israelites, shall be excepted (11:7). The agent of this mayhem is not easy to discern. Neither pestilence nor assassin—or perhaps both—it is revealed to the Israelites by Moses as simply "the destroyer" (12:23). In similarly apocalyptic passages (e.g., 2 Samuel 24:16, Isaiah 37:36) the Lord walks in the company of an "angel of death" whom he releases and retracts at will. But in the decisive scene of the tenth plague, the distinction between the Lord and his messenger is ambiguous. And while we are briefly confronted with the destroyer, it is thoroughly unclear whether this force represents a figure sent forth by the sovereign, an extension of the sovereign's will, or if it is, in fact, sovereignty itself: "For I will pass through the land of Egypt that night, and I will smite all the first-born in the land of Egypt, both man and beast; and on all the gods of Egypt I will execute judgments: I am the Lord" (Exodus 12:12, *New Oxford Annotated Bible*).

"Exterminating angel" is the term sometimes ascribed to God's agent of destruction. This is precisely the term invoked by Altamirano in reference to Martín Sánchez Chagollán (1901, 308), the most enigmatic figure of his literary work—indeed, of nineteenth-century Mexican literature in general—appearing in the final four chapters of the author's final novel, *El Zarco: Episodios de la vida mexicana en 1861–1863*. In many ways the allegory is not especially elegant. *El Zarco* is a historical novel, and its setting—1861 to 1863, the tumultuous years leading up to the French invasion and occupation of Mexico—could only through the most extravagant turns of rhetoric resemble the border conflict that defined the Israelite rebellion against Egypt. This aesthetic clumsiness aside, Altamirano hit the nail on the head in terms of the political allegory at work in this menacing image. For Martín Sánchez blurs the boundary between the sovereign and his messenger, to the point where law is neither deliberated nor applied but rather suspended, reduced to an immediate question of decision and judgment, well outside the limits of any covenant or constitution. *I am the Lord:* the plagues have nothing to do with justice. As Herbert May and Bruce Metzger, the editors of *The New Oxford Annotated Bible* (1973), convincingly put it, as early as the seventh plague (hail) we perceive that "the ineffectiveness of the plagues up to this point is not due to the Lord's weakness but to his patient determination to demonstrate his sovereignty" (77–78; see Exodus 9:15–16). The massacre of the first-born, as much as it anguishes the Egyptians, is meant for the Israelites. A promise (of security) and a threat (of untold suffering), it is both foundation and transcendence of the covenant that authorizes it.

In contemplating this allegory and its potential meaning in *El Zarco*, it is important to recall the demonic implications that accompany the idea of the angel. The Hebraic idea of an exterminating angel captures this etymological ambivalence. At once salvation and perdition, this angel is the figure who establishes the law by operating beyond the law. This is the case in *El Zarco*, and therein we find that Altamirano's demons were explicitly bound up with the delicate question of state sovereignty and the effective articulation of its covenant with the national population. Two figures emerge here, figures whose legacies still loom in the political conflicts that continue to beset a number of American nation-states: the bandit and the vigilante. Today we might call them guerrilla and paramilitary. In *El Zarco* they are called el Zarco and Martín Sánchez. Commentary on the figure of el Zarco is ample. Commentary on Martín Sánchez is fleeting at best. And yet it is Martín Sánchez who ultimately preoccupies Altamirano as he strives to sort out the contradictions of the mestizo state.

While structurally inferior to the earlier *Clemencia*, a novel that foreshadows much of its basic formula, *El Zarco* is Altamirano's most ambitious literary work. It is remembered today as a tale of national consolidation that pertains to a popular subgenre of its time: the bandit novel. Four major characters are lined up with more or less personal integrity; the darker-complexioned protagonists show themselves to be model citizens, with the blue-eyed and "impure" (1901, 164) white bandit and his blond lover cast in the most reprehensible of moral terms. After intrigue and high jinks, the good citizens marry, although, as we will see, it is not exactly in the happiest of settings.

The first chapters of what would eventually become *El Zarco* were drafted as early as 1874 (Sol 2000, 29); the manuscript was finished in 1887 (30) and submitted to the publisher in 1888 (Ballescá 1901, 7). The space in between is notable for its lack of a major civil war and is associated with the growing hegemony of the Díaz administration, the so-called Pax Porfiriana. An early supporter of Díaz, Altamirano developed a creeping unease with the Porfirian clique (among others, see Ochoa Campos 1986), but he never broke with the administration completely and was eventually appointed to a comfortable diplomatic post, first in Barcelona and later Paris. There is controversy around the meaning of this appointment, with scholars reading it alternatively as a political distinction (e.g., Chávez Guerrero 187), a personal choice (e.g., Sommer 1991), or a kind of soft exile (e.g., Rivas Velázquez 1992, 173). It was in Paris that Altamirano became ill. In 1893 he died of consumption while convalescing in San Remo. He never saw the publication of *El Zarco*, although he was paid for the copyright. Due to editorial carelessness, the manuscript went unpublished for over a decade, until 1901.[31] This means that the novel's gestation from idea to book spans a significant chunk—indeed, all but the last decade—of the Porfiriato. It thus traces a particularly intense period of nation-building, the very institutionalization of the mestizo state, marked, as Andrés Molina Enríquez puts it, by Díaz's commitment to *amificación*, that is, his talent for balancing political antagonisms and incorporating the former enemies of liberalism into the rapidly consolidating state apparatus (1909, 136; see also Hale 1989, 9).

The novel's very context, then, provokes its dominant interpretation today: we read *El Zarco* allegorically, as a lesson in a barbarous nation's process of civilization or as a wager on national reconciliation, what Doris Sommer has memorably called a "foundational fiction" (1991). The pedagogical intent of Altamirano's literary writings was well explained by the author himself as early as 1868 (e.g., *Obras completas*, 12:56) and has been extensively analyzed, indeed, beginning with Francisco Sosa, who described *El Zarco*, in the prologue of its first edition, as "instructive" (1901, 3). Operating within this framework, most readings of the text find in the love story between the "indio" Nicolás and the humble Pilar a didactic allegory of the formation of a new national spirit embodied by racially marked productive citizens. Sommer herself has described the work as one in a long line of Mexican novels that articulate "romance and nationalism," thus joining "a tradition of marriages between politics and passion" (1991, 231).

A number of critics, in one way or another, have followed suit (e.g., Cruz 1994, 73; Schmidt 1999; Conway 2000, 97; Ruiz 2005; Lund 2006, 91). Although suggestive and certainly not without merit, these interpretations of the novel in terms of national romance and reconciliation, made intelligible through the requisite formula of mestizaje, do not offer a satisfying explanation to a basic problem in the novel: in order to resolve the crisis of national disarticulation, Altamirano does not, in fact, turn to love. He conjures a vigilante.

Escalante blames the historically rosy treatment of the novel on Mexico's Jacobin tradition and its unwillingness to grapple with its own "despotism" (1997, 200). It may also be symptomatic of the ideological power and narrative force of mestizaje's immediate articulation to *amificación* that none of the contemporary national romance readings do anything significant with the figure of Martín Sánchez. This is despite the fact that he dominates the resolution of the narrative (see chapters 21–25).

Martín Sánchez Chagollán first interrupts the text at a key moment, when news of his existence throws a pall over the bandit dance party that provides the context for the long and colorful twenty-first chapter. It is surely no accident that the chapter is titled "La orgía" (The orgy). It is a depiction of the social chaos, moral depravity, and, most centrally, institutional collapse that Altamirano symbolized with banditry. Martín Sánchez, whose narrative function is to bring down the hammer of order, ends the fun. He does this even in absentia. His initial presence in the novel is purely narrative, a report: he arrives by word of mouth when "several bandits, disheveled and covered with dust" (1901, 296), burst in to tell their leaders that Martín Sánchez and his men have ambushed an allied group of twenty bandits, routing and hanging them on the spot. Alarmed, the bandits get serious and immediately begin to plot their revenge (297). So far we have learned little else about Martín Sánchez than that he is accompanied by a sizable force of about forty and that he carries "excellent weapons" (ibid.).[32]

The following chapter is dedicated to a brief biography of the vigilante. We learn that Martín Sánchez is a modest "campesino" (peasant or, more broadly, man of the countryside, without major landholdings) with no history of participation in the civil war ("sin antecedentes militares" [303]). Like all of Altamirano's masculine protagonists, he is noted to possess "Herculean biceps" (304). Significantly, given that the race–nation couplet exhibits considerable allegorical strength in the novel, he has a "dark complexion [orig.: *cara morena*]" (305). As if he appeared out of the pages of a Borges story, his "feline appearance" endows him with a "vague resemblance to the leopard (orig.: *vaga semejanza con los leopardos*]" (ibid.). His campaign against the bandits is waged in vengeance: his son and father were both murdered in a bandit raid (ibid.). Finally, it is essential to note that his actions go beyond himself and that he operates as a kind of populist, embodying a larger social frustration with the weakness and corruption of the state.[33] Or perhaps it would be more precise to say that he represents the wishful arrival of the sovereign in its purest liberal form: the enactment of a popular sovereignty through the embodiment of a certain social rage. The chapter ends with these words: "Bandits should tremble! The exterminating angel had finally arrived! . . . Martín Sánchez was social indignation incarnate" (308).

He is compared to Judge Lynch (ibid.). He rides with a posse (311). He wears black (ibid.). His vision of justice is Hammurabic: "An eye for an eye and a tooth for a tooth. Such was his penal code [orig.: *ley penal*]" (308). His authorization is explicit but vague; he has permission—granted to him by a local prefect—to "persecute thieves" but only "on condition that any criminals apprehended will be submitted to the relevant court" (306). The prefect also gives him a semiofficial title: *jefe de seguridad pública.*[34] But because the law of the state does not really apply to an exterminating angel, Martín Sánchez clearly operates in a juridical margin. With the words *Seguridad Pública* (311) emblazoned on their hats, Martín Sánchez and his men act exceptionally, issuing decisions on what constitutes justice: "The bandits [orig.: *plateados*] were cruel? He would be equally so. The bandits provoked terror? He would provoke equal terror" (308). Justice and vengeance are understood as one.

In the concluding chapters, Martín Sánchez is at the center of the action. When the hero, Nicolás, finally captures el Zarco, Martín Sánchez has plans to string him up immediately (317). Fortunately for el Zarco, Nicolás—a "good citizen" (328; see also 208, 220), Altamirano's symbol for the liberal ideal between state and subject—returns with "the authorities from Morelos," and Martín Sánchez is forced to let justice take its proper course. Unfortunately for Nicolás, the state is incompetent in carrying out its juridical responsibilities. The theme of corruption, abetted by the "disorder in which the country had fallen" (319), now intensifies, and we learn that "the bandit party . . . held great influence" (ibid.) and that "it held in its hands the life and interests of all who possessed anything, they were feared, and they achieved, at whatever price, their benevolence and friendship" (ibid.). The concessions to justice that come with a constitutionally ordered society become almost unbearable as el Zarco, using his powerful contacts, successfully executes a legal maneuver to have the trial moved to Cuernavaca (ibid.). We are not surprised when, during the transfer, he is easily rescued at the risky pass known as "las Tetillas" (320). The political resolution of the novel, then, depends on the intervention of a third, neither state nor regular citizen but operating on behalf of both: Martín Sánchez. There is, of course, a wedding, but the novel does not end on this note. Rather, the final scene is that of the wedding party as it happens to stumble across el Zarco's extrajudicial execution. Martín Sánchez apologizes to the newlyweds and suggests that Nicolás and Pilar move along. They do, momentarily horrified by the pleas for their intervention on the part of Manuela, Pilar's erstwhile best friend, the blond maiden who had once snubbed Nicolás as "that horrible Indian" (120). El Zarco is executed by firing squad, and then, brains spilling out, hung from a tree (334). Manuela begins to spit up blood and promptly dies—of shock, we suppose. The penultimate words of the novel belong to Martín Sánchez: "So bury her... and let's finish this job" (335). And the final words belong to the narrator, who speaks not of the nation's model civil union but of the exterminating angel and his host: "And thus marched away the terrible, grim troop" (ibid.).

Let us quickly return to Martín Sánchez's irruption into the narrative flow of the national romance. Recall the scene: it is the bandit camp at Xochimancas, a degraded space defined by a total lack of reason, where chaos, passions, mistrust, and greed govern. It is a space of disarticulation, a quality that seeps into all aspects of the camp and all human interaction that takes place there. Beyond the confusion between space and function (an old chapel, "once sacred," is now defiled by bandit lust, avarice, and mendacity [253]), this disarticulation applies all the way up to the horror of its aesthetic production, as we can see from this description of "bandit music" (a forerunner of the *corrido*, later romanticized as the people's music in the wake of the Mexican Revolution): "Manuela stared with horror; they sang a long series of songs, those irritating songs, chaotic, with no sense at all ... and that can't be heard for too long without intense irritation. Manuela was irritated" (272). Irritation—"fastidio"(and "fatigue," as some versions have it)—is the operative word here, the only possible reaction of the even semienlightened before this welter of "one hundred twisted mouths" (291). If Altamirano's goal is to write an articulate nation governed by reason, the bandit camp of *El Zarco* stands as a space of exception, disarticulate chaos without the possibility of any harmony. It is important that Martín Sánchez exacts his violence here, in the camp, a point on which Altamirano is explicit: "Who was this fearless man that had dared to hang twenty bandits in the very heart of their dominion?" (303). Only the exceptional figure himself can effectively enter into the space of exception.[35]

Who will emerge victorious in this struggle between competing exceptionalisms? Even the narrator pretends not to know: "Who would triumph? Who knows . . . !" (308). The literary result is in doubt, but the struggle is historical. "Rigorously historical" (303), like the figure of Martín Sánchez himself, who, we learn, joins the bandits el Zarco, Salomé Plascencia, and others as a character that Altamirano pulled from Mexico's recent past. Indeed, as Sol documents, Martín Sánchez figures in a number of accounts of the epoch.[36] In a semihistorical collection of war stories, *Los plateados de Tierra Caliente* (1891), Pablo Robles dedicates a chapter to him, called "Pueblos heroicos: Martín Sánchez Chagollán." The stories were published in 1891, and it is unknown if Robles and Altamirano would have drawn from each other in their corresponding portraits of Martín Sánchez, but it seems unlikely.[37] The almost exact correspondence between the two versions thus suggests a certain popular memory around the avenging angel, if not in the historical figure named Martín Sánchez then at least in the general type. Marked for death, it is the bandit gangs that give Martín Sánchez his nickname, Chagollán. Robles explains that prior to his vigilantism he was a silversmith, and the *chagollo* was the low-grade silver used to make counterfeit coins and iconic figurines for religious purposes, both referred to in popular speech as *chagollos*. The implication, says Robles, was that Martín Sánchez was a "militar chagollo"—fake, that is, "improvised" (1891, 142).

Far more important than the historical biography of Martín Sánchez, however, is the way in which his surprising dominance of the final chapters points to a political conundrum that was clearly on Altamirano's mind: how to square the liberal ideal of a voluntaristic and constitutionally ordered nation-state copula with a sovereignty that was ineffective in the face of, among other competitors, bandits?

Altamirano, who lived through civil wars and participated as a soldier in the national resistance (against French invasion) that provided the context for the proliferation of bandit gangs, was preoccupied with this problem throughout his writing life.[38] He addresses these concerns even more directly in his political writings. As early as 1861, within the context of a screed against Mexico's many institutional ills, he declares:

> On the outskirts of Mexico City there are . . . a thousand hordes of bandits that do not leave a single traveler unscathed, that murder foreigners and liberties alike, that intercept the mail. . . . Isn't it true that in the districts of Cuautla and Cuernavaca these bandit gangs number up to two thousand men, a truly terrible thing. (*Obras completas*, 1:75)

The menacing *condottieri* of Italy's Calabria are "Pygmies compared to the spectacular crimes of our bandits" (ibid.). A blow to national pride, the situation is enough to make "travelers believe that God has abandoned this country to the beasts and the bandits" (ibid.). Later, in an essay produced in 1867—the momentous year in which the Republic was finally restored and the liberal state far more precarious than the 1880s-era Pax Porfiriana—Altamirano takes up the issue head-on, in a passage that is particularly relevant when read in the light of *El Zarco*:

> Armed gangs are appearing everywhere, three, five, ten, twenty up to a hundred men that rob travelers, and whose appearance paralyzes agriculture and traffic, destroys commerce, at the same time reducing workers and proprietors to misery. A few months ago the roads were safe, thanks to the rural police [orig.: *fuerzas rurales*] that constantly patrolled them. Today, thanks to a wise measure on the part of the Minister of War, and one would have to be a Minister of War to produce such optimum results, the rural police have been suppressed, and as if by magic, the bandits appeared everywhere, not without giving thanks, from the bottom of their hearts, for the ministerial disposition that cleared the highways of all obstacles so that they could exercise their noble profession. (*Obras completas*, 18:104)

The first four lines of this citation serve as a kind of sketch for the social problematic that propels *El Zarco*: it is not just that the bandits are criminals but that they are gumming up the gears of capitalist expansion.[39] The early chapters of *El Zarco* are filled with references to the insecurity that stalks agriculture, traffic, commerce, and the highways, a threat to the lives and livelihoods of laborers and property owners alike. More bracing, however, and directly tied to the security of a market-oriented state, is the reference to the "fuerzas rurales" that defend against bandits. The invocation seems bland enough, but especially with historical hindsight, the reference today can almost be read as a provocation. Associated with the Porfiriato, which represents their heyday, these fuerzas rurales are remembered as the extension of Díaz's will, the feared Guardia Rural, or simply *rurales*. A kind of semiautonomous police force operating under the auspices of the executive branch of government, the *rurales* were responsible for policing the highways and, in general, quelling social unrest through intimidation. In practice they were more bumbling than their public image would suggest; nevertheless, because of their reputation for summary executions they stand as one of the great symbols of Porfirian authoritarianism and strong-arm politics.

A point that is often forgotten, and that Altamirano's 1867 citation helps us to remember, is that the *rurales* are actually a product of the much more scrubbed reputation of the Benito Juárez regime. Paul Vanderwood's classic study *Disorder and Progress* (1992) recounts this history. Altamirano is writing months after the liberal victory in the war against French occupation. Rural violence and pillaging are huge problems, with the state coffers and resources near, or even beyond, exhaustion. The situation was similar in 1861, when the ongoing struggle with the conservatives left the liberals in control of the state but not of the countryside. It is in this context that the minister of the interior at the time (coincidentally named Zarco) established the Rural Police Force under administrative control so as not to be contaminated by a military apparatus full of Juárez's political rivals. This first step resulted in a "hybrid federal-state police force" in which "militia-like" organs were run locally at the level of towns, with the federal "rural police" attempting to establish alliances toward "national unification and link rural districts to the capital" (Vanderwood 1992, 48). These first units, "undermanned and underfinanced," were "organized to guard the roads around Mexico City" (49). The effort then basically dissolved in the chaos of civil war. So when Altamirano, in his 1867 essay, refers to "fuerzas rurales," he is referring to this history. The border between these fuerzas rurales, semiautonomous and operating with relative impunity, and the "militia-like" vigilante organs of Seguridad Pública was blurry. These nebulous actors stand as the protagonists in the essay, titled, no less, "Policía"

(*Obras completas,* vol. 18). The police, agents of the lawmaking violence on which the capitalist state depends (Benjamin 1921)—and, make no mistake, Vanderwood's study is decisive in showing the relationship between these loosely organized security groups and capitalist expansion—are here independent of the state, indeed, something that the state has opted to "suppress" ("las fuerzas rurales se han suprimido") (*Obras completas,* 18:104). In short, the essay is not really about the police but rather about their absence. What Altamirano is speaking to here is the desperate situation in which national development must cede its security to the independent work of others: paramilitaries, or, in the words of Robles, "improvised" militias (1891, 142).

But this is just where things get extremely complicated. The problem of rural insecurity is not resolvable through a simple commitment to fund and arm a paramilitary force. The problem is precisely that these improvised militias were at the root of the bandit crisis in the first place: gangs of thugs and questionable characters were recruited by a bankrupt state to rout intransigent conservative strongmen who were still exercising authority in the countryside after the liberal victory in the War of Reform. But with the state out of money, how could it pay for these services? In a kind of security-oriented twist on the free-market relationship established between state and private enterprise in an ideal liberalism, the solution rests on the adage of laissez-faire: *let plunder.* Paramilitary victories would be accompanied by paramilitary banditry. Altamirano knows this all too well, as the editorial interventions that punctuate *El Zarco* make clear:

> The liberal troops, due to a lamentable and embarrassing error [amnesty], were obliged to accept the cooperation of the bandits in the persecution that they waged against the factionalist reactionary Márquez [a conservative general]. In their sojourn across the low lands [orig.: *tierra caliente*] some of these outfits were transformed into irregular but numerous groups, and one of these was led by el Zarco. (1901, 165–66)

Armed, hardened by battle, and unemployed, these groups of men reconfigured themselves into the *plateados* of Altamirano's novel.[40] To what extent Altamirano wants to demonstrate as much is unclear, but there emerges the brute fact that at the root of the bandit problem we find not shiftless youth but rather the state. And with this in mind, one cannot help but be somewhat unnerved by Altamirano's solution to this problem: "fuerzas rurales," that is, more paramilitaries. Neither moral nor juridical, the crux of the matter is political and rests on the difficult question of sovereignty.

A frankly incredible scene interrupts the climactic flow of the novel, and it is one to which we must now turn. The twenty-fourth chapter is called "El presidente Juárez." A scant eight pages, the chapter centers on the audience that the embattled president of the republic, Benito Juárez, grants to Martín Sánchez. Expecting to be snubbed, Martín Sánchez is pleasantly surprised to find the president "cool, impassive, but attentive" (322) and predisposed to help. His reason for the visit is to gain further and more authoritative legitimacy for his actions and, more important, to request support in the form of arms. Martín Sánchez puts it bluntly: "The first thing that I need, sir, is for the government to give me the authority [orig.: *facultades*] to hang any bandit that I catch" (323). He then elaborates his concerns regarding a corrupt official. Juárez never explicitly grants the right to hang, but it is understood that he will not hinder Martín Sánchez's efforts.[41] Martín Sánchez also requests arms, in response to which Juárez offers one hundred rifles. The culminating paragraph of the scene is a tightly knit expression of several of the key themes that define the novel: race, nation, law, republic. We read: "The one, dark, of pure Indian type, the other, yellowish, of mestizo and peasant [orig.: *campesino*] type; both serious, both grave, anybody that would have read a little ways into the future would have shuddered. It was the law of public health arming integrity with the ray of death" (326).[42]

This scene represents the political center of the text. Mysteriously, it is almost totally ignored in the critical bibliography around Altramirano, a lack that also applies to the figure of Martín Sánchez more generally. Its interpretations can be reduced to a handful. In "Altamirano y su nueva visión de la novela en *El Zarco*" (1992), Alejandro Rivas Velázquez reads *El Zarco* as a kind of protest novel, the product of Altamirano's increasing disillusion with the status quo. Within this context, Martín Sánchez—let us recall: the "indignación social"—is el pueblo that must step in and take back the basic tasks of justice that the state has proven unable to carry out. Escalante's 1997 essay (which I dealt with extensively earlier) moves in roughly the opposite direction as *El Zarco* is rethought in the terms of the juridical problematic that its narrative traces. Escalante criticizes what he reads as the "authorization" (199) of extrajudicial violence contained in the last sentence of chapter 24. He asks: "Would somebody actually dare to put *integrity* on trial? Would somebody actually dare to condemn a law, most of all when it's a law, as the text says, of *public health* [orig.: *salud pública*]?" (200, emphasis in original). What he shows us in answering these questions is a law (of "public health," even) that is not applied but simply attached to historical actors, embodied by them, thereby converting them from men into ideas—ideas free from potential prosecution and thus equally from responsibility (199). He understands this alleged circumvention of constitutional authority as nothing less than a "scandal" (ibid.) and calls Altramirano an apologist for despotism.[43] Finally, in a brilliant as-yet-unpublished manuscript called "Imagining Mexican Bandits," Amy Robinson offers a reading that outlines the moral order at work in *El Zarco* by thinking it in refreshingly political, rather than aesthetic or romantic, terms. Less concerned with the scandal of an apparent anticonstitutionalism than Escalante, Robinson focuses on the ways in which Altamirano attempts to craft a narrative of moral acceptability that can reconcile the contradictions of liberalism when confronted with historical conditions that its theories cannot adequately explain. She argues, "Nicolás and Martín Sánchez become heroes in spite of the corrupt state authority because the national problem is, in fact, the institution of authority's inability to define and enforce a national sense of right and wrong" (2003, n.p.).

Extremely suggestive, these readings cannot resist the temptation of associating Martín Sánchez with another entity, whether it be the people (Rivas Velázquez) or the state (Escalante). This kind of associative position was first articulated by Salvador Ortíz Vidales when he interprets the vigilante as "completely identical" to the bandit himself, el Zarco, based on their equally exceptional status vis-à-vis the law (1949, 36). Robinson complicates this relationship and formally associates Martín Sánchez with social banditry in general (and, by extension, el Zarco) but also places him politically in the terms of a "moral ally" to the chaste Nicolás (2003, n.p.; see also Sommer 1991, 226). Nevertheless, these attempts to locate Martín Sánchez within the neoclassical quadrangle of love interests (Nicolás and Pilar versus el Zarco and Manuela), or to reduce him to one of the basic political formations on the scene in 1860s Mexico, seem to fail to grasp the dimensions of his singularity within the narrative, suggested in the way in which his presence makes a mess of the structure of the plot. Yes, Martín Sánchez is exceptional—outside the law—like the bandit. Thus he might be a mirror for el Zarco. Or he might be the hammer for the ideal, law-abiding citizen, Nicolás, thereby operating as his other half. Or he might be popular rage, or he might be (a heretofore absent) state authority. But he is far more than any of these, which is another way of saying that he is reducible to none and transcends each.

Escalante, by paying ample attention to the encounter with Juárez, comes close to illuminating the true face of Martín Sánchez. But he also seems to go too far in reading the scene in palpably indignant terms, as the installation of the "ley de la selva" (1997, 199). But the "law of the jungle" is not at issue here; rather, what we are confronted with is the law of *salud pública*. On this point, the work of Rivas Velázquez is helpful. He leads us to a series of short essays by Altamirano, dating from 1880, in which he addressed these questions directly. Altamirano was writing for *La República* at the time, and the bulk of the essays appear as an epistolary exchange, made public, between him and Rafael de Zayas Enríquez, described as his "friend and disciple" (*Obras completas*, 19:46), who at the time was the director of *Ferrocarril*, a Veracruz newspaper. The point of debate between the two men is the legitimacy of the suspension of individual guarantees, also the central political issue of the meeting between Juárez and Martín Sánchez. Zayas takes a strong constitutionalist position against such suspension, among other reasons noting that it has traditionally been invoked for political ends, that is, for winning elections.[44] Altamirano, avoiding a direct reply to the 1880 case at hand, responds with a history lesson. Two elements of his response stand out. The first is that he makes a case in favor of consitutional suspension by pointing to the exact historical context that he will later stage in chapter 24 of *El Zarco:* the 1861 emergency of the triple threat of insurgent conservatives, the approaching French, and uncontrollable banditry (56–57). Reflecting on this state of emergency, he then contemplates the legal situation that Escalante criticizes, that is, the relation between the law and the "salud pública." Harkening back to the Roman legal tradition, he asserts that, in the face of foreign intervention or grave social crisis, the following imperative emerges: "The law is stored in a locked ark and nothing more is considered beyond the public health [orig.: *se guarda la ley en una arca cerrada y no se consulta más que la salud pública*]. Thus the government gains force, arming it with all of the rights and with all of the weapons of war" (57). Without the vitality of the national body, the question of law itself becomes academic; law can be protected by being temporarily suspended, while the forces of *salud pública* treat what an earlier Congress (of 1857) in a similar situation called "the gangrene that corrodes society," which can only "be extirpated by means of vigorous repression that, in order to be effective, needs to damage up to a certain point those precious freedoms [orig.: *garantías*] and expand, to a certain degree, the orbit of power" (cited by Altamirano in *Obras completas*, 19:52). It is only in these extraordinary circumstances, granted to Juárez as *facultades omnímodas* by the Congress in 1861 in the face of foreign invasion (the French, Spanish, and British were forcibly landing at Veracruz in order to collect debts), only in this state of exception, that a figure like Martín Sánchez can emerge. Although he may be the exceptional opposite of el Zarco, Martín Sánchez is not "the bandit." He is not the necessary counterpart of Nicolás. No, he is not even Juárez. He is the sovereign's messenger: the exterminating angel. He is the very expression of sovereignty.

Where, then, is the "scandal" of which Escalante speaks? Both he and Robinson are led to the conclusion that *El Zarco* should be read as making a favorable case for the existence and exceptional actions of Martín Sánchez, an interpretation shared by Rivas Velázquez. Indeed, there is universal critical agreement around this point (see, for example, Sommer 1991; Conway 2000, 98; Dabove 2007). Rivas Velázquez sees Martín Sánchez as the vehicle by which Altamirano can express a purer state of exception, one that will not degenerate into political opportunism:

> In 1861 he opposed suspension [of individual freedoms] due to the abuse of the power by members of the government, and in 1880 he supported such a measure hoping that this time it would work, but on the contrary, it was utilized for political ends. He was left with only the literary solution that he would offer in *El Zarco* several years later. (1992, 179)

Altamirano's suspension, in this interpretation, is populist: "the suspension of individual rights [orig.: *garantías*], . . . isn't taken in order to authorize greater powers for the men of the administration, but rather so that society itself could overrule them [the agents of the state], and without violating the Constitution" (181). For Robinson, similarly although less naïvely, the figure of the vigilante allows Altamirano to leverage a certain popular appeal around the social bandit, rearticulating this energy as a force for the reestablishment of social order and the state's authority (2003). A bit more shrill, Escalante is again scandalized by what he understands as a bald legitimation of despotism, the treason of the popular sovereignty supposedly embedded in the liberal republic's founding documents. Sol attempts to confront Escalante but moves too gingerly, missing his broader point about despotism and the liberal tradition by focusing on the narrow issue of whether Juárez's actions were technically legal (they were) (2000, 65–66).

Rereading the text in a more sympathetically postcolonial register, however, complicates these interpretations. Although there was certainly something attractive, maybe even necessary (see, again, "Policía," in *Obras Completas*, vol. 18), about Martín Sánchez for Altamirano, the text itself resists this easy reading. Paying attention to these subtleties may obligate us to rethink the nature of the political narrative that we confront in *El Zarco*. This becomes even more evident if we read it in the light of Altamirano's very existence as a man, which locates him smack in the middle of an extremely complicated set of political challenges in which he often played a polemical role. By the time that he finishes the novel, he is now a dinosaur of sorts, increasingly marginalized by the new mandarins of the rapidly consolidating mestizo state, some committed to a vigorous critique of the early liberal republic that he had helped to build, and he is certainly not happy about this fact. In his 1880 letter, he politely reminds his worried correspondent that his generation was locked in a fight to the death and that the liberal ideal had crashed no fewer than fourteen times: fourteen constitutional suspensions, fourteen states of exception (*Obras completas*, 19:51). Times were different, and times were not easy. A close reading of *El Zarco* seems to communicate this message, making it more difficult to see it as a simple case—whether romantic or cynical—for the violence of Martín Sánchez. Altamirano was well aware of the contradictions of sovereignty implicit in any liberal republic, and he knew that it was a much more complex phenomenon than the simple extension of the will of the state. Escalante, then, is hasty when he writes: "The secret of the pacification of Yautepec . . . resides in the National Palace" (1997, 200). It does not. It resides in Martín Sánchez.

Altamirano was known to be quick-witted and tough, but he seems unsettled by his own turn to the vigilante. Recall this odd line embedded in the passage that closes the key twenty-fourth chapter, the portrait of the meeting between the sovereign and his messenger: "cualquiera que hubiera leído un poco en el futuro se habría estremecido" (1901, 325).[45] While critics have wondered whether this "futuro" indicates the subsequent pages of the novel or the subsequent national history, it seems clear to me that it means both and that what gives the line its chilling quality is not its referential ambiguity but its equally ambiguous subject. The narrator does not speak of "cualquier bandido." It is simply "cualquiera"; *anybody* even slightly capable of looking ahead (toward the Porfiriato?) would have experienced a physical sense of foreboding at this transfer of sovereign violence. This does not seem to be the beginning of the road to happiness.

Then there is the spooky passage in chapter 23, "El asalto," in which Martín Sánchez and his posse are represented as living dead men, spectral figures imbued with the harbinger of death. The first time we meet their physical presence is at a crossroads ominously called "La Calavera" (the skull), described as a place that is "excessively sinister," an abandoned stretch populated by bandits: "They looked like ghosts, and in that roadhouse of La Calavera, and at that hour, when objects would take on gigantic form, and among those solitary hills, such a parade of horsemen, silent and scowling, more than a troop, they became a sepulchral apparition" (311).

A page later we read an absolutely crucial passage, one that I have never seen mentioned in any of the critical literature. It is suggested that there is suspicion around the actions of Martín Sánchez:

> He had already hung a good number of bandits [orig.: *plateados*], but they had also accused him, several times, of having committed abuses for which he was not authorized, since, as we have mentioned, he only had permission [orig.: *facultades*] to apprehend criminals and turn them over to the judges. But Martín Sánchez had responded that he only hung those that had already died fighting, which he had done as a lesson [orig.: *escarmiento*]. *In this it was very possible that he was hiding something,* and that he actually killed any bandit that he caught. (312, my emphasis)

The narrator goes on to mount a tepid defense of questionable relevance, noting that Martín Sánchez and his posse, in this scene, were not yet at full strength. This tangent regarding his actions, completely unnecessary to the plot, opens up the suggestion of two possibilities, indeed, probabilities. First, that he immediately violated his mandate and meted out vigilante justice against any bandit, on the spot (recall that he attempts to hang el Zarco extrajudicially [317]). And second, that his judgment was also immediate and that, along with bandits, he killed ordinary, if "suspicious," civilians.

Martín Sánchez was the Lynch law incarnate (308), and Altamirano indicates in other writings of the time that this is a form of law that should be resolutely avoided. In one of the essays from 1880, this one called "Ladrones y asesinos" and put forth to frame the debate on the suspension of individual freedoms, he vehemently defends the necessity of the state power to suspend "some individual guarantees, in light of the threat that weighs upon society, due to the bandits that infest the roads and to the impunity with which the juries afford them" (*Obras completas*, 19:15).[46] But in the same gesture, his liberal spirit compels him to cite Article 29 of the Constitution:

> In the cases of invasion, grave disturbance of public peace, or *any other* disturbance that puts society in great danger of conflict, the President of the Republic, in accordance with the Counsel of ministers and with the approval of the Congress of the Union and during *the recess of that body, the permanent council* [orig.: *diputación*] *can suspend the guarantees provided in this Constitution, with the exception of those that ensure life*, (ibid., 18, emphasis in the original)

Against Agamben, Altamirano's state of exception does not render the citizen *homo sacer* and thereby killable but must rigorously ensure life.[47] He continues: "So, now we can see that there is something before the *Lynch law* and the *primitive state* [orig.: *estado primitivo*] that can salvage public order and calm a society threatened by the impunity enjoyed by criminals" (ibid., emphasis in the original).[48]

Back to *El Zarco*. Perhaps the most prominent of all passages for a reading of Altamirano's ambivalence toward Martín Sánchez is the meeting with Juárez himself. Granted exceptional powers by the Congress, the figure of Juárez is a true sovereign in this scene, largely unfettered by the trappings of constitutionalism. He wraps up the meeting by thanking Martín Sánchez for his patriotism, noting that the country will soon be embroiled In a war against a foreign power and that only because of this has he looked favorably upon Martín Sánchez's audience. At the outset "cool and impassive," a cascade of reminders and disclaimers make Juárez's decision seem suddenly tortured, indeed hysterical. Here it is: "And know well, Señor Sánchez, that you carry extraordinary powers [orig.: *facultades*], but only under the condition that you work for justice, justice before all else. Only necessity can oblige us to use these powers [orig.: *facultades*], as they bring such great responsibility, but I know who I'm giving them to. *Don't make me regret it*" (325, my emphasis). The last line jumps out, but the whole passage is full of suspicion. No fewer than seven times does Juárez express preoccupation before what he is granting.[49] One gets the sense that Juárez had been down this paramilitary road before, which he had, and with disastrous results.[50] The narrator is indicating as much. Also, at the very introduction of Martín Sánchez's petition, which opens with a request for the right to carry out extrajudicial hangings, he adds this pledge: "And I promise to you, under my word of honor, that *I will not kill anyone except those who deserve it*" (323, my emphasis). One cannot help but hear the armchair psychoanalyst here, confronted with the neurotic "I do *not* hate my mother." The patient always also says yes. And in a security-oriented expression of what Foucault understands as the decisive gesture of liberal political-economy, the sovereign *withdraws*, suspending himself in order to let another enact his violence.

Finally, it is worth remembering again the novel's closing scene: any nation-state articulation here is full of ambivalence and trepidation. A criminal is executed on the threshold of the law. A wayward girl dies of fright. The hinge of this articulation—much less the Nicolás–Pilar copula than the solitary presence of Martín Sánchez—utters a last word, "enterrarla," before his "tropa lúgubre" marches off. There is no more sense that this is the end of paramilitary violence and gang warfare than that it might be the beginning. As much as finding its moral foundation, the nation seems to equally quake before its political reality.

To close this chapter, we should pose the question directly and ask about the racialization of this historical allegory. What is the relevance of the specifically constructed mestizo—"amarillento"—Martín Sánchez? Is it relevant at all? First and most immediate is its historical resonance. As John Tutino explains in his economic history of the era, the Martín Sánchezes of the world—the peasant capitalists, the modest landholders, the "rancheros"—were an important constituency of the liberal reformers struggling alongside and around Juárez. Why? Because joining with a powerful movement bent on land privatization and lending their arms to that movement was a way to gain allies toward the containment of "the protests of villagers who opposed the privatization of their community lands" (1986, 260). Moreover, besides an opportunity to expand their land holdings through the liberal reforms, rancheros would also be able to exploit more cheap labor as peasants lost their own access to land (ibid.). And then, drawing on Molina Enríquez's brilliantly influential racialization of social classes, Tutino reminds us that these rancheros were explicitly marked as "mestizo" (259). But all of this is merely descriptive; it is the discourse—symbols that articulate to institutions to stabilize the rules of the true—of race that is important in literary expression. The decisive point for reading the politics of race in Altamirano's novel is the fact that the mestizo was in circulation as the symbolic subject capable of lining up *campo* and *ciudad*, nation and state, of mediating the delicate negotiation between hegemony and sovereignty. Justo Sierra's iconic image captures the spirit of the time: the anti-imperial "guerrillero," fighting off French invasion, was the "mestizo," with "rifle at the ready" (1885, 316), that is, ready to defend the *patria* with whatever it takes.[51] Racially mixed, in between Spanish and Indian, a direct descendant of earth-shattering conquest, the racial symbol moves from the bland ethnology of a historical moment to a much more dynamic symbol of accumulation and consolidation, ultimately standing as a historico-political actor: the strong arm of liberal hegemony, between society and the state, neither police nor soldier, alongside the authorities, a paramilitary man. The paradoxically individualist guardian of the *salud pública*. The dialectic of mestizaje that speaks to a nation made whole retains within its major term the violence of state formation. The story of Martín Sánchez is the story of this historical unfolding.

Altamirano felt this burden. To be sure, one of its sources was the bandit. But the heaviest burden, explicitly thought by Altamirano, was the sovereign, that nebulous figure who can consolidate the rights of those ruled over or send forth unspeakable terror (Martín Sánchez is "terrible" [1901, 325]) and destruction. The place of sovereignty in liberal republics is ambiguous until it momentarily resides in the figure of the executive, showing its potential for menace. A careful reading of Martín Sánchez demonstrates that Altamirano was unsure about and uneasy with this contradiction at the center of liberalism and of Mexico's emergent mestizo state. And yet, like the god of the Israelites, it would seem that sovereignty needs its plagues. The bandits, a competing model of sovereignty produced for the state to exterminate, are expressed in these terms precisely: a *"plague of bandits"* (241, my emphasis). A byproduct of the very state that seeks their elimination, they ultimately become the prelude to the final plague, in which the state contracts out its sovereignty to another. The exterminating angel descends on the margins of the national space, and it is here that we are faced with Martín Sánchez and the symbols of race rendered raw, lashed to a legacy of paramilitarism in the Americas.

Chapter 3   **Misplaced Revolution**
Rosario Castellanos and the Race War

> Revolutions are cannibals, in the end they devour the revolutionaries.
>
> —ELENA GARRO, 1991

ONE OF THE MOST GRIPPING PASSAGES in *Oficio de tinieblas,* the 1962 masterpiece by Rosario Castellanos, comes in the novel's penultimate chapter. The Tzotzil Indians, around whose rebellion much of the story revolves, are in retreat, crushed by the crackdown of men with guns. Small bands of survivors, hungry and scattered, have regrouped at a mountain hideout, and although the mood can be nothing but grim, a kind of sacred ecstasy begins to seep into their exhaustion. The narrative itself signals this as it shifts back to the biblical tone that has defined certain chapters of the novel, a sonorous voice that was described, in the parlance of the time, as "popolvúhica" (Navarrete 2007, 39). Defeat becomes a ritual:

> Neither before nor today exists. It is always. Always defeat and persecution. Always the master who is not appeased by the most abject obedience or the most servile humility. Always the whip falling onto the submissive back. Always the knife lopping off the gesture of rebellion [orig.: *insurrección*]. In this eternity, the tribe's destiny is fulfilled. Because it is the will of the gods that the Tzotzils remain. (1962b, 360–61)[1]

The survivors congregate in a cave, and in the center of the cave they form a circle, and in the center of the circle lies the ark, and from the center of the ark arises the word: "the divine word . . . the testament of those who were and the prophecy of those who are to come . . . the substance [that] the soul eats in order to live. The pact . . . the bridge between humanity and the divine" (361–62). The build-up goes on like this for a while. Now "the

71

eyes that brim with tears can close forever. What they have seen is their salvation [orig.: *los salva*]" (ibid.). The tribal authorities open the ark. Salvation awaits. Peasant secrets, what Octavio Paz once called "a buried treasure" (1950, 66) for the "urban man" (65), are about to be revealed.

Let us delay this revelation for now, although it will not be difficult to hold the thought. This is because we've seen it all before, probably many times. *Al monte:* the place where Mayanist works, from *Men of Maize* (Asturias 1949) to *Men with Guns* (Sayles 1998), end up. The Mexican writer Gregorio López y Fuentes, though not precisely Mayanist, established the template for this neoindigenist trope by ending his brilliant 1935 social-realist novel *El indio* with its unnamed protagonist retreating to higher ground, maimed and suspicious, armed and ready to defend indigenous lands from the contradictions of agrarian reform (123). And whether the scene is tinged with optimism, as in Asturias, or ambivalence, as in Sayles, it is a convention to imbue the dialectic of indigenous defeat and perseverance with something unsaid, indeed, unsayable. Even back down from the mountain and in open dialogue with Paz's "urban man," the indigenous subject is constructed through this unknowable excess, with Rigoberta Menchú's closing words of her testimony standing as the most famous and obvious example of our time.[2]

I have no intention of offering a new (yet another) theory of the secrets. The objective of this chapter is to advance our understanding of the political intervention communicated through Castellanos's prose fiction, which to this day, and remarkably, has been insufficiently considered. Her refusal—maybe even deconstruction—of this Mayanist convention, somewhere between rancor and hope, in which secrets are suggested, is important in this sense. What does Castellanos do with this scene? To begin to seriously contemplate this question, we need to first understand her approach to race and its uncanny reemergence at the center of intellectual discourse in mid-twentieth-century Mexico. *Oficio de tinieblas* will be the text most centrally at issue here, but within the context of a number of works, by Castellanos and others, that helped shape the reinvention of the idea of race in postrevolutionary Mexico.

To begin, it will be helpful to consider the nature of the conflict that propels *Oficio de tinieblas* and that also propels the Tzotzils to the mountain cave. This conflict is a race war. It is, of course, a race war in the literal sense, insofar as the novel is set up within the terms of a long history of rebellions in southern Mexico that have entered the historical record as "guerras de castas."[3] Castellanos's basic trick in *Oficio de tinieblas* is to take elements from one of the more spectacular of these uprisings, the notorious Chamula rebellion of 1867–69, and transport them to postrevolutionary Mexico.[4] Specifically, the scene—while never precisely dated—is the 1930s. This is the high point of the so-called *reforma agraria*, the land reform that included elements of redistribution. Its realization, however partial, is arguably the central plank of the postrevolutionary state.[5] It is associated with the presidency of Lázaro Cárdenas, the great statesman of revolutionary national populism. Cárdenas himself makes a narratively significant cameo appearance in the novel, and his absent presence looms large throughout. An unabashed *cardenista*, Castellanos nevertheless produces the signature critical reflection on the era.

The interesting move here, from the outset, is the conflation of race war (generally affiliated with a social-political dynamic historically transcended by the Revolution) and revolutionary agrarian reform. There is, in fact, no significant race war, as *guerra de castas*, in the land reform era. But there is another kind of race war floating around *Oficio de tinieblas*, and the historical postrevolutionary Mexico in which Castellanos worked, that at once complicates the conventional idea of race and also anchors real racialization. This is the "race war" that Michel Foucault will outline and provocatively "praise" (65) in his 1975–76 lectures translated as *"Society Must Be Defended"* (1976). His argument is complex and extends over several lectures, but to reduce it to its points of greatest relevance here, we can begin by saying that what Foucault calls the "discourse of race war" (65) is the theoretical center of his case for historicism (168–86). Historicism, for Foucault, is the great opponent of the juridical-philosophical tradition of sovereignty, the rise of universalist and disciplinary thought that ends with the totalizing discourse of peace, that is, the word of the king (state, government, sovereign) that declares the land to be at rest and the people to be one (111, 172–73). Historicism confronts this tradition with, precisely, history: not the fantastically universal history of sovereign right but "counterhistory," the materially partial history that recites the infinite catalogue of national crimes that underwrites all declarations of right and peace (69–76). The discourse of race war, in effect, tells history from one side and is arrogantly transparent about this fact.

Foucault loves this, and it is clearly why he praises his own reconceptualization of race in these terms: his race war is the origin of the expression of the fundamental right to rebellion (1976, 110). He writes: "The people have in a sense never ceased to denounce property as pillage, laws as exactions, and governments as domination. . . . Rebellion therefore is not the destruction of a peaceful system of laws for some reason. Rebellion is a response to a war that the government never stops waging" (108). So, on the one hand, this commitment to rebellion made palpable in race war will underwrite the modern idea of revolution; but now, and paradoxically, it will equally underwrite modern governmentality. In effect, Foucault argues, race war will be quickly captured, biologized, and transformed into the racist discourse of the state (82–83, 216): "Racism is, quite literally, revolutionary discourse in an inverted form" (81). This historical and conceptual turn represents the emergence of biopolitics, the discursive food that nourishes the great ideological projects of the twentieth century (239–63). Note the key move: race war emerges as one side of decentered camps; now as race struggle (the legacy of biologism), race war finds itself imported into the center of state power. The discourse of race moves from war to struggle, precisely a "struggle for survival," no longer like a battle between warriors but rather like an organism that must be kept alive. Foucault writes: "And the hoarse songs of the races that clashed in battles over the lies and laws of kings, and which were after all the earliest form of revolutionary discourse, become the administrative prose of a State that defends itself in the name of a social heritage that has to be kept pure" (83; see also 65).

It's a nice line, but what should we make of these "races that clashed in battles over the lies and laws of kings"? Once you pose the question— What of these "races"?—and track the text for answers—What is the idea of race at work here?—you can pretty quickly come to the conclusion that Foucault is handling a naïve, even vulgar, philosophical conceptualization of race.[6] When he does pause to attempt a definition, he is uncharacteristically cursory, and we see that what he means by "race" is basically "group" (77).[7] And yet this superficiality around one of the more frustratingly complicated categories of our time has a surprising conceptual virtue. It loosens up the term and liberates race, to some extent, from the hegemony of self-evident reductions to genetic descent, skin pigmentation, national origin, and so on. *Race* is linked to *war,* and the copula *race war* emerges as a way of telling. *Race war* is a name for the order of historical discourse that says no to peace. The group inscribed by the race of race war, then, is the product of historical construction (a fictive ethnicity, in Etienne Balibar's well-traveled vocabulary) and marks its boundaries at a shared story of victimization. Note well: this is not simply a fancy way of denoting "the weak," "the meek," or "the oppressed," at least not in our conventional postcolonial understanding of social inequality. That one line, riffing on Proudhon—"the people in a sense have never ceased to denounce property as pillage"—can be misleading (although it is crucial; note the immediate link to land). In fact, Foucault's great example, his case study of race war in action and the power of historicism, is that of an obscure French nobleman systematically denouncing the political consolidation of the bourgeoisie (115–88). This not on behalf of the laborer, bereft of capital, but in defense of the rights of the aristocracy, a race of privilege, a race of plenitude, a race of kings.

Whether historically sustainable or not, in structural terms Foucault's trajectory raises a host of interesting questions, and, moreover, I have high hopes that it can help to open new paths in the field of inquiry at issue here: that is, I am betting that this framework can help complicate the generic binary of "mestizo e indio" and the metaphysics of mestizaje that order the study of the idea of race in modern Mexico. If Foucault's "race war" is the reconceptualization of society in a binary mode, as a fight between decentered camps (the spatial dimension stands out), I would propose that taking Foucault's genealogy literally might get us back to basics and bring into focus the thing upon which that splitting rests. Far from getting us "beyond" race, this move will return us to the origin of all race thinking: land. That is, land, its conversion into territory, its unequal division, its relation to labor, and the centuries-long violence that overdetermines the political necessities articulating these processes. The interrelation between race and this historical dynamic (sometimes called "territorialization") is extravagant in the national context of Mexico; and yet, in that same context, it has been extravagantly undertheorized. To begin, simply recall, once more, the long social history of guerras de castas. What are these race wars? Wars over race? No. They are wars over land . . . made intelligible (or not) through race.

Race is traditionally thought about in terms of people, but ultimately (and originally) its politics becomes comprehensible only when it is contemplated in territorial terms: race is always, more or less explicitly, the racialization of space, the naturalization of segregation. Race orders space, social space, from the common to the private, and this conceptual relation becomes the

major fault line of liberalism's ideological dissonance, where the reconciliation of basic human freedoms with capitalist expansion proves elusive.
There is no way out: the privatization of the countryside becomes the
contemporary language of an ongoing primitive accumulation, the race
war wherein one civilization is forced to recede before the cultural logic
of another. The emergence of modern Mexico experienced this process in
dramatic form: for individual rights to be fully realizable, the land must be
rendered individual. The conversion of this historical-political process into
a natural relation is what we call ideology, and the marginal corners of the
nation are where—as Marx once said about the "barbarism of bourgeois
civilization" (1852, 335)—the violence of its basic truth goes naked.

Think back to Luis Alva and Ignacio Altamirano. Taken together, they
sound out the limits of the liberal critique of race. Their solutions to the problem of cultural difference are ultimately technocratic, expressed through a
logic, however critical, of civilizational development: good schools can produce good citizens, and good laws can lead to social justice. And yet, within
their discourse, all of this progressive governmentality revolves around the
category of race and its immediate articulation to space. Alva and Altamirano offered up a thoroughly schizophrenic treatment of race, symptomatic of the liberal impasse around the topic, reified in the figure of the Indian.
So on the one hand, there is the project of talking about race, namely, in
terms of Alva's "raza indígena," as a kind of social problem to be solved. On
the other hand, there is real racialization, as the naturalization of the relations between man and land, of who belongs where and on what terms.

Alva's essays can be read as a kind of case study in how the former
becomes a way of simultaneously articulating and obfuscating the latter.
He speaks to the many virtues of the Indian, but ultimately calls colonization—another word for resettlement—the practical means for tapping
indigenous energy as the lifeblood of the mestizo state. Altamirano, for his
part, offers up a heroically modern Indian but must arm him with a paramilitary mestizo in order to portray the politics of his novel as even remotely
convincing. Martín Sánchez makes the scene, and ends the novel, as the literary expression of an emergent *guardia rural* charged with clearing space
and making the countryside safe for capitalist accumulation. The author's
own discomfort before Martín Sánchez, and all the tortured justifications
of his role in state formation, are indicative of the fact that Altamirano has
arrived at the ideological limits that demarcate the mestizo state.

All liberalisms must negotiate this contradiction between the affirmative rights of individuals or groups and the authority of capitalist penetration. And there are infinite historical examples of this contradiction's becoming particularly extravagant at its site of racialization. Mexican liberalism is no exception, and, like all liberalisms, the contradiction can be more readily sublimated, as ideology, near its center. Far from the front lines of rural rebellion, federal pacification, and local militias, the urban intellectual could look past the miserable exclusion of the urban poor from political life and imagine the forces of primitive accumulation as an integrative process of modernization, articulating the countryside to a universal project of nation. After all, the basic terms that the mestizo state must negotiate are evident enough: the rule of law and the rule of the caudillo; the rights of the individual property owner and the rights of the collective land users; in short, the struggle between modernity and tradition. But these contradictions become more drastically dissonant, and yet newly productive, as one moves further and further out toward and into the edges of capitalist expansion.

Castellanos is the great storyteller of the ideological dissonance that gets churned up with these conflicts as they fracture and complicate the modern processes of nationalization. In a way, she was destined to take on this task. She was born in 1925, and her Mexico finds itself at the other end of a historical process. Whereas Alva's and Altamirano's world sought to spark national development through privatization, the failure of this politics to uniformly break up the massive (and unproductive) estates now has to answer to revolutionary demands for land and liberty. The agrarian policy of the nineteenth-century liberals is best symbolized by the Ley Lerdo and its uneven attempt to extinguish the collective forms of land tenure, most famously the *ejido* system associated with indigenous communities.[8] Part of the work of the Revolution is to overturn this agrarian politics, ultimately leading to new legal protections for the *ejido*.[9] The indigenous communities, once forcibly displaced from their traditional lands, now find the state invoking their name to the tune of reparation, with promises to redistribute the holdings of large estates.

Moreover, given her obsessive literary thematization of Chiapas—Mexico's southernmost and poorest state—and her own biography, which runs directly through the region, Castellanos had a perspective on postrevolutionary national development that was at once immediate and oblique.

A backwater of the national scene, Chiapas is something like the "deep South" of Mexico, with all the discursive weight implied by such a term intact, and it is a convention to speak of the dynamic of its basic race relations, between indigenous peoples of Maya descent (mainly Tzotzils and Tzeltals) and the nonindigenous "ladinos," as a kind of apartheid.[10] On many fronts it represents Mexico's limit case for the effective articulation of nation and state, the exception that so often becomes exemplary, a place where ideological contradictions visibly fester as open wounds. It is famous today for the ongoing rebellion of the modern Zapatistas.[11]

Castellanos lived there until she was a teenager, in a family that was socially prestigious but often financially embarrassed. A well-known aspect of her life story is her relocation to Mexico City as an adolescent, precisely provoked by the *reforma agraria* that had made rural existence tense (her family had a ranch). By her own account, the move saved her soul.[12] Blessed with a devastatingly critical insight and the drive to cultivate it, she flourished in the big city, moving from a distinguished high school performance to ample opportunities for advanced studies (she earned a master's degree in philosophy) and engaging government work. It is fair to say that she pretty much hated Chiapas, or at best that she found it an inexhaustible source of frustration. This attitude comes through from her early correspondence with Ricardo Guerra beginning in 1950 all the way to her later 1960s reflections on her work there with a government agency.[13] But Castellanos was tenacious, and she was inspired to engage with her past more seriously.

At age twenty-six, Castellanos rediscovered her home state, although not at first by returning to it; in fact, the desire to return began to take shape from a very great distance, during a sojourn in Europe. It was in Paris, wandering around the Pre-Columbian room of the Musée de l'Homme, that she was startled, nearly moved to tears, when she unexpectedly came across a humble display on Chiapas. The ecstatic moment, however, was not provoked by an ethnological presentation of her childhood family. Rather, it was a presentation of the artifacts of her family's servants. Suddenly the so-called Chamula Indians, now resonating at the very heart of the world family of mankind, spoke to her in a profound way.[14] Although she invests no great reflection on the episode in her love letter, the moment is a fitting symbol for a transformation of attitude that would morph into literature, soon appearing as the collection of poems *El rescate del mundo* (1952), which deals with Maya themes in virtuous tones. The Indian, or at least his surprise appearance in Paris, had led her back to Chiapas.

The story has a familiar ring. In fact, it is the generic conversion narrative of the urban intellectual, struggling with alienation and inauthenticity, and the subsequent encounter with a recollection, the recovery of something essential that has been lost or forgotten. That is, Castellanos had the basic experience that grounds all primitivism, wherein the alienated modern subject is drawn into a moment of self-discovery through the recuperation of what Estelle Tarica (2008), taking a cue from José María Arguedas, calls the "intimate" other. In the case of Castellanos's own *petit récit*, it is striking to note how harmoniously her version resonates with that of the other great literary Mayanist of the mid-twentieth century, Miguel Ángel Asturias. Having left Guatemala as a young man, and shortly after publishing a eugenic tract on the alleged degeneracy of the Maya, Asturias would also go through a kind of conversion in Europe: first gazing at the Maya display at the British Museum, then in his work with the great Mayanist of the Sorbonne, Georges Raynaud, who went so far as to identify Asturias as a "real Maya" (López Alvarez 1974, 75; see also Harss and Dohmann 1967). He was not a Maya at all, but he would weave this identity into a project of national literature, becoming a sort of bard of Maya culture, spinning indigenous-inflected tales from a host of cosmopolitan cities.

This is effectively the opposite of the route that Castellanos took. Dedicating herself to the postrevolutionary project of nation-state consolidation, she actively sought to participate in the developmentalist approach to the still tenacious "Indian problem." Perhaps it is this more urgent labor—her direct contact with the excruciating work of ideological transformation, her firsthand experience confronting real poverty and the social problems that it exacerbates—that accounts for the critical edge that we can perceive in Castellanos relative to Asturias. Whereas Asturias's art can stand as a devastating indictment of the big themes of history (capitalism, imperialism, colonial domination), he nevertheless seems committed to remaking the Maya as the bedrock of the Guatemalan nation. His Mayanism thus runs from a selection of trippy stories culled from Maya myth to the great surrealist novel of modern Latin American narrative to, ultimately, a coffee-table book extolling the transhistorical "permanence" of Maya civilization.[15] By the end of his life he has adopted the self-styled nickname El Gran Lengua, the tribal storyteller (see Harss and Dohmann 1967). Castellanos, in turn,

takes only one tentative step down this road, represented by the poems collected in *El rescate del mundo*. But things quickly come apart. Eight years
later, in her story "La rueda del hambriento" (1960f), Castellanos would
confront us with a young, naïve nurse who has come down from the big
city to do rural social service and is trying to save an indigenous baby from
starvation. The Indians are not able to pay for services, the doctor thinks
it is a ruse, and the infant is near death. Frantic, the nurse rushes to the
baby's father, presses ten pesos into his hand, and begs him to give it to
the doctor. Passing a joint to his father-in-law, the man stares back at her,
expressionless, and then states: "The pukuj is eating my son" (147). The
mother, with "no sign of anxiety," confirms her husband's authority and
continues to patiently braid her hair (ibid.). Another couple of years pass
until the publication of *Oficio de tinieblas*, where Castellanos presents the
same Chamulas whose rustic display at the Musée de l'Homme so inspired
her a decade earlier, now as they crucify a young child.

Images like these have led to a generalized assessment that Castellanos's
narratives are trapped within an exoticist commitment to indigenous eccentricity, irrationality, and, ultimately, barbarism. But this interpretation fails
to deal with the complexity of her critical project. We can begin to give
shape to this project by pressing the comparison with Asturias one step further. And while their distinct national contexts of Guatemala and Mexico
cannot be easily compared in terms of their respective histories of the idea
of race and real race relations, Guatemala and Chiapas resonate in ways
both historical and cultural.[16] Indeed, "Mexico," in Castellanos's Mayanist
work, is almost universally used to refer to a distant, foreign place; and in
both *Balún-Canán* and *Oficio de tinieblas*, "Guatemala" stands as a sort of
escape route for the ladino protagonists, as a source of paramilitary forces
and a space of greater colonial purity in the face of Mexican land reform.
Both authors mobilize the specificity of the Maya world toward critical ends
aimed at the dominant project of nation-state articulation. If Asturias uses
a stylized indigenous culture in order to make a claim on a more inclusive
national identity, Castellanos stages that same stylized indigenous culture
as part of a larger problematization of the politics of inclusion that serves
as the ideological foundation of the mestizo state.

We can highlight this distinction, and the political stakes that emerge
from it, through a quick comparison of both authors' turn to myths of origins in their respective works. Take the opening passages of *Oficio de tinieblas*. The tone is biblical, a solemn invocation of the First Days. But right

where we would expect an Edenic idyll of preconquest plenitude, we find instead an origins story steeped in violent conflict. The novel begins with the words "San Juan, the Guarantor [orig.: *el Fiador*]" (1), the force that "was there when the worlds first appeared" (ibid.). That is, at the origin we find not a Maya god but a transculturated Catholic figure, the creator that will establish the signs. But "those called Tzotzils, the People of the Bat" (ibid.), cannot interpret the signs, and that "was why the other men had to come, later…as if they came from another world" (ibid.). Without a paradise to be cast from, the initial condition of the world is a relation between masters and slaves, and notably missing is the requisite story of deliverance from bondage. In a similar tale that opens Castellanos's short story collection *Ciudad Real* (1960c), called "La muerte del tigre," the once fearsome people of the "community of the Bolometic" (15) end as so many migrant laborers, a "race deformed" by "centuries of submission" (17). By the end of the story, they are literally wasting away under a plague of capitalism (27). The referent is clear enough: it is the trace of a politics of force, of military domination, that extends from the Spanish conquest to the liberal reforms to the conservative reaction against postrevolutionary land management. The origin of the tribe is nothing more nor less than the secret of primitive accumulation, the ongoing violence exacted against their existence. The common thread that unites these and other tales of origins that punctuate Castellanos's work is their immediate articulation to violence, conquest, defeat. In other words, for Castellanos, indigenous identity always emerges, indeed, can emerge only from this historical trauma. Although this refusal of indigenous autonomy is itself an easy object of criticism, it also exhibits the virtue of dismantling, from the outset, any temptation presented by a romantic indigenism.

Now compare, for example, the ahistorical logic of Asturias when presenting a similar narrative. Equally cognizant of and emphatic about the fundamental centrality of European invasion for the formation of modern Maya identity, Asturias nevertheless clings to the idea of a prior history that can somehow be reconciled with national modernity. A kind of mystical Maya thus underwrites, and is incorporated into, his contemporary Guatemala. The ruins of ancient Maya civilization become the bedrock of the modern nation. When this tale—first articulated in the opening story of his collection *Leyendas de Guatemala* (1930), titled, precisely, "Guatemala"—becomes the surreal epic of *Hombres de maíz*, his happy ending can only gesture toward the fanciful return to a nonexistent nonplace: the utopia of a

Maya renaissance high up in the mountains, cut off from the real world, that is, from the more productive lowlands and the more immediate politics of the nation-state.[17] With no precolonial fantasy to rely on, in the work of Castellanos there is no utopian space to look toward and return to. Ironically, it is Asturias, the Marxian-inflected anti-imperialist, who presents utopia and hope without historical ground; Castellanos, in turn, gives us history and politics. There are no ruins in Castellanos. There is only the grind of everyday poverty, political expectations and their deflation, fire, and transcultural accidents.

She was not always this gloomy. During the mid-1950s Castellanos became directly involved in the cultural politics of nationalization, and these years are pivotal for the critical project that emerges from her literary writing. In 1956 she took a position in San Cristóbal de las Casas with the Centro Coordinador Tzeltal-Tzotzil. An arm of the state agency for indigenous affairs, the renowned Instituto Nacional Indigenista (INI), the Tzeltal-Tzotzil branch was the first and most prestigious of several regional offices established around the country with the aim of incorporating indigenous populations into national life. Its task was ambitious, and although it failed to even come close to achieving its goal of modernization, its aggressive, systematic, and sustained communication with indigenous communities around San Cristóbal spawned decades of research. Evon Vogt called its arrival "the most important event to affect Indian cultures since the Conquest" (cited in Hewitt de Alcántara 1984, 58). This is an exaggeration; military inscription during various civil wars (including the Revolution itself), land expropriation (or its threat) during the nineteenth-century liberal reforms, and the intensification of migrant labor during the early twentieth century had considerably greater effects on the dynamics of everyday life in indigenous communities. But the hyperbole is useful insofar as it recognizes the impressive intellectual capital and creativity invested by the INI during those years.[18]

The entire context was invigorating, for Castellanos found herself on the crest of one of the more ambitious waves in the Mexican history of the relations between the state and indigenous communities. Recruited by the historian Gastón García Cantú, she was working under the aegis of figures like Alfonso Caso, Gonzalo Aguirre Beltrán, and Julio de la Fuente—in short, a veritable star's list of midcentury national anthropology.[19] Castellanos was charged with projects of intercultural communication and propaganda at the Centro Tzeltal-Tzotzil. Much of this was accomplished through puppetry: she authored a series of didactic puppet plays—on hygiene, commerce, national history, racial pride, and the like—and assisted in their performance in indigenous villages throughout the region.[20] Her task was hard but rewarding: long days and nights with a group of talented artists and linguists, excruciating efforts at conceptual precision in translating from Spanish to Tzotzil and Tzeltal, regular performances of her work that involved enthusiastic crowds. She was there to see the immediate results of her own participation in a battle against ignorance, disease, and cowardice. She was there to see the debates that would ensue between the Indians and the puppets. She was engaged in the realization of race relations.[21]

The idea of race itself, however, was conceptually stalled. In Mexican intellectual history, as we have seen, thinking about the idea of race, in one way or another, leads the thinking subject to a preoccupation with the Indian, canonized in countless essays with variations on the title *El problema del indio,* such that "raza" ultimately becomes a language for speaking of "the Indian." But this relation is ideological. Concerns with the "raza indígena" have always been a way of working through a larger concern with the nation, more precisely, the articulation of nation to state. The best thinkers of the Reforma and the Porfiriato, far from relegating indigenous civilization to hopeless degeneracy (as is often supposed), were anything from optimistic to determined about the eventual Mexicanization of the indigenous communities, mainly through institutional means both affirmative (scholarship programs) and prohibitive (police programs). The methods would transform over time, at least in theory, but the objective of assimilation would remain intact.[22]

This immediate link between *raza indígena* and nation is made clear by the theoretical refinements that would underwrite the work of the INI: on the one hand, from Aguirre Beltrán, the idea that the Indian problem was actually a regional problem wherein the elites of "dominant mestizo cities" (1957, 165) stood as an obstacle to the nationalization of the indigenous communities (Aguirre Beltrán cited Chiapas as a paradigmatic case [ibid.]); on the other hand, from De la Fuente, the idea that the "Indian" was not an ethnic category at all but rather a caste marker promoted by local elites in order to maintain a relation of domination vis-à-vis the indigenous communities.[23] These theses, which are explicit in taking the nation as their conceptual horizon (Caso 1962, 12) and in pointing to the long-standing "Indian problem" as symptomatic of a larger dynamic of exploitation, both historical (8) and economic (Caso 1955, 138)—in effect, as a

mestizo problem—would guide the work of the Centros. As a young aco-
lyte who had absorbed the tenets of the new anthropology and its political
activism, Castellanos would productively mobilize its premises and convert
them into literary material. But she transcends the mere aestheticization of
social-scientific theory. Indeed, one consequence of her prose fiction is to
illuminate theory's translation into a state-sponsored policy agenda and,
in so doing, to expose its fragility against the gravitational pull of racial
discourse: as the canonical racialized identity, the mestizo elites residing
in rural towns were, at most, a marginal object of the INI's work; it was
a Centro *Tzeltal-Totzil*, that is, a center whose referent was the specifically
indigenous communities.[24] The practical model ends up being one of inter-
lopers attempting to address what they understand as a specifically *Indian*
problem—what INI director Alfonso Caso calls "what are considered to
be negative cultural elements" (1962, 7)—when the theory prescribed a
wider and more "holistic" regional one (Aguirre Beltrán 1957, 165–66).
Moreover, while the INI model for thinking about the Indian problem as a
more nuanced indio-mestizo social relation holds the promise of emerging
from empirically grounded ethnographic work, the diagnosis and prescrip-
tion are surprisingly slight departures from the intuition of old liberals like
Luis Alva. Beyond the reversal on the virtue of communal property, which
was now to be promoted (Caso 1962, 10), and the prioritization of "per-
suasive" methods that seek acculturation "cordially" (Caso 1955, 143,
145)—in the words of Sol Tax, "We want to awaken hope" (cited in Caso
1962, 12)—the perceived problem of the indigenous communities is still
their alleged absence from national life, their segregation from and exploitation by mestizo society (Caso 1955, 144). The will to dominate of the
elite stratum of this social formation cuts off the Indian from the nation.
And here the reasoning turns into sand: *thus we must work to acculturate the
Indian.* Although centers of mestizaje—regional cities—have now become
conceptualized as an obstacle to nationalization, *mestizaje* as a cultural process—for anthropologists, acculturation—is still understood as an inevitable and ultimately promoted goal (Caso 1955, 1962; Aguirre Beltrán 1957;
De la Fuente 1965). What the protagonists of the INI have basically done,
then, is to take the outlines of liberal positive law and make them developmentalist. They were whistling the nineteenth-century tune, maybe in a
slightly more sophisticated key.

   And indeed, Caso's INI was not the first attempt at a formalized Indian
policy. Its modern prehistory can be traced through the universal education

and literacy plans (theorized but unrealized) of the nineteenth-century liberals that were aimed at a largely indigenous peasantry; land development schemes, from the Lerdo privatization act to colonization projects (equally unrealized) that were often explicitly proposed as modes of acculturation; and the nineteenth-century institutionalization of anthropology as a discipline that would take on the Indian problem as its raison d'être.[25] By 1910, a philologist named Francisco Belmar (also the chief magistrate of the Supreme Court) took the initial step toward institutionalizing the Indian problem as such.[26] He spearheaded the formation of the Sociedad Indianista de México, dedicated to applying new methods in sociology and philology to the question of how indigenous communities "evolve." In an interview, he explains that in some "regions of the isthmus, the Indians have evolved on their own" and asks, "How have they done this?" The objective of the Sociedad would be to foment intellectual collaboration on these kinds of questions, gain a deeper understanding of the Indian problem, and thereby guide state policy (*El Imparcial*, 1910a, 1). Its momentous inaugural conference was attended by a horde of dignitaries, including foreign diplomats; the dean of Mexican social history and minister of education, Justo Sierra (*El Imparcial*, 1910d, 1); and none other than Porfirio Díaz himself (*El Imparcial*, October 31, 1910b, 1, 10).[27]

This was in November 1910. It was colossally bad timing, although there seems to be something symbolically correct about the institutionalization of the Indian problem coinciding with the collapse of the very institutions that would prop it up. By the time the conference realized its first concrete "achievement," the headlines praising a senator and *hacendado* who had committed to a literacy program for his serfs had to share space with news of simmering unrest in Oaxaca, Chihuahua, and Quintana Roo (*El Imparcial*, 1910e, 1). Less than a year later, Díaz is on a boat to France. The coincidence, though, is suggestive: the formal institutionalization of the state's interest in the indigenous communities as a *racial* problem seems to run alongside the increasing tension in the countryside that would ultimately spill out into the great *national* crisis of the century.

Now, there is no special insight or scandal in noting the national concerns of an emergent indigenismo: the relation is widely known and universally recited. The reason I emphasize it is because, in spite of its self-evidence, this tight ideological articulation among race-thinking, nation-thinking, and the Indian as an analytical puzzle to be problematized still sits on the margins of the history of the idea of race in Mexico. What I mean to say is that while the relation is universally noted, it has been insufficiently thought through. In spite of everything, we still have the basic formula: race = Indian. Paradoxically, this seems to miss the basic impulse of indigenism itself. To understand the nature of the paradox, we need to return to the conditions of possibility of the INI, its prehistory, and theorization in Mexico's foundational *indigenista:* Manuel Gamio.

While Mexico's first attempt at formally institutionalizing the "Indian problem" accompanied the collapse of the political world that defined its basic terms, this was of course only the beginning. Beltrán's Sociedad, like the administration of Porfirio Díaz that supported it, was ultimately backward-looking, premised as it was on liberal boilerplate and clear lines of civilizational advance. But a more progressive revolution was already under way in the field of anthropology, one whose impact on the idea of race in Mexico must not be underestimated.

This disciplinary transformation arrived in the form of Franz Boas, the massively influential anthropologist associated with Columbia University in New York. Coincidentally, in 1910, the same year that saw the founding of the Sociedad, Boas was contracted by the Secretaría de Instrucción Pública to present a series of courses at the Escuela Nacional de Altos Estudios. In the wake of the successful XVII Congreso Internacional de Americanistas, hosted in Mexico City, much international enthusiasm had been generated around Mexico as fertile ground for anthropological research, with eager institutional support to boot. The year 1910 became even more momentous as the Díaz administration signed off on a cutting-edge consortium (including Columbia, Harvard, the University of Pennsylvania, and the Prussian government) for advanced studies: the Escuela Internacional de Arqueología y Etnología. Boas would become its second director for the academic year 1911–12. The Escuela itself ran into the same social upheaval that truncated the Sociedad, and for all intents and purposes it folded in 1914 (formally it limped along, through all kinds of revolutionary strife at home and World War I abroad, until 1920) (see Rivermar Pérez 1987, 103–10). Despite this short duration, the Escuela established the intellectual and institutional clout of the man involved in much of its research agenda and who transferred this energy into the establishment of anthropology as a modern science in Mexico. This was Manuel Gamio. Given that the central—indeed, almost total—preoccupation of Mexican anthropology is the study of indigenous Mexicans, it is fair to say that Gamio can also be understood as the starting point of modern indigenism in Mexico.[28]

Gamio was a student of Boas. His work and insights as a young practitioner were so impressive that the American archaeologist Zelia Nuttal recommended him to Boas with enough enthusiasm to promptly earn him a scholarship to study at Columbia beginning in 1909. When he returned home with his master's degree it was 1911, and he was just in time to continue his work with Boas, now at the Escuela and more than willing to continue the collaboration. As one of only two Mexican students participating in the Escuela, Gamio had ample exposure to international methods and paradigms, and he took advantage of the chance to apply their consequences directly to Mexico's tenacious Indian problem (see Rivermar Pérez 1987, 107–8).

Boas's intervention in the history of the idea of race is significant and it is ultimately here that Gamio cites his influence most consistently. Emerging out of the radical materialism that the Darwinian revolution had brought to the scientific world and the denaturalization of race that it implied, Boas is decisive in propelling the contextualist, or particularist, turn in anthropological studies.[29] Among his many contributions, his most important is the systematic rigor that he brought to the broad critique of race that was already afoot. In effect, Boas represents the crucial transition, still a foundation of contemporary multiculturalism, in thinking about human difference: from the fundamentally essentialist terms of race (as always ultimately rooted in descent, in man's relation to a genetic line) to the fundamentally contextualist terms of culture (as always ultimately rooted in human practice, as man's relation to the natural world). For Boas, every culture is complete, that is, corresponds to its environment. And every culture is in constant transformation, which is not to say evolution; cultures are not works in progress and are not moving from lower to higher. To claim the superiority or inferiority of identifiable human groups, from this perspective, is a social construction, a way of naturalizing historical accidents. Gamio brings this conceptual turn to Mexico: he helps to normalize a move from race to culture that was already apparent in some of the best thinkers of the Porfiriato.[30]

But as Boas's own work demonstrates, we cannot simply shake race by changing the terminology. In "Human Faculty as Determined by Race"

(1894), a watershed statement on racial discourse that would conceptually underwrite his most renowned work, *The Mind of Primitive Man*
(1911b), Boas concludes that all races are more or less the same in terms
of faculty and that it is cultural practices that should guide our study of
human societies. Nevertheless, he continues, it is the "white race" that
tends to produce the most geniuses and great men. So even while making
the case for culture, it is no surprise to find Gamio still trapped by a conceptual language that resonates race: he will study the Indian, and he will
talk about him in relation to the European, the creole, the mestizo, and so
on. Old racialized categories continue to guide his new culturalist work.
And within the parameters of his culturalism, the fundamental ideological
project will continue to be framed as the necessity to *forjar patria*, that is,
as we will see, to produce a national race. A certain disconnect thus arises
between teacher and student. For Boas, the basic tension exists between
race and culture, with the goal of displacing the former in favor of the latter. For Gamio, the fundamental tension exists between race and nation,
with culture operating as something like a mediating term, the bond that
will link the one to the other.

   This disarticulation between Boas's "race and culture" and Gamio's
"race and nation" is symptomatic of a greater tension that inhabits the
early twentieth-century field of anthropology in general. When Gamio
invokes the language of Boas, only to pivot toward the project of forging
a national race, it can at first come off as a puzzling contradiction or mis-
application. But it is again important to remember Roberto Schwarz and
the potential productivity of ideas out of place. Boas's thought brings us
toward a more systematic account of human variation and its coeval transformation. For Boas, any utility that race may have in speaking of human
types disappears once we begin to speak of the "quality" of a people: there
may be something biological to race, but racial inequality is historical.
Race "science," bent on demonstrating superiority and inferiority, confuses
race with history and civilizational advance with violence (1894). Writing from the institutional perspective of an emergent imperial power, Boas
has a vision of a particularist diversity that implies a multiculturalism that
destabilizes the idea of the nation, making it accidental, a modern form of
political hegemony as transient as all that have preceded it. For Gamio, to
embrace these premises would be an act of escapism. Writing at a moment
when the nation-state is now globally hegemonic and yet from the institu-

tional perspective of a nation-state trying to piece itself back together as a coherent politicoeconomic formation, it is no surprise that he privileges the nation form. If Boas represents the imperial interest in the exoticism of human diversity, Gamio represents the national interest in the acceleration of modernization.[31] In other words, there is a distinction in terms of the anthropological object itself: Boas travels to remote corners of the Pacific Northwest in order to bring back anthropological truths; Gamio travels to a suburb of Mexico City in order to identify national obstacles.[32] This disarticulation, of course, has nothing to do with the personalities of the two men in question or their willingness to think expansively and universalize their findings. It is the determination of local conditions that produce distinct notions of universality.[33] For Boas, this implies the human family and its infinite diversity of forms. For Gamio, this implies the national family and the need to forge its diversity of forms into an identifiable pueblo.

Gamio's lasting influence in Mexican anthropology stems from a number of important empirical studies, but outside of anthropological and archaeological circles he is usually, and correctly, remembered for the ideological contributions that he most fiercely articulated in his signature work, *Forjando patria*.[34] A strange and inspired text somewhere between a manifesto and an instruction kit, it was originally published in 1916, during the tumultuous first decade of the Revolution. Situated about halfway between Molina Enríquez's *Los grandes problemas nacionales* (1909; swallowed up by the Revolution) and Vasconcelos's *La raza cósmica* (1925; published in exile), it represents the great ideological statement of national culture from the early revolutionary period. It is in *Forjando patria* (1916) that Gamio articulates his central conceptual innovation, most clearly expressed in a chapter called "El concepto cultural." He begins by asserting that there is no such thing as innate inferiority, whether expressed as race or as culture. Every culture is accidental and specific, a "conjunto" (103) of ideas and materials. In Boasian terms, every culture is *complete*. He writes:

> Culture is the cluster of material and intellectual manifestations that characterizes human groupings; but it doesn't allow for speculation on gradations in terms of cultural superiorities, nor does it anachronistically classify peoples [orig.: *pueblos*] into learned and primitive [orig.: *cultos e incultos*]. . . . Every people [orig.: *pueblo*] possesses the culture that is inherent to its ethnosocial nature and to the physical and biological conditions of the land [orig.: *suelo*] that it inhabits. (103–4)

People, in their "ethnosocial nature," make culture in service of the necessities determined by the "ground" (or land) that they "inhabit." It's a problematic perspective for Gamio, for it would seem to make impossible any ethical notion of national "development." If every culture is complete, and if there is no innately qualitative distinction—the objective difference between cultural "manifestations . . . never connotes the specific quality of said manifestations" (105)—this then leads to a necessarily relativistic conclusion, that all cultures are effectively equal. Thus the ethical dilemma: How can modernizing development be justified? Development toward what?

The solution lies within the very terms of the Boasian outlook that Gamio is here misapplying, but productively so. Boas's anthropology teaches us that there is no innate inequality (thus race is displaced) and that there is also no adaptive inequality (thus cultural hierarchy is displaced). Each set of human practices that we understand as a culture satisfies its relations to its context. Contexts, however, are objectively different. And indeed, one can imagine an inequality of context. This is precisely the picture painted for us in Mexico's first neoindigenista work, Gregorio López y Fuentes's *El indio* (1935). The basic social problem at work in *El indio*, a kind of literary companion to *Forjando patria*, is the thesis that land cultivated by Mexico's indigenous communities is poor land. And this has nothing to do with the Indians, their cultural practices, or their innate abilities. It has everything to do with historical contingencies, a legacy of violent conquest, and the fact that this has created a response in which the indigenous communities avoid national development; that is, they avoid white people and the more fertile lands that white people have occupied. This narrative helps illustrate Gamio's equivocation, or correction, which is made subtly explicit at the point where he cites Boas directly. Taking up Boas's famous critique of race, as published in *The Mind of Primitive Man*, Gamio confirms that "assumed innate inferiority does not exist" between different cultural groups. But then, departing from Boas, he continues: "*except for that which is produced* [orig.: *sino que es producida*] by causes of historical, biological, or geographical factors [orig.: *orden*]" (1916, 23, my emphasis). Inferiority exists, but it is contextual: historical, biological, geographical. And with this we have exited the realm of Boas's critical position while nevertheless relying upon it. We can understand it as a misreading, willful or not, but the larger point is that here Boas has traveled to a new world, one with its own specific historical determinations. Bridging these worlds represents the center of Gamio's project.

The parameters of Gamio's diagnosis are now obvious: the indigenous communities of Mexico find themselves *out of context*. Their natural environment has been destroyed, and with that their cultural practices have degraded. Moreover, and already pointing toward the mid-century indigenistas, Gamio can bring a new theoretical language to the old conclusion that the indigenous communities are, in effect, alienated from the natural setting of modern life: the nation. Thus alienated, the Indian becomes denaturalized, the exception to Boasian universality. The Indian is degenerate. López y Fuentes again brings literary description to this idea. One chapter of *El indio* revolves around an impressive ritual, still popular with tourists, in which men swing around a tall pole (a *volador*) at frightening speed and height. But modern individualism and hard liquor have changed the dynamics of the ceremony, now reduced to brash oneupmanship and drunken risk-taking (1935, 57). Disaster ensues, and an Indian, thrown from the *volador*, ends up staggering around with his face literally torn off from the force of its collision with the ground (58–59). The metaphor of the maimed—a favorite of López y Fuentes—is more than clear: in modern Mexico, the cultural practices of the Indians no longer resonate, and with the coherence of their very identity shattered, they flounder, faceless, searching without goal for meaning. These Indians, in effect, are the indigenous communities that Gamio had portrayed at Teotihuacán, in a more scientific tone, a decade earlier.

Gamio's understanding of the Indian problem—impoverished context leads to a culture of poverty, further feeding impoverishment—should guide him to an elementary solution. The trick is not to change the people, a project that, as history teaches, succeeds mainly in provoking resistance and sowing resentment. The trick is to change the context. In other words, the terms of development need to be rethought. Gamio himself was not ready to do this: he prescribed schools, literacy and hygiene campaigns, the expansion of the Spanish language among indigenous communities, and a general intervention by experts, in short, a generic program of aggressive acculturation. He was also insistent and influential in championing what he perceived as the best aspects of indigenous culture, namely, artistic creativity. It was not until the mid-1930s that his friend and fellow Boasian, Moisés Sáenz, would come to a more elegantly contextualist solution to the Indian problem. Confronted with the fact that many of the villagers whose lives he was trying to modernize through schools modeled on John Dewey's "action" theory of pedagogy were quite content with their traditional ways of life, Sáenz concluded, "[As] far as change goes, I'd bet more on the road than the rural school to bring it about" (cited in Hewitt de Alcántara 1984, 15). While different sorts of pedagogical initiatives continued full force—up to and including Castellanos's puppets—Sáenz's comment crystallizes the common ground from Alva to Gamio to the INI's Centros: the indigenous communities need to be pried free of their isolation, put on the map, and integrated into the web of (commercial) relations that constitute the national community.

Equipped with the latest in anthropological innovations, Gamio stated a position on the Indian problem that was nevertheless not so far from that of Alva: methods and tone aside, they share the common goal of transforming the Indian's cultural practices. And if we pose the simple question of what indigenous cultural practices need to be transformed into, we can quickly arrive at another important element that links Gamio to Alva and the two of them to all who have ever proposed that the Indian is a "social problem" to be solved. It soon becomes clear that the fundamental object of their work is not really the Indian. Their preoccupation is the nation. Their language for approaching that concern is the mode of thinking about cultural difference in the modern world known as race. The "raza indígena," even dressed up as a set of cultural practices, stands as the glaring symptom of Mexico's failure to articulate nation and state.

This semantic slippage becomes apparent if we track Gamio's conceptual work around the race and culture relation with greater attention to the subjects of his prose. Both through the specific example of *Forjando patria* and through much of his life's work, Gamio gives the distinct impression that he is mostly preoccupied with the fate of Mexico's indigenous communities: *Forjando patria* famously opens with an evocative explanation of how the development of America's indigenous cultures was truncated; several of its most influential chapters—"La redención de la clase indígena," "Prejuicios sobre la raza indígena y su historia," "El concepto del arte prehispánico," and the like—are explicitly dedicated to thinking about aspects of the indigenous communities; he establishes a methodology for measuring indigenousness through a census; he serves as the director of the Instituto Indigenista Interamericano for eighteen years (1942–60); and he dedicates significant effort to hardscrabble fieldwork in an attempt to better understand the indigenous communities and the social problems specific to them, including intense lobbying for agrarian reforms that would improve their economic situation (see Lomnitz 2001,

252). And yet, at the crucial moment of making the cultural turn in think-ing about human difference, the Indian is not to be found. The move is not motivated by a plea to situate the Indian's place in world culture, within the universal family of man. Instead, it is about situating Mexico's place in the family of nations.

In setting the tone for "El concepto cultural," Gamio writes: "Any Mexi-can that has been in Europe or North America has encountered, without doubt, the qualification of an 'uneducated people' [orig.: *pueblo inculto*] with which they grace us over there. . . . The insult isn't worth screaming about, but it does move one to set the record straight" (1916, 103). The subject here is not the Indian, mired in poverty and isolation, whose worldview has been unfairly judged as "inculta." The subject is the worldly Mexican, trav-eling in Europe (or studying in New York), who finds his sensibilities upset when confronted with the dismissive snobbery of the pseudoenlightened (ibid.). This subject, in turn, stands in for "cualquier mexicano," although in reality this traveling Mexican can of course connote only a very limited, and very elite, sector of society. This is a decisive moment in Gamio's early work. The culturalist turn inspired by Boasian anthropology is not here put forth in order to rethink the ethical responsibilities that might govern the relations between the indigenous communities and the mestizo state. Indeed, Gamio is no more progressive than Alva (who invokes the justice of reparation) and Altamirano (who invokes his own biography) on this point. His motivation, made explicit throughout the chapter, is to rethink the nature of cultural hierarchies that place Mexico "below" the old bastions of cultural capital represented by Europe. The objective is to relativize, and thereby destabilize, that relationship: "We don't understand European art, we don't 'feel' it, one must confess as much; Europeans, for their part, neither understand nor feel our art" (107). The objective, in short, is to locate Mexico's place in and relative to Western culture: to *forjar patria.* And for anyone who might miss the not-so-subtle title, the original work carries an often deleted subtitle: *Pro-nacionalismo.* Mexico's great text on race, and its founding document of *indigenismo,* is about the nation. If the Indians are important, this is insofar as they can be brought into that political community.

Now, within the terms of the nation-building project, the Indian will be crucial, but not necessarily as Indian, that is, not as the symbol of a set of semiautonomous cultures whose historical motivations have, at different times and with variable intensity, been at odds with the project of nation. The Indian is important *as Mexico.* Indigenous communities will hence play a significant dual role. First, in the specificity of their cultural practices, the indigenous communities represent a source of cultural originality, the necessary ingredient of *mestizaje* that makes Mexico extra-European. Second, in their abject social condition, the indigenous communities function as the symbol of a national project of development as yet unrealized, but still very much in progress. The explosion of national culture in the wake of the Revolution confirms this indigenist dyad over and again and across the genres, from the visual arts to music to dance to literature. Although Alva made a ferocious case and Altamirano stood as the confirmation of a liberal model, it is only with the Revolution that the mestizo state and its cultural elite will begin to internalize a widespread feeling that the fate of the nation is also the fate of the Indian and that the Indian, in what Tarica would call an "intimate" way, is part of the national *us*.[35] The work of anthropology—in the literal sense, the ethnographer conducting field-work—is to foment the conditions of mutual understanding, to invoke and produce the "indigenous soul" (Gamio 1916, 25) that can make integral a nation struggling to ward off literal disintegration.

So this new language of coexistence, integration, and inner-indigenism is literally emerging out of an unprecedented explosion of national violence, the constellation of civil wars known as the Revolution. Gamio addresses this social spasm directly; indeed, *Forjando patria* is largely about how to harness revolutionary energy and invest it in a new national hegemony. For Gamio, the Revolution is an inevitable, even healthy, political upheaval that nevertheless needs to be reined in. The Revolution, as historical fact, is symptomatic of an ongoing social struggle, like Mariano Azuela's revolutionary "hurricane," a "natural phenomenon [orig.: *acontecimiento*], entirely natural" (Gamio 1916, 167). It is significant that, in order to explain this dialectic of justified protest and its productive transformation, Gamio will invoke a broader language of race. The Revolution, he argues, emerges out of atmospheric conditions: *"economic inequality between social classes, heterogeneity of the races that constitute the population, difference in languages and divergence or antagonism between cultural tendencies"* (167, emphasis in original). The Revolution, in so many words, is a race war. Recalibrating the nation in the wake of this outburst of social rage, and guiding it to a soft landing, will depend on a more profound understanding of the specific needs of this "heterogeneity of races that constitutes the population" (ibid.).[36] This heterogeneity of races, in Gamio's writings, is in reality more of a binary and most explicitly points to the presence of the Indian. Toward the end of the book, in a chapter called "Urgente obra nacionalista," he offers up a typology, describing various indigenous communities and the specificity of their relations with the nation at large. Most illuminating is when he turns to Morelos, one of the focal centers of Revolutionary activity, and proposes Zapatismo, in general, as a type of "legitimate" indigenous political practice ("indianismo," he calls it) (177). Three qualities of Zapatismo stand out: it is just; it is local; and it is temporary (177–78). That is, the state, through good Indian policy, must ensure that it is temporary and that the localism of its protagonists is integrated into the national web of economic and social relations (178–80).

All the way through the Porfiriato, Foucault's race war was never fully channeled into a thoroughly modern biopolitics of race. Even at institutional sites like Belmar's Sociedad Indianista or Boas's Escuela Internacional, the Indian still functioned as an alien being, something to be studied and understood. Policy generally reflected this discourse: the relation of the mestizo state to the indigenous communities was based on different forms of what Gamio correctly calls "cultural antagonism," whose expression emerged through an infinite interplay of invasion, rebellion, repression, negotiation, and abandonment. Uprisings, in turn, were articulated through the language of race war, not in any kind of anthropological sense (this race fighting against that one) but rather in the Foucauldian sense. That is, as uprisings from Julio López to Tomochic and back to Independence itself make clear, organized violence was grounded in the invocation of a counterhistory, a recitation of the crimes of the powerful and shared victimization that demanded restorative justice. The Revolution ostensibly ended this cycle. In keeping with Foucault's account, a hallmark of the modern state is the effective appropriation and internalization of the energy of race war, such that the struggle against the enemy becomes vigilance over society. The state maintains a state of war, now charged with extirpating the sickness that society itself produces (1976, 62). There is a trajectory of significant thinkers that alert the intelligentsia to this task as Mexico modernizes in the nineteenth century, from Gabino Barreda to Justo Sierra to Andrés Molina Enríquez. The Revolution would be symptomatic of their failure but would also establish the task for the postrevolutionary state that would follow.

Gamio's *Forjando patria* is the hinge from race war to state racism, which is not to say that it is any more racist, in the conventional sense, than the intellectual culture in which it resided. Gamio was sincere in his outlook, and there is no reason to doubt the depths of his concern for and affection toward the indigenous communities that he studied. But this in no way prevents his essay from executing the move to state racism in the literal, technical sense invoked by Foucault: he takes on the task of racializing the nation in a systematic, scientific language. And he links this language to concrete state policy. Most significant, and in keeping with revolutionary doctrine, is agrarian reform. A stake in the land will translate to a stake in the nation, leading to incremental social collaboration, transformation, transculturation, and, ultimately, production.

And there stands the Indian, still a problem, no longer the alien race to be defeated (pacified), now the very soul of the nation, whose sickness is the sign of the sickness that society itself produces. For about five decades, the postrevolutionary anthropological establishment in Mexico was generally optimistic about the possibilities of combating the ills of the countryside and making the nation well. Literary producers were less sanguine, and again we can turn to López y Fuentes and his role in ushering in the dark turn to neoindigenismo and its problematization of the mestizo state's attempts to guide the race war to a modern biopolitical agenda. *El indio* is a precise distillation of liberal unease as the politics of land reform begin to unfold. Revolution comes to the unnamed village that is the setting of the novel and agrarian reform begins to take hold, and along with it the emergence of paramilitary forces to retake "the former lands of the *hacendado*" (1935, 118), now in the process of redistribution not to the local Indians but to a new set of men with guns. The race war rolls on, and the project of integration is stifled by its deep-rooted history, where race cuts most sharply at the political division of space. The novel closes with an image of the unnamed protagonist, "el lisiado"—the maimed—on watch from his "hidden lookout." He represents "mistrust" itself, "spying on the highway—which is civilization. . . . Like all of his people, who only know that the *gente de razón* want to attack them; that in the hills and in the valley, hate, in packs, bares its fangs" (123). El lisiado inhabits, in one body, the painful contradictions of a misplaced revolution, and it is a fitting symbol that the thugs of unregulated land reform are called *guardias blancas*.[37] El lisiado stands at the intersection of violence and land that marks the space of race. That is, the Indian problem is the problem of the Indian's being caught at this point. El lisiado is the still incoherent national "us" that Gamio seeks to make whole. He has the head of a man and the twisted torso of a child, stunted in its development, a victim not of degeneracy but of history: he was disfigured in his youth by gold prospectors when he refused to reveal tribal secrets (16–22). The social mirror of *Pedro Páramo,* living rancor, he stands watch, waiting, bilious, a protagonist in the race war that roils beneath a postrevolutionary peace. Dealing with this is Gamio's challenge, a challenge that, four decades after *Forjando patria* and some twenty years after *El indio,* remains unresolved. This is what Rosario Castellanos discovered in 1950s Chiapas. *Oficio de tinieblas* is the great literary exploration of the race war without end.

More explicitly than any other modern writer, Castellanos captures these complexities in the Mexican race–nation dynamic. It is no surprise that we remember and love (or hate) Castellanos for her provocative portraits of indigenous Mexicans. Think of the lasting images that radiate from the pages of *Oficio de tinieblas:* the machinations of the ilol, the rage of the rebel, the transcultural comedies around the sacristran, the child of rape born under the sign of the eclipse, the crucifixion. But these fantastic evocations of indigenous life are only half the story, and in fact not even half the story. The Chiapas of *Oficio de tinieblas* is a totality, and at its center are neither indios nor ladinos but the routes and circuits that bind the two into one. San Juan Chamula over here, Ciudad Real over there: what brings these spaces into the novel, together, is precisely the superficiality of their segregation, their lack of disparity, their profound interconnectedness. As Joseph Sommers points out in the first substantial analysis of the novel, it is the "interpenetration" (1978, 87) and "interdependency" (82, 87) of the two communities that stand out, not their mutual isolation.[38]

As we saw earlier, with the creation myth that opens the novel, the beginning of the world invokes the Tzotzils and their conquerors as an internally volatile unity. And beyond the basic historically grounded facts that ladino children are raised by indigenous servants or that the economic basis of the region is sustained by Maya labor, even at the level of plot the interpenetrated social world is brought to the fore: the first narrative strand of the novel follows a group of indigenous women as the local political economy leads them from the village to the town and back again, introducing the events, transactions, and modes of intercultural contact that will put the larger story into motion.

The center of the novel, then, is the space in between, and the ambience of the story is that of one big contact zone, a totalizing landscape in which the various actors and communities are pulled together. The basic narrative movement traces the violence of this gravitational attraction (the women go to town to sell their wares) and the infinite means by which it is shattered and resegregated over and again (in town, custom dictates that they walk in the gutters). Put a different way, the novel stages the empirical reality of a desegregated world, then confronts us with the political forces that reassert the hierarchies of segregation. Race always returns to segregation, and the dialectic of resegregation that defines the cultural world of Chiapas can be illuminated if we simply trace race.

One striking example of the critical productivity of Castellanos's rigor on this theme is the complicated racialization of the Indians. Throughout the novel, the Indians are not Indians but Chamulas, the Tzotzils of San Juan Chamula. They become racialized, as Indians, only when appropriated as migrant labor, brought into industrial monoculture, and alienated from the land. There is a specific scene in which this happens, and it is worth recalling as an early sign of the subtlety with which Castellanos handles and problematizes race. Chapter 6 revolves around Pedro Winiktón, the judge, and his tenure as a migrant laborer on the farm of the progressive (a relative term) landowner Adolfo Homel. While there, Pedro Winiktón learns to read (through a program set up by Homel) and has a fateful meeting with "the president," whom, although unnamed, we recognize as Lázaro Cárdenas in a literary reenactment of his visit to the region, where he famously traveled to promote the revolutionary reforms. The significance of the scene is the way in which the experience conflates Pedro's *concientización*—his raised consciousness—with racialization, and that relation directly with the land. In addressing the workers, the president gives shape to the language of protest simmering inside Pedro, as yet inarticulate but now with a name and an objective: "justice." Here is how Pedro receives the president's promise: "Unable to represent it to himself in the abstract, Pedro linked it inextricably from that time on to a fact with which he had intimate and immediate experience: the possession of the land" (1962b, 52). But a problem immediately presents itself. Marked by suffering, defrauded of the land, living injustice, the race is apathetic, silent, hermetic, ultimately riven. Race, with all of its seductive powers to unite, reveals its true face as it divides. On the work gang, Pedro makes a remark on unfair treatment, to which somebody replies: "It was your fate to be born an Indian" (44). He reflects: "Indian. The word had often been thrown in his face, an insult. But now, spoken by someone of the same race, it served to establish a distance, to divide those who were united at the root. This was Winiktón's first experience of solitude and he could not endure it without remorse" (44–45). Even as race, the Indian is shattered, alone. Paradoxically, the "indigenous community," in Castellanos's work, is marked by its utter lack of common cause.

At the same time, the novel fairly oozes with the affirmative racialization of the ladinos, the Coletos who consume bottomless psychological capital concocting the most outlandish genealogies that certify their own racial exceptionalism, their direct descent from a race of conquerors, and their relation to the land as certification of this precarious bloodline. Manuel Mandujano, the unbridled priest sentenced to deliver the Indians from the demonic legion that every day infiltrates their ambivalently fanatic Catholicism, sums up the Coleto consciousness: "Pride in their ancestors, in their prosperity, in their race" (1962b, 98). The legacy of the "race" includes the exploitation of the Indians as a natural right: "Who would condemn someone for shaking a tree that belongs to no one in order to enjoy its fruits? Who could possibly take seriously the aberrant belief that trees are people and should therefore be respected as such?" (97). And yet, this racial "pride that had remained intact for centuries" is unstable: it "was beginning to crack only now" (98). Race masquerades as nature, but of course it is born and maintained through narrative. By nature race is indeed precarious, and as if to drive this point home, Castellanos populates her Coleto world with the questionable genealogies of social climbers, an alliance of illegitimacy bound by nothing more nor less than social class interests and the hysterical reaffirmation of racefulness. When Sommers calls the most ambitious landowner of them all, Leonardo Cifuentes, the very incarnation of the "dogmas of the landowning high bourgeoisie" (1978, 84), he elldes the fact that "high bourgeoisie" does not precisely define the elite center of the social world of Ciudad Real. An orphan who occupied his social position through an astute combination of politics (marriage) and ruthlessness (fratricide), Cifuentes spends much of the novel shoring up the insecurities around his origins, hosting social events, and outflanking rumors. The very expression of the race, he is also something of a monster within the aristocratic confines of delicate Coleto sensibilities. By the end of the novel, all eyes will turn to Cifuentes to save them from the threat of agrarian reform.

In the world of *Oficio de tinieblas* it is the top of the social hierarchy, the Caxlán, the white(ned) landowner—just like the elite national man in the Mexico of Gamio's *Forjando patria*—who stands as the protagonist of the race war. That which we readily identify as a guerra de castas turns out to be largely theatrical: a series of massacres dignified as a battle between warriors, much of it staged.[39] In other words, more than a historical fact, the race war is a way of telling. The Indians will be provoked, their response impotent, their descent upon the city fabricated, their defeat nearly total. There is an old ladino saying affiliated with the so-called guerras de castas of the Maya world about how "someday the Indians are going to come down from the mountains and slaughter us all." Castellanos is very consciously reversing the blood flow of this expression. It's about when whites attack.

The race war, then, is complicated—as we saw with Foucault—and in the context of Castellanos's postrevolutionary Chiapas, too often overwhelmed by the noisy discourse of guerras de castas. Naturally we reduce the novel's critical action, quickly and easily, to a conflict between ladinos e indios. This makes sense: there is, after all, an indigenous uprising, aimed, sort of, against the landowners of Ciudad Real. But this is not the essential struggle. The real conflict of the novel is elsewhere: not ladinos e indios but Chiapas and the state.

To miss this basic impulse of the novel can guide us to readings that miss its essential political dimensions. So, for example, focusing the conflict on the tension between Tzotzil and Coleto might suggest a "competing narratives" reading in which what is at stake is the intelligibility of two kinds of storytelling or, as Joanna O'Connell puts it, two different "modes of historical consciousness" (1995, 140). This interpretation is the weak point in her fascinating and still unsurpassed critical study of Castellanos, *Prospero's Daughter* (1995). She recalls that Sommers's influential outline maintains that, in *Oficio de tinieblas*, Castellanos confronts us with two ways of seeing the world. One runs through the Eurocentric vision of material history, the other through what we might call, from the perspective of this same Eurocentrism, "myth" (O'Connell 1995, 139–40). Sommers associates this latter way of knowing with the Tzotzils. This, for Sommers, presents a problem, something like the limit of Castellanos's critique. He accuses Castellanos of expressing the "experience" of the Tzotzils as "a vision that possesses the ahistorical quality of the eternal legend" (80) and claims that "this contradiction, seeing one of the cultures historically and the other not" (86), creates a host of formal problems for the novel that can lead only to "sociocultural pessimism" (88).[40] O'Connell wisely, and sharply, adopts the inverse of Sommers's proposal in her interpretation: if the Tzotzils inhabit a world of myth, we can equally understand history as a "code" (1995, 140) for a nonindigenous way of reflecting on the past. The Indians, as the old saying goes, become a people without history—a "race that has lost its memory," as Castellanos herself puts it—and Sommers criticizes Castellanos for banishing them to this realm.

Against Sommers, O'Connell's position is that we should not be tempted to empty this alternative epistemology of its truth value or, indeed, of its critical, even revolutionary, force. She writes: "Castellanos clearly represents the two communities as having different ways of understanding the past and of narrating their experiences, and thus of constituting their identities as groups, that is, as having different ways of knowing and telling their histories" (1995, 139). Nevertheless, and although this very well might be what Castellanos, the writer, is up to, O'Connell's account does not seem to get to the heart of the critical possibilities that emerge from *Oficio de tinieblas*. By noting the centrality of the problem of history, O'Connell has certainly located the political stakes of the novel. But her own critical move does not sufficiently problematize their implications. While pointing out a certain Eurocentrism around the value that Sommers ascribes to the representation of Tzotzil historical consciousness, O'Connell leaves his schematic interpretation intact. It is still a simple binary, a race war between ladino e indio, now with the indigenous way of knowing given new value as a nonhistoriographical way of talking about the past. The argument is largely semantic. What happens if we think about the race-and-history relation in different terms?

Two problems arise for the "competing narratives" thesis. The first is biographical and revolves around the question of how Castellanos approaches the politics of representation. The second problem is conceptual and has to do with the precise role of historical consciousness in the novel. The points are worth drawing out and considering one at a time.

To begin, we must first realize that situating the border of this truth-conflict between ladino e indio runs into a big problem: the fact that, in a very self-conscious way, half of the conflict at issue in this structure is pretty completely made up. Castellanos simply did not understand indigenous life and, unlike Asturias, did not pretend to take on stylized versions of its trappings (she never ran around calling herself El Gran Lengua). This, of course, does not present us with a literary problem: we are, after all, confronted with a work of fiction. But it is certainly a political and social opportunity for problematization, that is, for reflection on the sociopolitical operations of her fictional narrative. Indeed, she herself was explicitly self-critical about this fact. She was frustrated by the Tzotzil language and never learned it, and her later regret was not this failure but the fact that she had never taught her Tzotzil maid how to read and write in the language of the national future, that is, Spanish.[41] In 1965 she would reflect on her days with the puppet theater in an essay called "Teatro Petul," where she states: "With them, with the Indians . . . our problem was the same as that of the anguished contemporary man: that of incommunication" (299).

Indeed, biography represents something of a stumbling block for thinking about Castellanos's work and its critical possibilities. The impediment usually arises before the question of how to reconcile her literary indigenism with her participation in the institutional indigenism of the state.[42] She was open about her commitment to developmentalist progress, and her interviews and opinions often express an attitude of vulgar paternalism toward indigenous Mexicans. In a widely cited passage from an interview with Emmanuel Carballo, she states:

> The Indians are human beings absolutely equal to the whites, except that they are relegated to an especially unfavorable circumstance. Since they are weaker, they can be more evil [orig.: *malos*]—violent, betraying and hypocritical—than the whites. . . . It is necessary to describe how this misery has led to the atrophy of their best qualities. (Castellanos 1965, 422)

Although it is easy to lose the critical function of this statement—the refusal of a romantic Indian—it is nevertheless bracing in its condescension.[43] Very much a creature of the INI, in a nutshell Castellanos felt that mainstream Mexican society owed a debt to the Indians and that this debt should be repaid by lifting the indigenous communities out of poverty. At the same time she believed that indigenous Mexicans, in order to survive, would need to be willing to integrate into national society, this perhaps at the expense of their cultural specificity. At the INI office in Chiapas, indigenous education was a means toward the ends of acculturation. It is not surprising, then, that we can find confirmation of these publicly expressed attitudes in her literary writing. And indeed, ample critical work has been advanced along these lines.[44] But literary discourse is a cauldron of contradictions and the novelistic form a kind of laboratory for their experimentation. Perhaps it should be equally unsurprising, then, to discover how drastically Castellanos's fiction precisely complicates, even resists, this standard indigenist narrative of social progress that underwrites the mestizo state.[45]

Take, for example, these two versions of the same story. The first is recounted by Tarica, who summarizes an enthusiastic letter written by Castellanos while working in Chiapas. A Maya servant woman, gravely ill, had been abandoned by her employer, who feared having to shoulder the costs of a funeral. The local INI office takes up the servant's cause, ensuring that she be nursed back to health. The servant eventually regains her strength. The employer now reappears, demanding compensation for accumulated debt. The INI intervenes, pays the debt, and Castellanos triumphantly reports that the indigenous woman "now has somebody to defend her. The debt was paid and the girl [orig.: *muchachita*] is free" (in Tarica 2008, 149). Tarica goes on to conclude: "Every word in Castellanos's narration of these events reveals the INI's perspective regarding the need to civilize and modernize not just Indians, but an entire regional culture based on a quasi-feudal system of servitude" (150).[46] By no means an unfair assessment of the narrative at hand, this kind of doctrinaire ideological commitment to the INI and to the simplicity of its social outlook does not line up with the vision that emerges in Castellanos's novels and stories.

In fact Castellanos retells the exact same episode in a short story called "El don rechazado" (1960d). The piece is narrated as the first-person account of a male anthropologist working for a fictional version of the INI's Centro Coordinador in San Cristóbal de las Casas, the municipal center of highland Chiapas. It goes like this: The anthropologist encounters a sick Maya woman, Manuela, basically dying in the street, accompanied by a newborn baby and her adolescent daughter. They are transported back to the mission, where the woman convalesces. While she is there, social services move in. They secure a spot for the older child at a local boarding school, but the mother resists because this will deprive her of the daughter's labor and, ultimately, result in lost income. The anthropologist agrees to compensate her losses by paying whatever income the daughter would normally contribute. Manuela does not really understand, and the interpreter reports her response as follows: "If you want to buy her daughter, to have as your lover, she's going to demand in return a jug of booze and a bushel [orig.: *dos almudes*] of corn. She won't give her up for anything less" (160).[47] The anthropologist tries to explain, but only succeeds in raising Manuela's price for the girl. Negotiations stall. Someone suggests to the anthropologist that he seek to become the newborn's *padrino* (godfather), a status that would put him in a position of greater trust. He starts paying extra attention to the baby, brings toys, and so on. The day comes for Manuela to choose a godparent. She names Doña Prájeda. Doña Prájeda? Doña Prájeda is her *patrona*, her employer, the one who, as the anthropologist, incredulous, puts it to Manuela, "sent you to the stables so that your child would be born in filth? The one that threw you out into the street when you most needed her help and consolation? The one that hasn't stopped by the mission, not even once, to ask if you lived or died?" (162). A couple of days later, Manuela is strong enough to leave the mission. She returns to work for Doña Prájeda.

It's a strangely didactic parable, not one of Castellanos's best unless we understand its narrative voice in the terms of parody. The closing lines address the reader directly, and it is impossible to tell if the exhortation, placed in the mouth of the anthropologist, is earnest or ironic (although it is probably earnest). Announcing a critique of the expectation of gratitude that is a major theme in all Castellanos's work, he warns us not to write off Manuela as ungrateful.[48] He reminds us that four centuries of abuse have made her people instinctively mistrustful. He says that only if we keep trying can things ever change for the better, even if we have to do so in the face of repeated failure. And then he ends with this unanswerable question, grounded on the everyday failure to communicate: "What I want you to tell me is if I, as a professional, as a man, did something wrong? There must have been something. Something that I didn't know how to give them" (163).

This is Castellanos's ethical demand: for the necessity (but impossibility) of intercultural communication and the equal necessity of striving to transcend that impossibility. Her literature reflects this. She does not shrink from an attempt to represent, knowing in advance that this representational effort will fail. Chiapas is a race war, impossible to overcome or effectively mediate, equally impossible to escape.

Consider one of Castellanos's most memorable, and most thoroughly analyzed, literary creations, the relationship between the unnamed narrator (a young girl) and her nanny (nana) that dominates about two-thirds of *Balún-Canán* (1957), the semiautobiographical novel that stands as Castellanos's first major work of prose fiction. The canonical reading of this relationship proposes it as a narrative of female self-discovery, wherein the ladina girl must move beyond dependence on her indigenous nanny in order to realize her agency, her voice, her authorship: the novel closes with the girl literally beginning to write. A clear homology is set up: in the world of the novel (and the social world to which it responds), both women and Indians are oppressed.[49] The logic of the novel thus empowers women at the expense of the Indians (e.g., Tarica 2008, 137–82). This has always struck me as a simplistic reading that leaves out some basic points. For one, it seems to evade the overdetermining context of the relationship between the narrator and her nanny: the arrival of revolutionary agrarian reform and the subsequent uprising against the family ranch. Neither the nanny nor the narrator are protagonists in this political struggle, but both belong to communities that have opposing stakes in its outcome.[50] Add to this the fact that the girl does not really move beyond, or "outgrow," her nanny in any kind of organic or progressive sense: Nana is beaten with a comb and banished from the house by the girl's mother for reporting bad news that later turns out to be prophetic (the girl's younger brother dies, either struck by malaria or eaten up by sorcerers, depending on the perspective) (1957, 225–28). Finally, there is the chilling penultimate scene, which effectively forces a rereading of the entire novel.[51] Strolling around town with a new handler, by chance the girl encounters her old nanny on the street. The girl hurries toward her, ecstatic. But the nanny is unmoved. And then we cannot be sure if it is even the nanny at all. Here is how the chapter ends: "But the Indian watched my running approach, impassive, and gave no sign of welcome. I walk slowly, slower still, until I stop. I let my arms fall, demoralized. Never, even if I found her, will I recognize my nanny. It's been so long since they separated us. And besides, all Indians have the same face" (285).

Castellanos is cagey, and it is quite evident that to read this turn as a blunt expression of racism would be a mistake. In setting up the ending on this deflating note, the narrator speaks not to the civilized versus the barbarous (in Castellanos's writings, everybody is barbarous) but rather to a world's investment in colonial relations of power. Everything must now be understood—that is, read again—in this light: suddenly the homology of oppression between (white) woman and Indian (servant) in the figures of narrator and Nana is completely degraded; narrator and Nana can no longer be understood as collaborators that grow apart; Nana is not training the narrator in the arts of second sight and alternative epistemologies; the narrator, ultimately, is taking these from her. This entire world's investment in colonial relations of power, then, must extend to Castellanos herself. The penultimate scene of misrecognition leads to a brief passage in which the girl-narrator begins to write (286), and this chronology is not to be overlooked. For this transition—from racist worldview to the emergence of writing—is pure Castellanos, the problematization of the project of writing itself, of the writing subject, the one whose literary material rests on occupied land.

Castellanos is a participant in the reformation of the mestizo state, in its postrevolutionary incarnation, and she is a sincere advocate for its politics of integration, materialized in agencies like the INI. If the law of the state is premised on mediation, inclusion, and rationalization, Chiapas, her literary invention, will be the quicksand into which this law sinks. In Castellanos's Chiapas, indigenous peasants are always on the verge of (failed) uprisings, landowners are always marshaling their forces, and both sides are provoked by weird rituals and small acts of hysteria. This should not be confused with lawlessness. In fact, it represents an order, the order of *Balún Canán*, and this law is expressed neither by an emissary of Lázaro Cárdenas nor by a state functionary, neither a landowning caudillo nor an Indian rebel. The law is stated by Nana. It is the law of historical rancor: "It is evil to love those who order, those who possess. Thus says the law" (1957, 16). By the end of the story, the Indians have burned the ranch.

On to the second problem. O'Connell is right to point out that history is at stake in *Oficio de tinieblas*. Moreover, let us recall that, if we take Foucault's narrative seriously, race war is expressed as a mode of historiography. In O'Connell's model, however, this historiographical conflict is not so much historical as it is ethnological. Different ways of knowing are associated with discrete communities whose difference is defined by sets of differential cultural practices. But going back to a point that O'Connell makes earlier in her book (1995, 136), it seems productive to assume that the Chiapas of Castellanos needs to be read as a totality, as a single, if internally complicated, piece of a larger political struggle. Read in this light, the conflict over history becomes more palpably national, linked immediately to the modern problem of race, which ultimately, in appropriate resonance with the context, has to do with race war. Put another way, I maintain that although the Coletos and the Tzotzils may have different versions of events, and different modes of telling, they are united insofar as they tell history from one side, a history of victimization.

A series of confrontations shifts the center of the political critique embedded in *Oficio de tinieblas*. The most illustrative, and also representing the high point of the novel's ideological struggle, is the meeting between Fernando Ulloa — a government geographer, in the highlands to rewrite the map — and the leading lawyer of Ciudad Real, Virgilio Tovar. It is relatively late in the novel, and a group of Tzotzil women, affiliated with an upsurge in ecstatic mysticism, have been arrested, seen their village burned, and been dragged through town, nearly lynched, and eventually put on trial for some sort of charges (blatantly unconstitutional) that basically amount to the worship of false idols (231–37).[52] The village men (who were away during the attack and subsequent arrest) march into town and ask Fernando for help (238). Fernando, in turn, goes to see the lawyer Tovar (239).

Tovar's message to Fernando is a justification of the trial of the Tzotzil women, an argument that expresses the logic of the unequal relations of power that exist between the landowners of Ciudad Real and the Tzotzils of San Juan Chamula. He begins by explaining that the problem with the indigenous women on trial is not religious but rather political and that the political charge is sedition (240). The problem is not false idols; the problem is masses of Indians gathering in one spot and carrying on in ways that the Coletos cannot precisely grasp. This has happened before, he continues, and the historical ledger demonstrates that these kinds of indigenous mobilizations inevitably end with an attempt to harm the ladino landowners. Read the history, he says: 1712, 1867, 1917 (242).[53] The terms of the interactions between ladino and indio are a relation of war. The Coletos are accustomed to the ideological work of producing this relation.

Fernando's position represents a state project struggling to harness this polemical energy: Mexican history is inarticulate. The Chiapas of 1712, 1867, 1917, is a world unto itself, barely national, as much a part of Guatemala as anything else. The Revolution, in this sense, changes the terms, and its work of national articulation will be decisive. Ciudad Real is part of Mexico, and Mexico is governed by the rule of law (242–43). As Fernando will later put it to the governor, the law can redistribute the land without violence (245; see also his conversation with the landowner Leonardo Cifuentes, 149–56).

Note well: Tovar has laid out a historical case, and Fernando has responded with juridical discourse. This will be crucial. Tovar's history — a series of dates, a list of accidents — now coalesces as a concrete reality: "Would you defend the person who murdered your father, raped your sisters?" (237), he asks. Fernando's response—"Things may have happened that way in the past, but that is no basis for declaring that they will happen the same way today" (ibid.)—is ethically correct, but it lacks visceral appeal, to say the least.

Just beneath Tovar's historical narrative resides a political subtext, and it is in this scene that it will now come out into the open. If the indigenous mobilization around mystic ecstasy represents the threat of organized insurrection, the racist worldview of the Coletos presupposes that this kind of project cannot be carried out by the Indians alone. That is, they need a third party, "una voluntad oculta" (236), to pull off a coordinated attack against the interests of Ciudad Real. Fernando, obviously, has been cast in this role. Tovar communicates this widespread suspicion to him directly (241). From the Coleto point of view, the plan of the state is to provoke the Indians with promises of land, incite a riot, send in federal troops, occupy the area, and break the regional hegemony of Ciudad Real. The terms of the ideological disarticulation are set. On the one hand, communicated by Fernando, is the juridical discourse of overarching sovereignty, justice, and ultimately peace. On the other hand, communicated by Tovar, is the historicist discourse of local complaint, injustice, and ultimately war.

Each man represents an ideological position, the one incommensurable with the other. In Fernando's world of state power, policy, and positive law, good rules can produce good results. In Tovar's world of local struggle, custom, and natural law, the ends justify the means. Fernando's ideological claim is that if you apply the law, justice will follow; Tovar's ideological claim is that the law is a foreign power, and a bloodbath will follow. When Fernando says, "The Indians' guilt cannot be based on prophesies," Tovar's response measures the dimension of this ideological gulf: "No one is prophesying. We are remembering" (237). And then, not without heat: "Usted no entiende esto" (This is what you don't understand) (ibid.). Tovar's memory is a history of siege, of decentered camps, of one side in a race war. And with this confrontation between geographer and lawyer, it begins to become clear that the Indians, paradoxically, are not the opponents here.

A less nimble writer might leave it at this and then proceed to "reveal" Tovar's position as "mere" ideology. Historical facts could be trotted out, showing on the one hand the justifiability of indigenous uprising in the face of overwhelming oppression and on the other hand the likelihood that what history recalls as "indigenous rebellion" can be better understood in terms of self-defense. And this would not be historically inaccurate. Nor would anybody be too surprised: the vast majority of Castellanos's readers, if they know anything about Chiapas at all, associate it with power structures both archaic and hard to move. Representing a rustic elite committed to a kind of semifeudal existence and a self-righteous view of history would be unilluminating, and the plot would be preordained: the ideological veil would be lifted, land reform would be realized, justice would be served. A talented postcolonialist, committed to the problematization of self-congratulatory truisms, Castellanos refuses this kind of hollow fairy tale. And as it turns out, between the two ideological positions put into play against each other here—revolutionary peace versus historicist war—it is Tovar's counterhistory, the prose of race war, that more efficiently produces the lay of the land. That is, Tovar's worldview is more compactly articulated to the naturalization of history. While representing this history falsely, its representation nevertheless corresponds to a certain actuality. And the actuality is this: Fernando Ulloa is, in fact, inciting the Indians to rebellion (303–4, 327, 346–47). The opponent has been flushed out: not the Indians, the enemy is the state.

And with this we arrive at the center of the principal political narrative of *Oficio de tinieblas.* It represents Fernando Ulloa—the character most intimately linked to Castellanos's own life experiences—and his education in ongoing colonial relations of power. It represents the truth that all decolonized nations know: even propelled by the enthusiasm of revolution, we cannot simply slam on the brakes and throw the colonial project into reverse. As readers of a novel whose voice is generally in the third-person omniscient, we perceive this from relatively early in the novel. It is very clear what justice means for Fernando: restoring the Indians' rights over the land (149). It is equally clear what justice means to his primary indigenous interlocutor, Pedro Winiktón, the judge: "He saw the Caxlán impaled; he saw fire running through the streets of Jobel [Ciudad Real]; he saw the Ladino throng bent low [orig.: *humillándose*] beneath slavery's whip" (24). When he returns home from the plantation with a new language with which to speak justice, the people of the village see the road ahead, and they are afraid:

> To say justice in Chamula was to kill the patron, to raze the hacienda, to
> lie in ambush for the police, to resist the merchants' abuses, denounce the
> *enganchador*'s manipulations, avenge the mistreatment of children, the rape

of women. To say justice in Chamula was to keep a vigil, day and night, sustained only by the promise of a faraway man whose good faith no one had yet put to the test. It was preferable to remain silent. (54)

Fernando departs the novel as the accidental leader of an ineffectual indigenous uprising, doomed to failure before it even begins. The trap closes: he can flee and be executed by the Coletos for the political treason of insurrection or stay and be executed by the Indians for the incompetence of false promises. He starts to think through his options, in search of the loophole, the escape route, the compromise: "Because there must be a way out. It wasn't logical for things to end like that" (347). But he quickly catches himself: "Must be . . . logical. . . . And [he] burst out laughing" (ibid.). If this lament for logic, shortly before he is lynched by the Coletos, certifies Fernando's descent into the irrational, it also means something more. Like Foucault's laugh, it is the moment of realization that another reason has triumphed and that he finds himself the protagonist of a misplaced revolution.

The discourse of race war has material effects, and *Oficio de tinieblas* hypnotically traces its slow transformation into the racist discourse of the state. The rebellion unfolds quickly and violently, and it is crushed in short order. The revolutionary state, completely outdone by the Coletos, abandons the Indians. It is an extremely complex postcolonial scene, masterfully portrayed through Castellanos's dark prose. The upshot is that the revolutionary state, in the figure of Fernando, has shown up to recolonize the local colonizers. And the *patrones,* a social class protecting property interests, invoke a counterhistory precisely through the language of race.

While the lawyer Tovar articulates the most sophisticated expression of this discourse, there is a more active protagonist of this counterhistorical move. This is Leonardo Cifuentes, the none too subtle villain of the story, who at the end emerges as the local caudillo prepared to restore justice, order, and peace (356). With all of the different notions of justice floating around the novel, it is his that prevails. The distant and twisted descendant of Martín Sánchez and a striking figure worthy of more analysis than he has received in the critical bibliography on the novel, Leonardo will stand as the author of the final enigma of *Oficio de tinieblas.* His triumph is secured by a declaration of martial law, with its corresponding militarization of space and its enforcement through paramilitary fighters (271–72, 353). With his opponent, the state, now exhausted, it is precisely at this moment that Leonardo Cifuentes (whose initials he shares with Lázaro Cárdenas) will succeed in harnessing the race war and recentering it as racist discourse.[54] With the establishment of law and order, society no longer needs to be defended against an invading enemy other (the state); society must be defended, as Foucault puts it, from itself, from the sickness that it itself produces. This sickness is now (again) the Indian, and plans for its surgical removal are drawn up.

The plans come in the form of written instructions authored by Leonardo, and they are completely insane. Resonating with the old juridical language still customary in Ciudad Real (see Castellanos 1960e, 533–37), they are bombastically titled *Ordenanzas militares.*[55] We do not get to read these ordenanzas, and they will not be carried out to their conclusion, but we glean their methods and objectives as Leonardo communicates their contents, first to his lover and then to the local governor. The ordenanzas, normally a set of guidelines governing military rights and responsibilities, end up being a kind of catalog of all of the little genocides that traverse Mexican history: massacre, deportation, colonization.[56] The moment of concocting the genocide document is also one of the clearest expressions of the race war itself. Leonardo: "[The Coletos] don't want an Indian to die any more than they want their herds of cattle to be diminished. They feel that their Indians are something that belongs to them and they don't fully understand that the government has taken them away. And that's why, as I've said many times, the Indians must be finished off" (338). In other words, the race war has fast-forwarded to its endgame, biopolitics, where what is at stake is naked life and the state takes on the task of permanent purification by directing *ordenanzas militares* at society itself. And my association of Leonardo with the "state" here is not accidental. For it is precisely at this point in the novel that Leonardo, with ordenanzas militares in hand, championed from Ciudad Real to Tuxtla as a promoter of justice and peace, sees his future in politics and realizes that he must begin to carve out his niche within the Party, the institutional revolution whose advances on the region he has just rebuffed (353).

Finally, we still have the Tzotzils, *al monte*, in the cave, kneeling before the ark. Let us recall that we were on the verge of secrets revealed, the first step on a long road to regeneration from the latest cycle of exhaustion and defeat. We were at the point where "eyes that brim with tears can close forever. [For] What they have seen is their salvation" (362). The ark is opened, and the word is brought forth. It is only a couple of lines, worth reciting in full: "And there remains exposed, like a communion wafer, the page that an unknown hero rescued from the catastrophe. The first page, on which a title flames: . . . Ordenanzas militares" (ibid.; 364 in Spanish).

This is a surprising, and perplexing, turn of events, and there is no self-evident way to understand the reappearance of the ordenanzas militares as the sacred word of the Tzotzils. It could be the latest way of destabilizing the ontology of indigenousness, of suggesting that what we understand as Indian has no pre-Columbian foundation, that it is irreducibly the result of transcultural violence. Another common reading is to note that the Indians are illiterate, see the written word as Caliban saw the books, and suggest that only when the Indians know how to read the signs will they be able to effectively advance their own cause.[57] But this seems a little too didactic: *Oficio de tinieblas* is not much of a bildungsroman. I confess that I do not know what the scene means, but there can be little doubt that Castellanos wants it to be significant: beyond its position as the denouement of the entire story and her recourse to images of sacred documents throughout her work (see *Balún Canán* [1957], *Ciudad Real* [1960c]), the moment of the Tzotzils' converging on the cave is described as a "búsqueda de la tiniebla" (1962b, 363), thus resonating with the stark Catholic ritual of defeat that gives the novel its title. But to my knowledge, Castellanos never explains the ordenanzas militares and their appearance as a sacred text. In attempting to make sense of it all, we might begin by recalling that the readers of the novel are not the fleeing Tzotzils. We are the readers. For better or for worse, Rosario's Indians are not the subjects of a rebellion but the objects of a race war between powers that alternatively fear them and take them for granted. No Indians in Rosario's world—real or fictional—will read the title that flames. The title is meant for us, as subjects of a modernity constructed and, indeed, maintained, on ordenanzas militares.

Chapter 4 Elena Garro and the Failure of Alliance

Unity is always effected by means of brutality.

—ERNEST RENAN, 1882

It's natural that they would do the hanging now if you were the ones doing it before.

—ELENA GARRO, 1963

A STRIKING CONVERSATION from Elena Garro's 1963 novel *Los recuerdos del porvenir* captures the basic problem that guides this chapter. The novel tells the story of Ixtepec, a small town under military occupation in the wake of the Mexican Revolution. While ostensibly in place to restore order and enforce a newly aggressive national secularism, the federal army's unstated purpose in the town is to snuff out the increasingly radicalized demands around agrarian reform, in other words, to crush the politics of zapatismo.[1] Most of the novel's land activists are peasants racialized as "Indians," so a crucial scene in the narrative is the iteration of each dawn being greeted by the spectacle of dead Indians hanging from trees (92–93). The families that constitute the novel's protagonists—an impotent confederacy of petit-bourgeoisie and decadent aristocracy—are troubled by this. When one of these characters comments on the barbarism visited on the Indians by the military commanders, it sparks a memory in the adolescent Isabel Moncada. She remembers the kind of morality tales that her parents, uncles, and aunts—those now scandalized by the general's violence—used to tell that inevitably ended with an Indian executed as just punishment for one alleged transgression or another (103–4). Then, with provocative intent, her brother and double, Nicolás, blandly offers up a cynical truth, rendered here as a question: *If you yourselves didn't care about killing Indians before, why do you object to the general doing it now?* (104).[2] Surrounded by uncomfortable guests, his father explodes with vociferous justifications, none of which seem to ease the tension: it was a different time; there was a war; it was too damn hot; and so on (ibid.).

Nicolás's question—the critical heart of the book—gets under our skin and irritates his parents because it shatters the fairy-tale logic that links community to national formation by forcing memory onto the scene: Why do you care today when—don't you remember?—you didn't care yesterday?

Garro is often remembered, both from her literary work and from everyday life, for these kinds of provocations. She is infamous for her erratic behavior around the student movement of the late 1960s, a sacred cow among the Mexican Left, and in later years dismissed it as unrealistically ambitious, socially destabilizing, and subject to manipulation, calling it "una cretina huelga de estudiantes" (a cretinous student strike) (interview with Verónica Beucker in Beucker 2002, 44). And yet she was interrogated by the authorities and accused of being a communist agitator in the wake of the 1968 massacre at the Plaza de las Tres Culturas.[3] In fear for her life, she held a press conference prior to her arrest in which she accused a host of prominent intellectuals of egging on the student movement and then slinking away when the violence erupted (see Ramírez 2000, 49–54). What actually transpired while Garro was under arrest is still exceedingly murky, but whatever the case, the episode helped consolidate what became a "leyenda negra" (Melgar and Mora 2002, 7) around the writer.[4] As Margo Glantz testifies, the years did nothing to diminish Garro's larger-than-life stature: "Anytime that she is mentioned at a conference, provocations spark and rumors spread" (cited by Beuecker 2002, 45). Against state orders she fled the country and proceeded to live much of the rest of her life in self-imposed exile. When she moved to Cuernavaca in old age, a parade of interviewers invariably remarked on her small apartment shared with a considerable army of cats. In a late interview she praised the dictatorship of Francisco Franco and speculated that Adolph Hitler was a Jewish necromancer (interview with Lucía Melgar in Melgar and Mora 2002, 269–73). Often read as an outstanding point of reference within a broader Latin American critique of masculine domination, she rejected any association between her writing and feminist discourse, stating that women simply work with ideas invented by men (in Beucker 2002, 42; see also Lopátegui 2002, 247). She claimed that her greatest ambition was to be poor (in Melgar and Mora 2002, 15), and yet she was unfazed by criticism of her tastes for Chanel and expensive furs.[5] Some suggest that her mental state was never entirely stable. When she was interviewed in 1964 as a potential witness in the investigation of the Kennedy assassination (she was said to have been at a cocktail party with Lee Harvey Oswald), a CIA agent noted on the report: "She is also nuts."[6]

There is a strong counterdiscourse working against this portrait, one nourished by something of a boom in studies on Garro and the republication of her works, alongside the appearance of previously unpublished work, that has emerged over the past decade and a half.[7] This renaissance of interest in Garro can at first come off as a surprise—there is nothing comparable, for example, around Castellanos—but is explainable through a confluence of factors. First was the opening of a sizable archive of Garro's manuscripts, private papers, and correspondence acquired by Princeton University from Garro's daughter, Helena Paz Garro, and made public in 1997.[8] Shortly thereafter, and with some fanfare (and scandal, too), Paz Garro published her *Memorias* (2003), a massive kiss-and-tell on the midcentury intellectual, cultural, and political scene in Mexico, revolving around everybody's favorite literary soap opera, the complicated relationship between her parents. Finally, and I would say perhaps most significantly, a generation of young scholars has begun to revisit Mexico's literary history outside of the shadow of 1968. Concerns over Garro's political loyalties have begun to cede before the blunt fact of her literary talent. And with this kind of postideological research, a much more complex picture has emerged around, precisely, the political implications of her writings and her life.

Whether Garro was insane or misunderstood, her eccentricity, flamboyance, and at times even courage in the face of authority helped turn her critical voice into an unpredictably formidable one.[9] Race is an important theme in her writings, and her ability to effectively match the evocative metaphor with the cutting turn of phrase make her works essential reading for the critique of racial discourse in modern Mexico. I would go so far as to argue that even though, by her own account, her stories are about the persecution of women in Mexican society (in Beucker 2002, 42), race is the central category for a political reading of Garro's narratives; perhaps it would be better to say that we cannot fully appreciate her critique of masculine domination without special attention to her engagement with racial discourse. For example, in a comment regarding her activism around land reform in the 1950s, she speaks of the violence committed against *agraristas* challenging various privatization projects that inevitably lead to the displacement of the rural poor, making explicit the fact of its unequal division along the lines of race: "They kill all of them. Not us [orig.: *nosotras*] because we're white [orig.: *güeras*], but yes, them" (in Melgar and Mora 2002, 244). And even though the surrounding remarks about the Jews during World War II show that she was more than just a little unhinged, it is interesting, and I think significant, that in explaining her engagement with the classic texts of international socialism she takes special notice of Moses Hess, "el profesor de Marx," as "the one who invented the race war" (in Melgar and Mora 2002, 269).

Like Castellanos, Garro was preoccupied with race, and this preoccupation led her to contemplate the condition of indigenous Mexicans, along with the material effects of racial discourse more broadly. Her approach to the topic, however, could not have been more different from her colleague's. She was not an institution builder or even an institution collaborator, and her access to channels of state power was at once privileged (she was married to Octavio Paz) and problematic (she was married to Octavio Paz). But she shared with Castellanos the obligation to wrestle with the thorny topic of representation embedded in the "problema del indio." Between the two writers, their distinct representational strategies show the impossibility of ever getting the Indian question "right," and both deserve praise for their backbone in nevertheless making the attempt in the face of this political quagmire.

In Mexican discourse and society, the generic role played by the Indian is that of a silent and inscrutable being, almost part of the setting until provoked into violent action. This stereotypical image is of course absurd, and, as we have seen, it is a convention that Castellanos's prose works hard to overcome, or at least problematize. Her Indians are unusually noisy, and both of her major novels—*Balún-Canán* (1957) and *Oficio de tinieblas* (1962b)—present an indigenous protagonist who attempts to mobilize the tools of liberal development (education, literacy, land reform, legal discourse) only to be rebuffed by the high walls of the modernizing polis. Frustration builds, and arms are taken up. Her psychologically complex indigenous characters, while often proposed as an important advance within a larger trajectory of indigenismo, were nevertheless criticized as Western literary creations that were hardly believable, especially at the level of their often high modernist language, resonating with speech patterns reminiscent of sacred texts.

Garro goes in the other direction, precisely exaggerating the silence of the conventionally silent Indian. Even more predictably than among Castellanos's interlocutors, Garro's aesthetic stance has also led to criticism in the form of accusations that she diminishes the presence, or at least the agency, of the Indian within modern Mexican society. On the contrary, I propose that it is the other way around: Garro's silent Indians call special attention to the politics of race and the attendant marginalization of indigenous Mexicans within those politics. Moreover, the silence makes their moments of speech all that more politically charged and, ultimately, effective. Like the whiplash comment that closes Castellanos's *Balún-Canán*, about how "all Indians have the same face," the constant presence of "indios callados" in *Los recuerdos del porvenir* is clearly mobilized by Garro as a strategy for critical reflection on social injustice and racist hierarchies.

These were real concerns for Garro. In the 1950s she became a known sympathizer with and active supporter of a militant group of agrarian activists led by Rubén Jaramillo and centered in the historically restive state of Morelos. Idiosyncratic as it was, this work left a profound effect on her, and by the 1960s she was sacrificing much of the momentum around her literary production in order to take up land reform activism. In a wild interview with Lucía Melgar near the end of her life, Garro speaks of being struck by the comment of Enedino Montiel Barona, one of the leaders of the group, whom, under the duress of interrogation, she cites as having said: "Excuse me, sir, but in Mexico the Indians have no government" (in Melgar and Mora 2002, 243). She is reciting an old cliché here, but whether it was actually spoken by Montiel Barona or is in fact another in a long history of Garro's dramatic flourishes, the recollection is clearly reflected as a motivating image in *Los recuerdos del porvenir*, a work that has more than a little resonance with the Jaramillista movement and its persecution.[10] And the stakes could not be more significant. Two years after the publication of the novel, Garro reports, Montiel Barona and his wife, Antonia, would both be kidnapped, flayed, and killed by state-sponsored thugs (Melgar and Mora 2002, 246).[11]

The relatively common complaint, then, that Garro "excludes" the Indians from the world of *Recuerdos*, especially if we are reading the novel's setting, Ixtepec, as a metaphor for the nation, or "silences" them in its narrative voice, seems misplaced (see Portal 1980; Kaminsky 1993a, 151; Gladhart 2005). The invisibility of Garro's Indians is a staged invisibility, a clearly visible invisibility. And in this it is neither a value judgment nor an ethnographic description but rather, as Kaminsky puts it, "structural" (1993a, 86), a foundation of the novel's critical operations. Moreover, it is difficult to see what the novel could gain, aesthetically or critically, from a surely awkward presentation of any "authentic"—which is to say, ethno-graphic—indigenous point of view. As the case of Castellanos suggests, any kind of modernist stylization would certainly expose Garro to an entirely new round of criticism. All things considered, and returning to Kaminsky's point about the structural nature of silence, it is important to recognize that the Indians in Garro's works are not merely silent but "callados," shut up, as if by an oppressive force. And yet they do speak, as we will see, in moments of high critical impact.

This is certainly the case in Garro's best-known work, a masterpiece of short fiction called "Es la culpa de los tlaxcaltecas" (1964b). Usually placed within a canon of early examples of magic realism, the story is probably better described as existentialist surrealism in which a complex interplay of perspective, historical context, and psychological drama converge to create a harrowingly complicated narrative landscape.[12] The story bounces around from 1950s middle-class urban Mexico to a small rural village in Michoacán to ancient Tenochtitlan during La Noche Triste, or Night of Sorrows, when Cortés escaped the Aztec city in a battle that became the very definition of a bloodbath, especially for his indigenous allies. This chronology and these settings are often mixed as the Noche Triste erupts into the contemporary Federal District, at least in the mind of the protagonist. The plot is a love story that centers on Laura, a repressed middle-class housewife, and her descent into madness, or perhaps her ascent from madness; it's hard to tell. In the grips of a possibly abusive—and absolutely tyranni-cal—husband, Laura is beset by memories of the love she left behind, her *primo-marido* (cousin-husband), also known in the narrative as "el indio."

El indio is a phantom presence throughout: when Laura's car breaks down, el indio approaches, in arresting anachronism, wounded and toting a spear, leaving her white dress stained with blood; as Laura convalesces from a nervous breakdown, a maid spies el indio at the window and, upon inspection, finds only traces of blood on the sill. His three extended dialogues with Laura are ghostly, and it is never clear if he actually exists outside of her head. Traditionally read as an allegory of the Mexican form of masculine domination known as machismo (e.g., Duncan 1985; Montes Garcés 2007), in which a young woman finds no space for agency in a society where all social power accrues to men and unhappy women are diagnosed as hysterics and medicated accordingly, the story is also, and most critically, about race. It is el indio, specifically, who tells us this in the most direct way. In the first passage in which he speaks, in response to Laura's confession of "betrayal," he takes her hand and says, "Está muy desteñida, parece una mano de ellos" (It's very faded, it looks like one of their hands) (Garro 1964b, 13). Through this encounter—perhaps a memory, perhaps a dream—we learn that Laura, like Malintzin,[13] has left her home village and her *primo-marido* accompanied by a man of power. But even in a story whose obvious Malinche metaphor so explicitly reflects on problems of gender and modern society (see esp. Messinger Cypess 1991), Garro is careful to make clear that these problems can only be made fully intelligible by bringing the complications of race onto the scene. Space, as the national relation between *ciudad* and *campo*—with the former resting on a conquest (Tenochtitlan becomes the Federal District) and the latter representing the partial nature of that same conquest—is racialized, and this race–space relation is what brings new political weight to the conservative melodrama that is la Malinche's allegory of fallen women. The city, gazed upon by the Indian subject, from which that same subject has been expelled, is where the elusive promises of a mestizo modernity, the whitening of Tenochtitlan, come to the fore. The racial fracture at the heart of mestizaje is thus a central concern spoken by the experience of the campo, a space whose modern race registers "Indian": *parece una mano de ellos*, that is, in the pigmentocratic logic of race, a whitish hand, *desteñida*, not us, not ours, from somewhere else. The mestizo state claims a nation, but the race war rolls on.

This book has been preoccupied with the relations between race and space in modern Mexico, and Garro's greatest novel, *Los recuerdos del porvenir*, reveals itself as an especially attractive context of analysis for the critical possibilities of literary discourse in this area. If the strength of Rosario Castellanos's prose fiction is the way in which it highlights the complications around racial discourse and state policy within the specific context of Mexico, Garro's work is even more aggressive in problematizing the terrain where race meets space most explicitly, that is, the nation-form as a universal category for political organization. Indeed, the scene from Garro's novel that opens this chapter—"Es natural que ahora cuelgan ellos si antes colgaron ustedes"—points well beyond its own traumatic context, all the way back to a modern foundation of the problematic: Ernest Renan and his well-known 1882 speech "What Is a Nation?"

A French philosopher, historian, and essayist, Renan delivered "Qu'est-ce qu'une nation?" at the Sorbonne in March 1882. It was later published in his *Discours et conférences* in 1887.[14] Even though geopolitically decontextualized, as a philosophical statement the piece captures much of the conceptual problematic around the nation-form that Mexican intellectuals needed to confront both before and after the Revolution. Renan's argument still resonates for its precocious formulation of the thesis that something like a narrative structure—one productive of history—undergirds the affective identification on which all nations rest. This narrative production of the nation, Renan explains, emerges dialectically out of the tense relation between memory and forgetting. But the movement that enables an answer to the question "What is a nation?" is not simply the conscious organization of memory and forgetting into a social or political relation that can emerge as nation. Rather, the fundamental movement of Renan's critique rises out of the idea that the nation demands that its originary forgetting be, like Freud's totemic meal, precisely forgotten. It is by calling attention to this fact that Nicolás's intervention and Garro's novel can be understood as something of a scandal.

Renan considered his sermon on the nation the pinnacle of his career. In *Discours et conférences* he writes: "I have weighed every word of it [the nation essay] with the utmost care: it is my profession of faith in all that concerns human affairs" (cited in Chadbourne 1968, 100). In order to properly frame the critical possibilities and limits of the idea of nation that emerges from Renan's argument and to understand the political significance of Garro's confrontation with it, we need to rethink the lasting influence of Renan and the return to his theorization of the nation in the human sciences today. This will entail returning Renan to the Hegelian assumptions that informed his work.

Modern invocations of Renan tend to either occlude or take for granted the historical dialectic that orders his thought, in the process converting what he himself considered one of his most important and provocative intellectual efforts into a set of relatively bland conventions. The list is a prestigious one. Hannah Arendt, exemplifying a move common to political philosophers, uncritically takes up Renan's voluntaristic definition of the nation as a "daily plebiscite" (1982, 19), making it the ground from which to launch her famous critique of imperial expansion and promoting it as that which imperialism ultimately destroys (Arendt 1951, 125 et passim).[15] Decades later, in the work that would at once enable and provide fodder for a generation of postcolonial historiographers, Benedict Anderson draws from Renan's idea of national forgetting in order to invoke his influential theory of "imagined communities" (1991, 6). Finally, Homi Bhabha opened his widely cited 1990 anthology *Nation and Narration* by reproducing the essay, helping to make it a kind of touchstone in the postcolonial reconsideration of the nation-form. Although the inclusion of Renan's essay at the very front of *Nation and Narration* goes largely unexplained (only the immediately following essay by Martin Thom treats it extensively), an important reference to it in Bhabha's own contribution, "DissemiNation," speaks to the attraction precisely for its implicit relating of the nation-form to the problematic production of national narratives (1990, 310).[16] All of these readings take Renan's insights in new directions, and yet none of them adequately traces the dialectical movement by which Renan arrives at his narrative of nation as both "soul" and "daily plebiscite," a movement that potentially blunts its critical edge.

As a positivist whose historicism could never entirely shake itself free of a Hegelian idealism, Renan does not surprise us in reproducing many of Hegel's ideas of nation, albeit in a more sophisticated dialectic. These include the necessary naturalization of the relations between humans and history that Hegel called "spirit," Renan "soul" or even a "spiritual principle" (1882, 19). But clearly, Renan is not merely aping Hegel. What is the difference? A fundamental difference is Renan's much more focused and necessary engagement with race.

For Hegel, race is a shifty term. He most directly addresses the concept in *Philosophy of Mind* (1830), where he states: "According to the concrete differences of the terrestrial globe, the general planetary life of the nature-governed mind specializes itself and breaks up into the several nature-governed minds which, on the whole, give expression to the nature of the geographical continents and constitute the diversities of race" (§ 393). Race is a function of geography ("the concrete differences of the terrestrial globe"), and although this is a promising start, reducing race to mere description—"Man is implicitly rational; herein lies the possibility of equal justice for all men and the futility of a rigid distinction between races which have rights and those which have none" (§ 393 Zusatz)—it quickly descends into the quintessential expression of Eurocentric thinking, where the "essential" differences of race are further subdivided into "local or national minds" (§ 394 Zusatz). To understand the specificity of these local nations carved out of the major races, we need to turn in part to "natural history" (context) and in part to the "philosophy of world-history" (conquests), which can yield conclusions about "the world-historical significance of races" (§ 394 Zusatz). Race as physical description is at the same time race as historical achievement. Eurocentrism aside, the distinction is an important one (it underwrites Boas's innovations), but in the writings where one might expect Hegel to mobilize race more critically or even just pragmatically, for example his *Philosophy of History* (1835), its function seems to be that of an occasional stand-in for nation, people, tribe, and so on. In other words, Kant's late eighteenth-century attempt to pacify race and convert its menacing voracity into a rather narrow empirical concept seems not to have gained much traction in continental philosophy during the subsequent decades.

Renan will attempt to make more concrete, political sense of race. By 1882, the stakes are much higher. These stakes break in two directions. First, and most obviously, race had become a science, with its rationalist aura enlisted in the service of naturalizing all sorts of conquest and exploitation, such as colonialism, imperialism, and slavery. But these extra-European concerns are not the concerns of Renan. The explicit concern for him was the political mobilization of race within Europe, namely, the project of annexation following the Franco-Prussian war, which left border regions such as the Alsace vulnerable to expropriation and absorption into larger projects of nation-state. The intellectual justification for annexation rested on race, that is, an idea of racial commonality in which the "German race," which would allegedly include a majority of Alsatians, should be reunited as a single nation. Renan, in the name of France, perceived the need to take a stand, against race. This is the meaning of the passage in which he mocks the annexationists and racial expansionists, stating: "Human history is essentially different from zoology, and race is not everything, as it is among the rodents or felines, and one does not have the right to go through the world fingering people's skulls, and taking them by the throat and saying: 'You are of our blood; you belong to us!'" (1882, 15).

Renan's discourse on the nation, then, is in fact also about race. Indeed, in 1882 it can be read as a sharp critique of race science in an age of theories of racial purity and emergent practices of eugenics.[17] Race and its relation to nation will be of tantamount concern to Renan. As he put it, reflecting on

the importance of his "What Is a Nation?" speech, "When modern civilization has foundered as a result of the fatal misunderstanding of the words:
'nation,' 'nationality,' and 'race,' I hope that these twenty pages will be
remembered" (cited in Chadbourne 1968, 100). He opens his argument by
calling the supposed association between race and nation a "mistake": "Race
is confused with nation and a sovereignty analogous to that of really existing
peoples is attributed to ethnographic or, rather linguistic groups" (1882, 8).
And later, at the end of the crucial first section, in which he outlines the
origins of the nation form, Renan restates the question of relating race to
nation (12). As I will argue here, it is precisely at the theme of race that
the resolution of his dialectic—the forgetting of national forgetfulness—
comes into play with full force. My claim is that tracing the vicissitudes of
race through his argument can unlock the dialectical action through which
Renan imagines the nation. This is worth some explanation, because it is
crucial for reading Renan against Garro and resituating his idea of nation in
the Mexican scene.

Race marks an organizing distinction in Renan's argument, at once
enabling his critique and weakening its power. The distinction begins to
take shape when Renan invokes two kinds of contexts for the appropriation of the idea of race, each corresponding to a certain practice of historical investigation. On the one hand is the anthropological perspective, for
which race is a physiological concern akin to zoology, related only to the
history of the human form as a kind of animal. On the other hand is the
historical perspective, related to the history of languages, culture, and, ultimately, politics (14–15). It is the first of these practices alone, he argues,
that provides a defensible homeland for race. Race's legitimacy in history
can be found only in the widest historical sense, the "history of humanity" and its taxonomic and physiological preoccupations that reduce race
to questions of "real descent" (14). In terms of the cultural concerns that
must, explicitly or implicitly, guide the history of political action and the
practice of philological investigation, race loses all force because the cru-
cible of primordial descent that could be imagined as productive of racialized human origins is "massively prior to the origins of culture, civilization
and language" (ibid.). Race may be relevant to Kant's conceptualization of
"natural history" (what Renan here calls "zoology") and its inquiry into
"humankind," but it is distinctly irrelevant to political history. For Renan,
the two are—or should be—separate. Race, insofar as it enters the history
of political forms, such as nations, does so not as cause—nations do not

emerge from races—but as effect—race is an idea often wielded by nationalists. He concludes: "Race, as we historians understand it, is therefore something which is made and unmade" (ibid.). Race is not natural and thus should not naturalize the nation-form.

For an analysis of the modern nation-form, the idea of race now stands as an elaborate, if powerful, fiction. At the same time, however, Renan does not entirely abandon the notion that there is something like race, an empirically grounded, scientific concept, even if in the modern world its actual referent is to be unearthed only paleologically. Thus, while explicitly confronting and undermining the fantastic mobilization of race in nationalist discourse, he still clings to what he calls the "fact of race" (13): that is, the objective existence of Kant's norm, the fact of discernible and hence classifiable differences between human groups, organizable into something like families.[18] The critical force of Renan's invocation of race emerges when he accepts in principle Kant's norm of racial difference—hereditary descent—and then argues that this norm shatters within the territorialized nation (13–14). All nations are an impenetrable mix of families; there is no nation built upon a "pure race"; *all nations are racially heterogeneous, hybrid, mestiza, mixed* (14; cf. Gamio 1916).

Although Renan was repeating an idea hit upon long ago by Johann Gottfried von Herder (precisely in response to Kant) and reiterated by the Comte Arthur de Gobineau in his "Essay on the Inequality of the Human Races" (1851), the point here can be converted into a critical one, made in the wake of a century of race-guided slave debates and during an age of intensifying race science and attendant ideas of degeneration and national purity. Whether Renan even could have followed through and gone all the way to radically destroy race is a question impossible to answer (Boas, for example, could not pull it off either). But the fact is that he did not. Indeed, precisely at the very enunciation of his most aggressive move—the apparent delinking of race from nation—he leaves intact the impulse to naturalize hierarchies that is central to all race science. Again, when he attacks race, his target is not the idea as such (even as a scientific concept) but rather the way in which it becomes confused with and muddles the question of what constitutes a nation. We can conclude that, within the context of national formation, Renan is concerned primarily with the intrusion of the fact of race. The national production of race, then, is to be read only as a kind of perversion. This is to say that he excludes from his horizon the ways in which the nation-form, at once a political project and an affective community, produces a feeling of nation that may in fact enable the very idea of race in the first place: the English race, the Mexican race, the German race, and so on.

This brings us to the brink of a historiographical mess. So for Renan, the nonracial character of the historical trajectory of the nation form assumes an idea of what race is: family, tribe, genealogy (1882, 13–14). But then, given that the course of history's empires preceding the rise of the modern nation destroys precisely these lines of descent (ibid.), it is equally clear that the "ethnographic argument" (14), in historical terms, is at best a canard: "Ethnographic considerations . . . played no part in the constitution of modern nations" (ibid.). What is the proof? The fact that all nations are hybrids.

Thus Renan's recourse to race must presuppose, prior to the historical emergence of the nation-form, precisely the ethnographic argument that he wants to displace, the existence of something like singularity of origin, that is, something like a purity of tribes before everything was mixed. Left unconsidered—and this is crucial—is the dialectical reversal of race and nation with and through actually existing "hybridity." Indeed, left unconsidered is the fact that the modern idea of race rises within, not against (and certainly not before), the national-racial mixing with which he confronts it.[19] In other words, he stops, just before his critique gets really sharp. Declaring the baselessness of "pure race" for any "politics," he promptly reasserts the hierarchical gesture that is precisely the program of all racist politics: reiterating Gobineau without citing him, he concludes that advanced nations are superhybrid nations, "those where the blood is most mixed" (ibid.).[20] The invocation of mixture requires the metaphysical ground of an absent purity. The terms are simply inverted against the purists—the best nations are here the most mixed—and the same familiar names end up atop the hierarchical family of nations.[21]

But let us remember Renan's dialectic and its play on forgetfulness. The role of race is decisive here because Renan himself believed that it is precisely the racially plural and mixed origin of all nations that is "forgotten" in the formation of national homogeneity, hegemony, solidarity (10–11). The point here is to call attention to the way in which Renan reminds us of a forgotten dialectical history of contradiction and synthesis . . . and then asks us to forget about it once again. The strongest nations, he maintains, are not only the most mixed on empirical grounds, but also those that have forgotten their heterogeneous and fragmented origins (ibid.).

They feel homogeneous, fraternal, national. Race, for Renan, is fluid; it is always being made and unmade. But this position does not allow us to outpace race, because right here something like a logic of race reappears sentimentally: now as a spiritual principle, a moral conscience, in short, a soul (18–20).[22] Nation, then, does not rest on or emerge out of any history of "pure race," that is, lineal descent; but, even for Renan, it feels as if it does. It should feel, following Étienne Balibar's analysis of the production of national "fictive ethnicities," like one big national family. Most important, the national-familial affect rests on another level of amnesia: the forgetting of the violence that made what was once heterogeneous now more or less homogeneous, national. As Renan puts it, "It did not occur to anyone that the origin of all this [the coherent nation form] was a conquest" (10–11). This necessary forgetting is what Renan is getting at when—in an argument still familiar to us today—he raises the specter of reparations for historical crimes and declares, seemingly without ironic intent: "*It is good for everyone to know how to forget*" (16, my emphasis). Everyone: Slavs, slaves, Jews, Arabs, Indians, everyone. And this everyone includes us, his audience.

Both Benedict Anderson (1991, 199–201) and Homi Bhabha (1990a, 310) make admirable contributions to Renan's confusing invocation on the need for the French to have forgotten certain protonational massacres (1882, 11). Neither, however, compares that passage with the one just cited here—"It is good for everyone to know how to forget"—which illuminates the meaning of the former passage on the relations between conquest and nation: national solidarity must be based on a natural unity, not a conquest; it is this violence that must be "forgotten." Thus arises the risk of extrapolating Renan's argument into a postcolonial scene where, in the decolonized world—most of the world—we must go beyond Anderson's insight that this "forgetting" is often a discursive conversion of foundational interethnic warfare into foundational "fratricide." The conquest of Mexico or U.S. westward expansion or South African apartheid is, even today, simply unthinkable as fratricides. For the terms of the national narrative, they must be forgotten in a different light.

Decontextualizing Renan, however, has an important virtue: it exposes the limits of the Hegelian dialectic that orders his thought. For we can now perceive a cunning shift that structures his argument, wherein his powerful opening moves cede almost all of their critical ground. Whereas he begins by announcing the basic structure of forgetting that resides at the heart of the nation-form, by the end of the essay this forgetting is forgotten, with the dialectic of memory and forgetting converted into memory and sacrifice (19) and, most important, memory and consent (19–20). Forgetting, in other words, becomes the sublated part of the dialectic, incorporated by and transferred to the higher ground of "consent." The nation no longer depends on forgetting: in the last instance, it depends on a "tangible fact, namely, *consent*, the clearly expressed desire to continue a common life" (19, emphasis in original). Renan famously concludes: "A large aggregate of men, healthy in mind and warm of heart, creates the kind of moral conscience which we call a nation" (20).

Read as a cipher for Mexico, Garro's Ixtepec is many things, but it hardly emerges as a large aggregate of men, healthy in mind and warm of heart. Renan suggests that this aggregation, this national *feeling with*, consent, emerges not from racial, linguistic (1882, 16–17), religious (17–18), dynastic (12–13), economic (18), or even territorial (30) commonality but rather from what we might call "history," the consolidation of competing narratives into a unified national narrative: the dialectal sublation of forgetting into a common past worth fighting and dying for in the future. The nation's condition of possibility, then, is also its greatest potential weakness: for the genealogical practice (in the Nietzchean sense) of historical investigation may oblige us to remember too much (11). Why do we remember Zapata, the mortal enemy of the state, and not Calles, the very author of Mexico's so-called perfect dictatorship?

This is what *Los recuerdos del porvenir* is about. By this I do not mean to suggest that it is a work of historiography or historical fiction or that it should necessarily be read first and foremost as a "historical novel." As Amalia Gladhart puts it, "If *Los recuerdos del porvenir* is a historical novel, it is so in the broadest sense of the term, as a novel that is set in an identifiable past" (2005, 93). It is ultimately a novel of ideas and their political stakes, in which its complex and multilayered meditations—on time, gender, language—swirl around and are grounded on the problem of the nation, Mexico, and its desperate production of a "large aggregate of men" working in a common time, on a collaborative project, on the same page.

The narration of Renan's dialectic—from the play of memory and forgetting to the "tangible" consent that is productive of national history—is not so much the organizing structure of Garro's novel as the object of its critique. And its movement is explicitly articulated here, emerging in the context of a national community (perhaps we should say a modern national community) in the process of formation through (like all national communities) the expression of violent force, the "deeds of violence which took place at the origin of all political formations" (Renan 1882, 11). In Garro's Ixtepec, however, the violence of nation is not banished to a remote and forgettable past: it is palpable and ongoing.

This is the nature of the national problem as expressed through the prism of Ixtepec. It is a pueblo that does nothing but sink into confused forgetfulness: Were we Maderistas or Zapatistas? Was Madero a traitor, or did we betray him (e.g., Garro 1963, 71)? Was Zapata a pirate or a saint (e.g., 73)? And so on. It is a pueblo that does nothing but forget but cannot banish to the forgotten its conditions of possibility.

One of the more memorable lines of the book speaks to this unforgettable condition: "A los mestizos, el campo les producía miedo" (The countryside made the mestizos afraid) (26). The novel's complex narrative device, a source of controversy in critical readings of the work, makes this passage at once ambiguous and cutting. The narrator is "the pueblo," Ixtepec itself. But its narrative voice is inconsistent. At times, such as in the lyrical opening pages, it appears in the first-person singular *(yo)*, evoking the pueblo as physical space, an aggregate of houses and streets, at once an abstract territory and a material place. At other times it appears in the first-person plural *(nosotros)*, evoking the pueblo as nation, as an "aggregate of men" speaking together in chorus, as if from a common soul. And yet another layer of complexity emerges here, for the game of inclusion and exclusion of the plural pueblo is ambiguous, making it difficult to tell who exactly is inscribed by "us."

These cloudy borders around the collective narrator are present throughout the text. A nice example comes during an argument among the chastened petit-bourgeois families, once community leaders and now supplanted by the military occupation, regarding the recent political history of the country. The scene is set with the families standing in a relation of implicit otherness to the pueblo, the passive voice of the impersonal reflexive structure indicating the action: "During the evening in don Joaquín's house, chairs *were relocated* to the hallway, the lamps *were lit* and trays of drinks and sweets *were prepared*" (69, my emphasis). *Los indios* are twice indicated as marginalized figures, thus also implicitly standing outside of the narrator's discursive terrain at this juncture and resisting any temptation to make them the self-evident collective receptacle of the authentic pueblo (ibid.). The narrator, then, is embodied as the physical town, Ixtepec—"the obtuse shapes of the mountains that surround *me*" (70, my emphasis)—which observes its inhabitants. A moment later, however, in the midst of a debate around the role of Madero in the Revolution, the narrator seems to take on the role of the interior voice of the families as a political entity (71–72), while the Indians are objectified as so many stray dogs, creatures who "in their misery and pariah status" are "equal to the millions of Indians, brutalized and made landless by the government" (72). And then, suddenly, the collective voice, apparently embracing all Ixtepec, as a totality, erupts into the text as the narrator leaves behind its territorialized quality (as the physical town, Ixtepec) and becomes community, invoking an "us" whose subject is unclear but whose embrace would seem to include the families we usually observe, with the narrator, from the outside: "'The gunmen!' The word, still new, left *us* stunned" (72, my emphasis).

"A los mestizos, el campo les producía miedo": the social objectification of the Indians (a "problema social") is here applied to *los mestizos,* whose referent is Ixtepec's leading citizens but whom Ixtepec nevertheless often seems to perceive as something outside of itself. What is it about the countryside *(el campo)* that the mestizos fear? The pueblo-narrator elaborates: "It was their legacy, the image of their pillage. They had established the violence and now they felt themselves in a hostile land, surrounded by ghosts. The order of terror that they had established had impoverished them. That was the origin of my deterioration" (26–27). Then an anonymous voice lashes out against the fear, hostility, terror: "'Ah, if we could just exterminate all the Indians! They are the shame of Mexico!' The Indians remained silent" (27).

Let us quickly remember Renan: the nation, while never of pure race, realizes itself along the lines of something like a national race, that is, having forgotten its heterogeneity, it feels like a race. The racially marked language of the passage just cited highlights this as a problem for Garro. But it is a delicate point, so we should proceed with caution. The "fear" ("el campo les producía miedo") of which the narrator speaks stands in homologous relation to what will be referred to, in a later passage, as the "shameful origin [orig.: *origen vergonzoso*]" of the "mestizo" (1963, 72). This racialized space—campo, mestizo—linked by fear and shame and, to tie it all together, pointing back to an "origin," is a tightly wound network of signifiers, all socially and historically charged and worth disentangling.

First, at the most archetypical level of race, is the Malinche myth, the birth of the nation in the form of the symbolic first mestizo, a child of conquest representing a simultaneous beginning and end of three worlds.[23] The second layer: Mexico, then, is born of tragic consequences, but this tragedy is the result of desire, even pleasure, as Malintzin takes Cortés as her lover and actively participates in the fall of Tenochtitlan. The origin is shameful and speaks (deceptively) of betrayal. This fear-inspiring *vergüenza* (shame) has nothing to do with any sort of genetic sickness in the form of degeneracy brought forth through promiscuous mixture: Garro is not a follower of Agassiz, Morton, Galton, or the tenets of National Socialism.[24] Nor does it have anything to do with an epochal inferiority complex that might be construed as afflicting all Mexicans, made symptomatic in gross caricature and pathetic aping: these were the preoccupations of many more prominent writers who surrounded her and ones that Garro— always a problematic political figure—meticulously transcended.[25] The shame of the mestizo state is its origin in transgressive libidinal pleasure, a crime of passion that, from Aristotle to Freud, has gone insufficiently dissimulated or, in Renan's terms, forgotten. This is all somewhat obvious and, frankly, old news. But it brings us to the third point of resonance, which is the decisive one for Garro. Mestizaje produces originary *vergüenza* and even fear insofar as it represents nothing less than the racialized mark of national identity, that which gives the nation its first-person plurality: what the midcentury anthropologists had sought to foment, what Gamio and Vasconcelos had already proposed as a "pure" mestizaje, what before them Molina Enríquez had theorized as the secret to Mexican state power, and what before him Justo Sierra had identified as the very embodiment of the national family.[26]

By 1963 for Garro to say "mestizo" is not to name a caste; it is rather to name a social and political class, the one that articulates most effectively and *affectively* the problem of hegemony and sovereignty, that is, nation and state. In this sense, it is significant that Garro invokes the "origen vergonzoso" not in a scene of illicit romance but rather in the context of a comment on state formation and its reracialization: "In truth they were surprised at the bloody friendship between the Catholic Porfiristas and the atheist revolutionaries. *They were united by voracity and the shameful origin of the mestizo.* Between the two they had inaugurated a barbarous era that was without precedent in my memory" (72, my emphasis). In other words, for Garro, *mestizo* is simply another way of saying "Mexican": it is the binding agent that unites state, nation, and identity. And to say "Indian" ("los indios calla-ban"), while perhaps not reducible to extra-Mexican, is to say something else and marks a problematic internal exterior ("el campo") vis-à-vis the national family ("mestiza"). It is to name, precisely, the people of exception, of the "campo," those who experience most directly the menace of national consolidation in the form of "pillage," "violence," and "terror." With com-parable discursive violence, we shift the voracity, indeed, the desire of this excessive encounter with the other onto the "shameful origin" that lies in Malintzin's bed, some four centuries past. Garro indicates that the living origin is the condition of the present, diagnosable not in a preoccupation with national psychology but rather in a material voracity unsated. The embarrassing mark (racial, reproductive, *embarazoso*) is a mark of national identity whose ground is an obvious and continuous violence.

The narrator resents this and holds no illusions about a mythical ori-gin: it speaks of a barbarism "without precedent in *my* memory," expelling the "mestizos" (remember: Mexico) into a world of "*their* pillage" where *they* will be "surrounded by ghosts" (my emphasis). This history of racist violence realized in land expropriation denotes a history that the pueblo, Ixtepec, wants to forget. The narrator-pueblo laments: "All of my splendor fell upon ignorance, on a refusal to look at me, on a voluntary forgetting" (118). The pueblo as nation wants to forget, but it can't. The reminders are constant, as no one can escape the menacing images of human beings hung from trees (e.g., 75–92). Likewise, the conglomeration of petit-bourgeois and semiaristocratic families that anchor the novel, beyond hav-ing their sensibilities upset, are in their own way victimized by the same process of primitive accumulation that besets and kills the *agraristas*. And yet the clear and necessary force that could expel the invading federal army is revealed as an impossibility in the face of the cowardice and class con-sciousness of the families: their inability to form a natural and, indeed, national alliance with their other, the Indians and activists.

I argue, then, that the novel's sharpest critical edge is not the narration of a nation of marginals (women, Indians, prostitutes, clerics, decadent aristocracy) allied for a revolutionary moment against state-military power (cf. Franco 1989, 133–34). To the contrary, it narrates a kind of disgust—even shame—in the face of the utter failure, incompetence, and indeed, his-torical impossibility of this necessary alliance. This is clear from the outset and is precisely the meaning of that weird moment at which the narrative voice seems to evaporate and we hear, quite plainly, the voice of Elena Garro, conspiracy theorist:

> The newspapers spoke of the "Christian faith" and the "revolutionary rights." But between the Catholic Porfiristas and the atheist revolutionaries they had prepared the tomb for agrarianism. It had been less than ten years since the two factions had agreed upon the assassinations of Emiliano Zapata, of Francisco Villa, and of Felipe Angeles, and the memory of the revolutionary leaders was still fresh in the minds of the Indians. The Church and the Government fabricated a cause to agitate the discontented peasants. (1963, 154)[27]

Not a revolution but a trick, the (soon-to-be) failed union of rich and poor, mestizo and indio, rests on a distraction: "There were conflicting interests and the two factions in power agreed to throw themselves into a struggle that offered the advantage of distracting the people [orig.: *el pueblo*] from the one point that had to be concealed: the redistribution of the land" (153). With a kind of bait and switch, all eyes turn elsewhere: "Religious persecution!" (154).

What is the nature, then, of the frontier that divides this nonalliance, the relation between the leading families and the Indians that surround them, *callados*? If it is defined by something like disinterest, this feeling is certainly not mutual. Although the Indians—except for brief, but telling, glimpses of the indigenous point of view—maintain their role of general inscrutability, the mestizo elite is consistently and explicitly perturbed by their other. While on the one hand the dead Indians provoke expressions of regret and shock among the leading families, on the other hand the live Indians inspire nothing but paranoia in the literal, Freudian sense: the families demand expressions of love from their oppressed other; any other expression (for example, indifference) is immediately interpreted as hostility, betrayal, indeed hate.[28] The momentous scene bringing together Elvira, Conchita, and their Indian servant, Inés, is illustrative. The townspeople's plot to rescue the insurgency has been outwitted by the military when the reticent Conchita informs her mother that their servant is a sergeant's lover:

> Elvira raised her eyes and prepared to say something terrible but at that moment the beautiful Inés reappeared, carrying with reverence the sparkling tray as if it held the heart of a sacrificial victim. . . .
> "We're screwed . . . ," said Elvira when Inés disappeared behind the door.

"We can't fire her," Conchita responded laconically.

"No! . . . Can you imagine the reprisals? These Indians are traitors." (1963, 258–59)

Much like the inscription on the rock that famously ends the novel, this dialogue is usually read as a verifiable indictment, with its implications logically, and predictably, extending outward: as Amy Kaminsky writes, the conspiracy is "brought down by those who are even less visible than they [the mestiza-bourgeois women]: their Indian servants" (1993a, 84). Nothing in the text, however, beyond this scene of high paranoia, directly implicates Inés—the indigenous servant, *callada*, unknowable, impenetrable, part of the background, a prop—as the rat informing on the conspiracy. Indeed, as Kaminsky's own effective approach to the gender politics in the novel suggests, we should exercise caution. Read within the terms of what Kaminsky calls "residual authority," the scene lends itself to a Eurocentric discourse—amply nourished by Ixtepec's families—on the treacherous nature of the Indian, here residing behind the conspiracy's collapse. Read within the confines of the text, however, Inés just as smoothly becomes an iteration of el indio Sebastián—whose torture and execution inspired Nicolás's question with which I opened this chapter—whose only explicit crime is a refusal to recognize the words of his master (1963, 103–4). In the world of the novel, we simply do not know Inés's role in the counterinsurgency—she may or may not have been in on it—just as we are not equipped to judge Sebastián's guilt or innocence.[29]

Indeed, consistent with the novel's generalized critique of the town's inability to recognize its enemy, it is Rodolfito Goribar—the land-grabber mobilizing his connections and abetting the federal army—not the Indian servants, who stands as an equally plausible source of the leak. In their last conversation together, in which they discuss a plan to save the priest, the Moncada siblings have this premonition, which turns out to be prophetic: "'If something goes wrong, Rodolfito will cut a deal,' they said, prophetic" (264). Whether Rodolfito was let in on or cut out of the plan and how he found out about it if he was not, is left unstated. The suspicion around Inés can still hover. And this, of course, is the point. The coloniality of power, once unleashed, oscillates wildly and spins out of control. As Castellanos so powerfully thematized in Chiapas, one cannot simply open an escape hatch and begin anew at this or that opportune moment. This is the utopia of the leading families, their dream of a convenient solidarity in the face of the irrational, or perhaps excessively rational, brutality of the nation's articulation to state power. In response to Nicolás's question—"Why do you care now when you didn't care then?"—his father, exasperated, asks for understanding: "We are a young nation [orig.: *pueblo*], still turbulent [orig.: *en plena ebullición*], and all of this will pass" (104). "Un pueblo joven," without enough time to forget. Or, for Renan, without enough time to forget the obstacles to hegemonic consent. Garro here brings to the fore the durable nature of these obstacles.

The failure of alliance and its deferral to the ordering of a certain national vision, I maintain, is the fundamental historical-political critique of the book.[30] Its thematization emerges at all of the novel's key turns, most often allegorized in the leading families' cowardice, their decision to "remain silent"—a never-ending refrain—in the face of mortal danger to their very existence as a community. Let us consider its rhetorical trajectory and political implications in the text.

The critique begins to take shape as the savagery of the parasitic relation between the state's military and Ixtepec's landowners erupts with full force. It is in the pivotal eighth chapter that the local opportunist, Rodolfito Goríbar, most explicitly teams up with General Francisco Rosas to crush the potential radicalization of agrarian reform. This entails hunting down and hanging the activist Ignacio and four of his companions, "anonymous Indians" all (1963, 92). The pueblo-narrator concludes the episode: "We never mentioned him again. After all, it was just one less Indian. As for his four friends, we couldn't even remember their names. We knew that soon other anonymous Indians would occupy their places in the branches" (92–93). Again we must gingerly read the narrative voice, which here clearly speaks for the mestizo elite. This is because the response to the murder of the activists is not uniform, and not all social classes appear to be as interested in forgetting the atrocity as the elite families.

In a scene that reads as an indicator of the petit bourgeoisie's failures to recognize resistance that will later define the entire second half of the book, the response to the assassination on the part of the horrified leading families is to do nothing. This stands in contrast to the response of the town's working-class prostitutes and their live-in guest, Juan Cariño, an eccentric whose stentorian pose earns him the nickname El Señor Presidente. While the leading families cower, only the slightly deluded Juan Cariño takes an ethical position, actively leading Luchi and her "muchachas" to

General Rosas's garrison in order to answer "violence with violence" (87), by which he means that he will challenge the general politically, with the action of speech.[31] He is of course mocked, more by the pueblo—"'Would you like to join this demonstration?' We laughed and answered Juan Cariño's invitation with insults" (ibid.)—than by the soldiers, who are momentarily shaken by his protest (88). Indeed, his is the only response involving action. The leading families respond by not responding. Matilde is "embarrassed" at the thought of how this must look to the visitor that she is hosting: "This time it would have led her to blame one of her friends and she preferred to remain silent" (82). Elvira and Conchita wonder if the Indians really deserve this kind of treatment and dispense displaced blame (ibid.). Doña Lola Goríbar, mother of Rodolfito, complains of the lack of pastries at breakfast (the baker is the assassinated Ignacio's sister): "The just must pay for the sins of the sinner" (84). Ana Moncada frantically attempts to shield her daughter Isabel from the news, while her husband, Martín, sinks into a morass of lost memories, hoping aloud in front of his servant to be able to retrieve the bodies for proper burial (85). Félix, the servant, responds: "'Maybe they would return them to you, sir, they always have greater respect for the well-dressed man,' said Félix, knowing what it means to walk barefoot" (86). But despite the suit and the respect that it allegedly conjures, Martín and his social class remain mute. A good liberal and committed Maderista, he shows that his sympathies for his Indian servants cannot coalesce into political action. Far from demanding the return of the cadavers, he simply awaits the general's permission to retrieve them. The prostitutes, too, are fearful, but nevertheless stand their ground with Juan Cariño. No one from the upper classes joins them in their effort. And although the protest comes to nothing, the chapter ends with the prostitutes on strike, barring the soldiers from their business. Besides the agrarian activists themselves, theirs is the first direct line of resistance—isolated and partial—against the military occupation.

By the second half of the novel, we find Ixtepec mobilized, in "revolt" [orig.: *sublevación*] (247). The churches have been closed and worship suspended by the revolutionary Calles regime, orders carried out in Ixtepec by the military occupation (157). This becomes the cause that unites rich and poor (158), and the town begins to make plans, conspire, and turn its silence against the occupiers: "Ixtepec slithered away [from Rosas] like a snake. . . . People came and went paying attention to neither [the soldiers] nor their suspicions. . . . I knew that behind their innocent faces they were spying on the soldiers. . . . Ixtepec's mockery was the origin of his [Rosas's] fall" (182–83). Investigating the mysterious disappearance of the sacristan's body (a victim of political assassination), the military officers find themselves driven mad by an impenetrable wall of silence: "The soldiers found themselves defeated by the silence of Ixtepec. What could they do before those innocent faces? Before that village, in the morning, radiant, and at nightfall, dark and shifting like quicksand" (187). This passive-aggressive attitude culminates when the leading families throw a party for Rosas, a ruse for whisking a persecuted priest out of town and out of danger (191–221). The alliance, however, is ultimately as weak as its silence. As a thousand untraceable whispers reveal the plot—perhaps reducible to the machinations of Rodolfito, perhaps to Inés's revenge against her employers; we never find out—the conspiracy is broken by Rosas and a number of Ixtepecos are executed.

This is the context for the novel's suspended climax: the rebellion of a respected family's daughter, Isabel, and her love affair with General Rosas that becomes the center of the last eleven chapters of the book. Easily read as a kind of Malinche allegory, the logic of the text takes it well beyond these parameters. Whereas the dominant narrative on Malintzin has her acting as Cortés's translator and lover, enabling the conquest, hastening the fall of the Mexica, and bearing the symbolic "first mestizo," the most direct result of Isabel's treason, clearly demonstrated in Kaminsky's (1993a, 1993b) pioneering readings of the text, is the fall of the invader through the collapse of his sovereignty. The problem with reading Isabel as a reiteration of Malintzin is that this approach quickly leads to speculation around questions regarding her love for Rosas, the assassin of her brothers, and the nature of her treason. In short, the homology drives us to ask: how could she? But just as the precise nature of the historical Malintzin's motivations are irretrievably lost, the text gives us very little to go on regarding Isabel's romantic fascination with Rosas. Moreover, the terms of the question repeat the bewilderment of Rosas himself: "How was it possible that a decent young woman would lie in his bed after what had happened to her family?" (1963, 250). And this, of course, is the question on the lips of all Ixtepec in its rancor toward this "ungrateful daughter" (283).

The critical force of Jean Franco's reading of the Malinche myth is here worth remembering, for it is applicable not only to Inés but also to the figure of Isabel. Franco makes the center of her critique the absurdity of the very terms of the "treason" thesis: Malintzin's "situation neatly illustrates the thoroughly gendered inflection of terms such as *loyalty* and *treachery*" (1999, 71). It is difficult to ascertain precisely what Malintzin, an object of exchange, the daughter of a civilization victimized by Mexica expansion, could have betrayed. In effect, it is only with the rise of nationalism, its concomitant essentialization of race, and its retroactive appropriation of symbols of origins (e.g., the indigenous civilizations upon whose defeat it depends) that Malintzin begins to be understood as "traitor."

Garro seems to be up to something along these lines. Taking the bait of the "How could she?" question can blind us with its melodramatic force, thereby obscuring the political critique lodged within the novel. How and why Isabel falls for Rosas is never explicitly stated and is left as opaque as the workings of love itself.[32] Her political motivations, however, are at once clear and pragmatic. From the beginning, Isabel—along with her brother and double, Nicolás—stands apart in the novel as a figure imbued with a modern restlessness. She yearns to escape the prison of provincial Ixtepec and resents the limits of her gendered (subordinate) social role (1963, 24). She would thus seem to be susceptible to the seductive power of a supposedly modernizing state, its forces of individualization, and the possibility of escape, represented by the figure of Rosas (see Gladhart, 106). More important, however, we should recall that her political habitus is also, in relation to that of her fellow Ixtepecos, modern. She stands as a kind of mirror, mocking Ixtepec's commitment to traditions of euphemism, its secrets and its shame, its silence and its cowardice (e.g., 1963, 239). Stigmatized by an active beauty that her mother interprets as evidence that Isabel was conceived in lust (238–39), she possesses an acute perception of the town's realpolitik combined with an impatience for hypocrisy and social artifice. It is thus not surprising to find at the origins of her affair with Rosas—regardless of the mysteries of desire that convert it into something like obsessive, if ambiguous, love—an act of resistance, a tactic to further a strategy of rebellion.

It is at the tense dance party, thrown as a distraction while conspirators attempt to usher the priest to safety, that Isabel's actions begin to take center stage. Astute and observant, she is the first to smell a rat, sounding the alarm as Rosas begins to recede from the party, receiving news from field officers and checking his watch: "Isabel, very pale, went to look for the lady of the house. 'Who knows what's going on . . . ?' the young woman whispered in doña Carmen's ear" (200). Distraught, the hostess asks Isabel what to do: "'Delay them!' begged Isabel" (ibid.). As the leading families—the hosts of the party—hesitate, Isabel rises to the occasion and insists on a dance with Rosas: "Flushed and with her eyes fixed on the general, she seemed adrift in a blood-soaked world. Francisco Rosas looked at her obliquely, without daring to utter a word" (201). *Without daring to utter a word.* Her delay tactics can last only so long, but her potential power over Rosas is here suggested in their first contact. With the conspiracy defeated and the fate of her brothers still unclear, a situation that Isabel is the first to perceive and admit, Rosas appears at the Moncadas' home to call on their daughter: to Ana's horror Isabel "disappeared with him into the darkness" (238).

Is this part of a desperate battle to save Isabel's brothers? Or is it a betrayal? Although the text never answers this question for us, the objective result of her actions plays out over the following chapters. It is with Rosas's seduction of Isabel (or is it her seduction of the general?), almost immediately regretted, that the torment and fall of Rosas begins to unfold. And, contrary to the intentions of Isabel, the general's motivations are explicit:

> He wanted to know and make Ixtepec know that in Ixtepec all that mattered was the will of Franciso Rosas. Hadn't they been laughing at him for months now? . . . He then turned to Isabel, who waited mute and standing in the middle of the room. "Now they will know that I share my bed with the woman that hurts them most," he said to himself. (245)

The desire for sovereignty is clear: *en Ixtepec solo contaba la voluntad del general Francisco Rosas.* If the sovereign is he who decides, then Rosas's project is not confirmed but rather annulled by Isabel as she methodically reduces him to indecision and doubt.[33] He orders her to strip, she does, and then he loses himself in her "obstinate eyes": "Isabel obeyed without replying and Rosas, intimidated, blew out the lamp; in the bed he found himself next to a strange body that obeyed him without saying a word. The morning light found him defenseless. . . . He wanted to leave the room, which had become asphyxiating" (ibid.). This game, whose stakes are not at first clear, continues for the rest of the novel, with Isabel's "ojos obstinados," her creepy obedience, her active silence, her occupation of Rosas's room all converging to methodically reduce the general to tatters, blotting out his romantic memories of revolution (personified in the figure of his escaped lover, Julia) and overwhelming his sovereign force. Where he had assumed that his conquest of Isabel would represent complete triumph (244), instead "there no longer remained any space for him, nor for his past, he was drowning. . . . 'She occupies the entire room,' he said to himself, and in that moment he realized that he had made a huge mistake" (246).

By the end of the novel, the collapse of the general's sovereignty provoked by Isabel plays out in the most literal terms. With Isabel's invasion and occupation of the general's most intimate space, he begins to recognize her as a kind of double for her brother, Nicolás (247), on trial and sentenced to die for participating in the rebellion. Taking advantage of his torment, she wins her brother's freedom, and Rosas orders him to be secretly liberated on his way to the killing grounds (276–77). Just as the executions reach completion, however, Nicolás returns of his own volition to demand that he, too, face the firing squad. The sovereign pardon is rejected, and with it Rosas's power evaporates in a fit of regret: "'He didn't accept my pardon. . . .' He went pale and smacked his thigh with the palm of his hand" (286). If the Moncada doubles—Isabel and Nicolás, whom, Kaminsky explains, must be recognized as the "the primal couple in this novel" (1993a, 94)—represent the love and commitment at the heart of revolutionary action, it is with the death of Nicolás that the general—now clearly delirious—sees in himself the death of revolution itself: "He thought that he was about to cry. . . . Why did he always have to kill what he loved? . . . The Moncada children had shown him a world of companionship and when he entered into it, unsuspecting, they snatched it away from him and left him alone once again, turned over to the nothingness of his days" (1963, 287). Remembering "the treacherous words of Isabel and the proud face of her brother," he vows: "'I will never again pardon anybody'" (ibid.). But he will never have to: his power of sovereign decision deflated at its most basic gesture (the pardon), he roams the remainder of the novel drunk and depressed before mercifully being recalled by the revolutionary government (292).

If the copula of nation and state represents the modern articulation of hegemony and sovereignty, the fall of the general, the local sovereign, represents a momentary loosening of this articulation and a potential crisis of state power. A fissure opens up, a historical opportunity that may or may not be filled by political action, the emergence of a moment in which national hegemony—the terms of horizontal identification that Renan calls "consent"—may be renegotiated. It is, in short, a historical fracture

waiting for revolution. This opportunity, for Garro's generation of critical revisionists, was the Revolution and its aftermath, and Garro clearly
understands it as an opportunity missed. Again, the failure of alliance provides the thematic ground of Garro's critique.

Ixtepec, in its drive to forget, misses its historical moment. It does so by
completely misidentifying the enemy. The last chapters of the novel see all
of Ixtepec enraged and in protest. In these tumultuous scenes, the crowd
rallies around the imprisoned Nicolás, the macho hero, converting him into
a revolutionary martyr and eagerly awaiting his salvation by the rumored
approach of a mythical *cristero* rebel, Abacuc.[34] This popular rage, however, is not directed against the forces of oppression that beset the town:
the general and his troops are not expelled, and there are no calls for the
sinister Rodolfito to be brought to justice. Rather, the protest quickly and
violently turns its attention to Isabel. With a newly perverse hegemony,
Ixtepec, as nation, solidifies its identity by consenting to despise its marginalized other: "Only Cástulo [an indigenous servant] wanted Isabel to rescue
the life of her brother; all Ixtepec wanted her to expiate its [or her, or their]
sins" (1963, 284). If the disjunctures of race and nation produced a terrifying campo whose solution is found in a wishful "extermination of the
Indians," here the disjunctures of gender and nation—"an aggregate of
men"—produce a blindness that allows the march of primitive accumulation to continue unfettered while all Ixtepec rises in one voice against the
betrayal carried out by its "hija ingrata." Without even taking up Franco's
insight in asking on what terms we can begin to think of a betrayal in this
context, the political catastrophe is obvious. With the general beaten down
by Isabel, the pueblo fails to articulate her rebellion, opting to remain
silent, absorbed in its task of forgetting: "Sometimes outsiders don't understand my exhaustion and my dust, perhaps because there is no longer anybody to name the Moncadas" (292). And here we find a kind of sad Rena-
nian nation wherein unity is not merely effected by means of brutality: the
unity of Ixtepec is the same thing as brutality. Or, perhaps more accurately,
brutality appears capable of producing national hegemony, with "unity"
merely standing alongside it as an empty slogan. With Ixtepec tacitly consenting to the arrival of new generals, the expansion of Rodolfito's lands
continues, as does the hanging of more Indian activists (ibid.). As for
Isabel's rebellion, it turns to stone.

In the novel's famously disconcerting ending, Isabel, having driven the
general from the town while also being seduced by him, is transformed into

a large rock—whether symbolically or literally (*piedra*, many critics note, is slang for "prostitute") is unclear and unimportant—at once a monument to her treason and the foundation on which Ixtepec rests (ibid.). The *malinchista* allegory asserts itself, pointing to the "weak weapons" (bodies, silence) that at once limit and enable women's political agency in the national (indeed, protonational) scene. With more skepticism of Garro's project, it can be argued that the ossification of resistance suggested by the stone stops history in its tracks, rendering null any progressively revolutionary discourse, critical or not. Both of these readings are good readings and may in fact be the right readings. But a sympathetically postcolonial reading must look for the critique and its object housed in the novel.

As Kaminsky (1993a) argues, the dead, unmoving time that defines Ixtepec would seem to equally immobilize revolutionary action. This is what I believe Franco is getting at also when she concludes that, for Garro, "Women do not enter history—only romance" (1989, 138). More explicitly, Kaminsky sounds a note of disappointment that Garro "undermines the old plot but puts nothing but silence in its place" and that "no one refutes the final words of the novel. . . . Offering nothing in its place, Garro all but silences the muted voice of resistance" (1993b, 109–110). But precisely on this lack, I maintain, the novel sharpens its critical edge: far from silenced, the voice of resistance is ours, as active readers, to unveil. By offering no self-evident alternative narrative, no user-friendly manual of appropriate world-historical action, Garro's novel avoids the trap of the object of her critique: the desire for a fantastic narrative of overcoming in a context that she precisely wants to criticize for failing to overcome the forces of oppression and, ultimately, segregation. In this sense, the idea that she "produces a *new* national narrative" that highlights ambiguity over closure (Gladhart 2005, 102, my emphasis) is equally dubious. The only national narrative evoked here is a very old one, the narrative of postrevolutionary malaise, already apparent (and equally ambiguous) in Azuela and Vasconcelos, which is the novel's most conventional point, a precise reiteration of the generic mark of the *novela de la Revolución Mexicana* in general.

But Garro moves a step beyond mere malaise, and the impulse of her novel is important for the critical possibilities of literary discourse because it confronts the subtle workings of race in a society premised on a racial contract of acculturation and fusion. Alliance fails, and the boundary that marks this failure is traced along the bright line of actually existing segregation. In a Mexico where the Indian had been ambivalently internalized as the essence of the national identity (Villoro 1950), the mestizo elite can still find no common cause with real indigenous communities and their struggles for land rights. The novel's conclusion speaks to this impasse.

Now we realize that Isabel-as-stone, the daughter of the mestizo state serving as the foundation of the indigenously named Ixtepec ("Here I am, sitting on this apparent rock" [1963, 11] are the novel's first words, uttered by the narrator-Ixtepec), is inscribed with Isabel's shame: "I am Isabel Moncada. . . . I caused the misfortune of my parents and the death of my brothers, Juan and Nicolás. When I came to ask the Virgin to cure me of the love that I have for General Francisco Rosas, who killed my brothers, I repented and I chose the love of the man who destroyed [orig.: *perdió*] me and who destroyed my family" (292). The inscription, however, is not a confession but a testimony, interpreted, translated, and immortalized by the bedazzled Gregoria, the maid who ultimately does the bidding of popular conservatism, first dragging Isabel to face the crowd and later obliging her to seek succor before the Virgin.[35] Moreover, the words are inscribed on a monument. And if we have read the novel carefully, we must read the stone in the context of Garro's unyielding critique of monumental history, the history that Renan signaled as crucial to the formation of nations, the dialectical hinge that converts forgotten foundational violence into consent. Far from a confession, then, the inscription is an erasure, blotting out Isabel's political action, and her humiliation solidifies Garro's repudiation of the petty nativism and class consciousness of Ixtepec, Mexico.

And again, this is an opportunity missed. A couple of concluding details help to emphasize the point and to reveal a glimmer of how things might have been. Wary of the mob, Gregoria escorts Isabel the long way around the town, out into the campo, where the mestizos are afraid, and there they come across the decrepit "hut" of "the wisest and most courteous of my neighbors" (290), as the narrator puts it. This is Enedino Montiel Barona, named for Garro's fellow traveler in the world of agrarian activism, he of "excuse me, sir, but in Mexico the Indians have no government." With his home reduced to "a heap of stones" and all of his pigeons dead (290), his human interaction with Ixtepec's *hija ingrata* is as natural and as pure as the humble meal that he can offer the weary pair: "a stack of tortillas, a little salt, and a gourd of fresh water" (ibid.) With an ethical immediacy that can make common cause unfettered by class prejudice, Enedino's precious generosity stands in naked contrast to Ixtepec's mendacity and neurosis, its failure to see anything but its own embarrassment, and not even that.

Isabel's petrification might be a monument to her own transgressive desire, and her foundational position might stand in homologous relation to the mestizo state, born of Malintzin's sins. The fundamental object of critique, however, is not women's agency or lack thereof. It is not even state-military power as such. I maintain that this object is the glue that holds the mestizo state together: Garro's own social class, its cowardice, its exclusive (and exclusively violent) nationalization, its historical opportunity missed.[36] Through Isabel, this is all that it will see: Ixtepec, from its Nahuatl roots, is an "obsidian hill" (see Boschetto 1989). The mestizo state, as it gazes on Isabel's shame, will find only its own contradictions, its failures, its indigenous self, reflected in black. And this missed opportunity can be symbolized in a mistake: the mistaking of the state monumentalization of Zapata and Madero for the real and necessary lasting alliance, solidarity, between two revolutions—at once materialist and idealist, about land and about justice—in the formation of a nation that succeeds not in forgetting but rather in stopping the reenactments of its own foundational rituals of violence.

Acknowledgments

WRITING A BOOK can be a lonely road, but I've been in good company the whole way. Most of all I was surrounded by the love, support, inspiration, patience, and affirmation of Sarah Elizabeth Hultgren Lund, Benjamin Weldon Lund, Natalie Elizabeth Lund, and Ingrid Rose Lund. I owe them everything.

Friends and colleagues helped me in ways large and small. Peter Hallberg is always a voice of good sense, eloquence, and friendship on which I rely. Nacho Sánchez has been a consistent interlocutor from the outset of this project. I owe eternal thanks to the infinitely generous María del Pilar Melgarejo; chapter 2 emerged out of a conversation with her, and she has been a dedicated reader and critic at various stages of this book. I have depended on Amy Robinson for lots of good ideas and historical confirmation. Salomé Aguilera Skvirsky has been a great friend and a fair critic; her advice sharpened several points in this book. Erin Graff Zivin helped me get moving on chapter 1, which in turn helped me frame the problematic of the book. Many thanks to Koichi Hagimoto and Aarti Madan for keeping me connected to reality; more thanks still to Aarti for her archival work on chapter 1. The good advice of Betina González-Azcárate enabled the completion of chapter 4, and her constant enthusiasm for collaboration kept me in good spirits during the final stages of this project. Mabel Moraña and Gerry Martin have been inexhaustible sources of mentorship and dialogue; I can't thank them enough. Thanks as well to Richard Morrison at the University of Minnesota Press, and his reviewers, for taking interest in the project, not to mention their advice and patience; and to Alicia Sellheim, Nancy Sauro, and Sallie Steele for their help with the manuscript. Many others, with a reading here or a comment there, have assisted me in more ways than I can recall; some who come to mind as I write this include Bram Acosta,

Susan Andrade, Jerome Branche, Hannah Burdette, Juliet Lynd, Anne Garland Mahler, Malcolm McNee, Giuseppina Mecchia, Dierdra Reber, Karen Stolley, Joel Wainwright, Christine Waller, and of course my students at Pitt. Finally, I would like to remember two people who left us in recent years. Beyond e-mail correspondence, I never met Professor Charles Hale, but his work on nineteenth-century Mexican political culture made the first half of this book possible; I wish I could have thanked him in person. Without the initial guidance of Professor René Jara, I never would have made it to this project at all; I've thanked René a thousand times, and I am honored to do so once again.

The University of Pittsburgh has supported me and my family throughout this entire project. The arrival of the Pitt Humanities Center was a godsend; it provided me with time, funding, and, most important, a space of interdisciplinary dialogue; warmest thanks to Jonathan Arac and Todd Reeser for their work and support. The Center for Latin American Studies at Pitt is a perennial source of generosity; special thanks to John Frechione for his relentless encouragement. I am also indebted to the University Center for International Studies, the Dietrich School of Arts and Sciences, the Nationality Rooms Program, the Department of Hispanic Languages and Literatures, and the office of N. John Cooper, the Bettye J. and Ralph E. Bailey Dean of Arts and Sciences. These resources allowed me to travel several times to Mexico City, where I relied on the assistance of researchers and archivists at the Instituto Nacional de Antropología e Historia, the Archivo General de la Nación, the Biblioteca Miguel Lerdo de Tejada, and the Instituto Mora; special thanks to Lorena Gutiérrez and Dalia Hernández, who helped me navigate the Hemeroteca of the Fondo Reservado at the Biblioteca Nacional de México. I am grateful for support from the Richard D. and Mary Jane Edwards Endowed Publication Fund.

I wrote the final version of this manuscript overlooking the hubbub of the most beautiful street in the world, a community governed by the Little Blonde Girl Army and their allies; to Niña, Jon, Carole, Kate, Amelia, Don, Mel, Emily, Roy, Jack, Maggie, Lilah, Lidia, Zamby, Zuky, and Lampy (and the dozens more whom I cannot fit in here) . . . thanks for filling my office with the spectacular sounds of joy.

Notes

Introduction

1. The prenational history of *mestizaje* in Mexico is profoundly complex, and the nature of the relation between the so-called society of *castas* and racial discourse in modern Mexico is controversial. An account of this history and the debates that surround it—which are unfolding as I write this—falls outside of the parameters of this book. The foundational study for the modern discussion on race and *mestizaje* in New Spain is Mörner (1967); there is ample recent work, and a short list of what I consider some of the most illuminating studies in this booming field would include Cope (1994), Lewis (2003), Katzew (2004), Restall (2005), and M. Martínez (2008).

2. Molina Enríquez's key text is called *Los grandes problemas nacionales* (1909). In it he makes the first systematic attempt to understand Mexican social history, especially the problem of land development, in terms of race. See Basave Benítez's excellent study (1992) for an efficient review of Molina Enríquez's basic precepts.

3. Rather than amass citations as the basis for these premises, I can note three sources as indispensable to my thinking about race in this project. Henry Louis Gates Jr. and Kwame Anthony Appiah's edited volume *"Race," Writing, and Difference* (1986) is a watershed in the poststructural turn around critical race studies and the mobilization of literary discourse as not simply reflective but moreover productive of race. Etienne Balibar's idea of "fictive ethnicities" (1991) is essential for understanding the relations between race and nation. Alongside these I place Claudio Lomnitz's *Deep Mexico, Silent Mexico* (2001) for its history of the anthropological institution in Mexico as a kind of intellectual machine for the production of national identity. This last work has been especially important in helping me to sense the historical shape of the conceptual innovations of the first two insofar as it highlights the role of intellectuals and their institutions engaged in the actual work of making race and, moreover, in the precise national context that had captured my interest.

4. The social-political typology within which I place the writers most at issue in this book can be compared with, and certainly owes a conceptual debt to, Ignacio Sánchez Prado's idea of the "nación intelectual," which he describes as "un conjunto de producciones discursivas, enunciadas sobre todo desde la literatura, que imaginan, dentro del marco de la cultura nacional hegemónica, proyectos alternativos de la nación" (a complex of discursive productions, enunciated above all from literature, that imagine, within the frame of hegemonic national culture, alternative projects of nation) (2009, 1). But there is an important difference. The writers at issue in this book are not in the business of imagining alternative projects of the nation, at least not in any explicit sense. Often radically critical, they are by no means cultural radicals, and their critique of racial discourse is largely aimed at the production of a more just hegemony.

1. Colonization and Indianization in Liberal Mexico

1. In Mexican cultural politics, the category "mestizo" refers to an individual of mixed-race ancestry, generally assumed to be indigenous American and European; the presence of Africans in Mexico suffers from a profound historical erasure (see Martínez Montiel 1994). Mestizo is also the long-standing favored racialization of national identity. See, among others, Villoro (1950), Basave Benítez (1992), and Tarica (2008). The more important category for this chapter is "indio." By "the Indian" *(el indio)* I refer to the outcome of a historical trajectory of identification that depends on a colonial gaze backed up by force: one that dialectically homogenizes (the monolithic Indian) and produces difference (distinct indigenous communities). The Indian thus functions rhetorically as both emblem and social relation. I place "the Indian" in quotation marks here (and note that their use is implied henceforth throughout the book) to gesture toward this complex history, and I maintain the term, however problematic, because it resonates with the language of the historical context that forms my object of inquiry. In doing so I attempt to invoke the referential ambivalence of the Indian, at once indicating subjects and communities so (self-)defined, as well as the sociohistorical processes through which those subjects and communities enter into discourse.

2. But it did not change everything. On the nineteenth-century origins of Mexico's postrevolutionary discourse on race, see Villoro (1950, 209–23), Stabb (1959), and Powell (1968). The Porfiriato was briefly interrupted by the presidency of Manuel González, who was in office for about three years between 1880 and 1884. The years are correctly absorbed into the Porfiriato given the continuity between the policies and efforts of the González and Díaz administrations.

3. During the late nineteenth century, Mexican liberalism, as Hale (1989, 23) explains in his influential study of the topic, became confused with a larger philosophical current of positivism and ossified into the ideological underpinning of a state party obsessed with the twin projects of pacification and modernization. Within

the specific context of Mexico, liberalism must always be understood as resonating with this history.

4. Capitalism is one of many "modes of production." See Wolf (1982, 73–79) and, for the specifically Latin American context, Laclau (1971). The heterodoxy of "Mexican liberalism" is especially useful as a case study in this sense, because it so blatantly emphasizes, over all other ideological aspects of liberalism, its articulation to the development of a capitalist mode of production. It is thus that we end up with the oxymoronic "conservative liberalism," so important to Mexico's political history, as a guiding set of policy initiatives that prioritize state-protected capitalist development as a product of liberalism's ideological role in the formation of a state party.

5. This process began formally with the Constituent Assembly of 1856–57, the installation of the Constitution of 1857 and subsequent Laws of Reform, and the presidencies of Benito Juárez of 1858–63 and 1867–72. Sebastián Lerdo de Tejada took over the presidential reins and, despite governing in tumultuous times, succeeded in institutionalizing a number of liberal precepts. In a chaotic three-way fight for executive legitimacy, he was overthrown in a rebellion led by Porfirio Díaz in 1876. While anathema to the more orthodox Juárez in many respects, it was precisely under the long presidency of Díaz that Juárez's legacy, and the so-called Reforma period associated with his leadership, would be canonized as the authentic origin of Mexico's effective political culture.

6. This social, political, and historical dynamic was dramatized through the popular "bandit novel," a literary form that, like the cultural elite to whom it corresponded, tended to flatten the heterogeneity of resistance to state domination into generic "banditry." Luis Inclán's *Astucia* (1865), Manuel Payno's *Los bandidos de Río Frío* (1889), and Ignacio Altamirano's *El Zarco* (1888; published posthumously in 1901) are the classic texts of the genre. But perhaps Heriberto Frías's *Tomochic* (1893), something of a literary failure, in explicitly resisting the banditry of its local rebels, most successfully captures the brutal edge of the pacification of rural Mexico. It should be noted that the consolidation of Mexico was a transhistorical project and that the contours of "unpacified" territory correspond suggestively, if imperfectly, to the "margins of empire" that dogged Spain, as explored in David Weber's exciting study *Bárbaros: Spaniards and Their Savages in the Age of Enlightenment* (2005).

7. *Colonización,* in this sense, conflates the tension that Hannah Arendt (1951, 132–53) draws between imperial expansion and the popular sovereignty of the republican nation-form. Whereas Arendt proposes that the former can only corrode the latter, the Mexican case shows how the basic structure of the former can and does, in fact, operate within the latter.

8. Moisés González Navarro opens his classic study of the topic with this succinct definition of the politics of colonization: "Población escasa y deficiente, y tierra abundante, fértil y baldía, eran las dos premisas en que se basaba la necesidad

de atraer la inmigración extranjera que pasara de la potencia al acto las legendarias riquezas del país" (Scarce and deficient population, and abundant, fertile, and untilled land; these were the two premises in which was based the necessity to attract foreign immigration that could take the legendary riches of the country from the potential to the actual) (1960, 1). (Unless otherwise noted, all translations are my own.) Porfirian colonization was a return to an idea that had been promoted by statesmen since before the war of 1847 and the subsequent expropriation of Mexican territory by the United States in 1848. Hale lists the following as crucial in terms of state policy: the 1846 formation of a "government colonization bureau"; an 1863 wartime decree authorizing "the occupation and alienation of unclaimed lands"; and explicit colonization laws of 1875 and 1883 (1989, 235). See also González Navarro (1960). For a discussion of *colonización* within a wider historical context linking it to Spanish imperial expansion, see Katz (1991).

9. See Craib (2004, 166) and González Navarro (1960, 16, 18–20 et passim). González Navarro explains that indigenous use of lands declared *baldíos* was often dismissed as only itinerant occupation by "salvajes," the common term for nonsedentary indigenous communities (ibid.). As Craib points out, the premise of this logic of civilization through settlement—that indigenous groups were already itinerant *before* the onset of modern state formation—is "open to question" (ibid.).

10. The break-up of indigenous communal lands—the *ejido* system—into private farms began to take serious legal shape in the 1850s with the introduction of the liberal reforms and the Ley Lerdo of 1856, which formalized the attempted privatization of indigenous communities. (New safeguards for the *ejidos* were put into place after the Revolution, and their cancelation in the early 1990s has been a rallying cry in activism against the North American Free Trade Agreement.) By 1900, the intensification of expropriation of indigenous lands was a historiographical and critical commonplace, receiving comment in prominent places such as Sierra's *México, su evolución social* (1900–1902) (see Powell 1968, 29). The quick articulation of "rural violence" to "indigenous rebellion" is a difficult issue. As Hale correctly states, "Observers in the capital tended to refer to all rural rebels as Indians" and "were poorly informed and largely insensitive to the variety of rural protests and to the range of grievances they entailed" (1989, 222–23). That said, whether or not particular rebellions were authored by protagonists who could be identified empirically (biologically, culturally, etc.) as indigenous, the fact is that the nineteenth century witnessed a metropolitan *production of indigeneity* precisely by conflating rural violence and Indian identity. State and press organs worked hard at propping up this discourse. For one example, see Vanderwood (1998) on the 1892 uprising at Tomochic.

11. At its most primordial, the nineteenth-century version of the *problema del indio* has to do with the fear of violence and with a certain anxiety about the threat

(real or perceived) of leftist doctrines that were believed to be floating around the countryside. Separating the underdevelopment of indigenous communities as a *social* problem from their potential rebelliousness as a *political* problem is difficult.

12. "Primitive accumulation" is Marx's name for the appropriation of resources, potentially convertible into capital, by use of force. A quick outline of primitive accumulation is a key strategy for Marx in destabilizing the "idyllic" origins of capital in the works of political economists such as Adam Smith. Primitive accumulation attempts to explain the fact of pre-existing "masses of capital and of labour-power in the hands of producers of commodities . . . an accumulation not the result of the capitalist mode of production but its starting point" (1867, 713). In short, it can be understood as "nothing else than the historical process of divorcing the producer from the means of production" (714).

13. See Stabb (1959, 407–12) for an efficient introduction to these works. Prieto comments on the indigenous condition in a number of his *costumbrista* travel sketches. Pimentel's study is called *Memoria sobre las causas que han originado la situación actual de la raza indígena de México, y medios de remediarla.*

14. See Caso (1958) and Favre (1998). See also the opening pages of Tarica (2008) for a more elaborate definition of indigenismo, including consideration of its oppressive and emancipatory legacies. In literary studies, it is common to distinguish between social realist or surrealist indigenismo (1930s–60s) and Romantic *indianismo* (associated with the nineteenth century), the treatment of an idealized Indian as a subject of literary works. Contemporary indianismo often refers to indigenous-led rights-based political movements.

15. Cf. Leticia Reina and Cuauhtémoc Velasco's idea of "reindianización," which, conversely, refers to the tenacity of indigenous communities in resisting the liberal drive for "homogeneización de sus pobladores" (1997, 15) in nineteenth-century Latin America.

16. Spencer, alongside Auguste Comte, was the great positivist source for much of late nineteenth-century Latin America, and his influence was especially felt in Porfirian Mexico. Alva was a dissenting thinker in this regard. The basic distinction can be drawn around their invocation of a general "law of progress." They concur that a universal law of progress limits the effects of individual human actions. For Spencer, the motor of this law is struggle, and he used it as a case against state intervention in social affairs. For Alva, on the contrary, the law of progress is something that humans must strive to properly harness, and this can be accomplished not through the individual but through the collective, whose spirit is captured by great leadership, whether in the form of a man or a state (*El Monitor Republicano*, October 12, 1893). On the topic of progress, if Spencer is Darwinian, Alva is Hegelian. Alva understood Darwinian struggle as a cheap philosophy of the social sphere that merely justified the exploitation of the weak by the strong (*El Monitor Republicano*,

November 9, 1893). Constant was a Swiss-French political philosopher and a hero to the Mexican constitutionalists. Alva applies many of his teachings on government, especially regarding the division of powers that should undergird a modern republic. Although he departs from Constant's support of a neutral or mediating monarchical power within republicanism, he shared Constant's elitist thesis that modern societies required stable representatives to effect good political practice. For an informative introduction to Constant's thought and its reemergence today, see Rosenblatt (2004, 2009); for Constant's impact in Mexico, see Hale (1968, 76 et passim).

17. *El Siglo Diez y Nueve* announces that it has received the first copy of Alva's *Museo de la Casa* on November 19, 1881: "Dicha publicación está consagrada á las familias, y será una enciclopedia popular y económica para uso de las señoras, los jóvenes, los labradores y los comerciantes en general, pues se ocupará de diferentes materias propias a la instrucción y recreo de las familias" (This publication is directed toward families, and it will be a popular and economic encyclopedia to be used by ladies, the youth, workers, and merchants in general, since it deals with diverse topics relevant to family education and recreation). *El Nacional* makes the same announcement on November 20, adding: "Si el papel fuera mejor, lucirían los grabados que contiene el *Museo*" (If the quality of paper were better, the engravings contained in *El Museo* would sparkle). On December 4, *El Siglo Diez y Nueve* announces receipt of the third issue. Other than these references, I have been able to find no trace of this publication in several major Mexico City archives.

18. *Tomochic* was the first major blow in the form of protest writing to rattle the Porfiriato. In stark detail, it told of the destruction of a small village and its inhabitants at the hands of federal troops. An embarrassment for the government, it was picked up by opponents as an example of Porfirian tyranny. In a critique of "peace" as promoted by the Porfiriato, Alva writes: "Y nuestro ánimo se llena de horror y nuestro corazon se entristece, al pensar y al presentir que se repetirán las sangrientas y horribles escenas de luto y desolacion de Tomóchic y Temosáchic" (And our spirit is filled with horror and our heart is saddened, upon contemplating and foreseeing that the bloody and horrible scenes of mourning and desolation of Tomochic and Temosachic will be repeated) (*El Monitor Republicano*, October 28, 1893).

19. Sierra's concluding sentence of his contribution to *México, su evolución social* (1900–1902) is famous as a cautious expression of the political establishment's growing unease over the permanent presidency of Díaz: "The entire social evolution of Mexico will have been vain and fruitless, if it does not lead ultimately to liberty" (cited in Hale 1989, 11).

20. Although Daniel Cosío Villegas accurately associates the constitutionalist arguments of the anti-*reeleccionistas* as the nascent platform of the Revolution, he somehow misses Alva in his remarkable history of the Mexican press. Thus Alva, especially with his prominent perch at *El Monitor,* should stand alongside Emilio Vázquez as constructing the groundwork for the fundamental plank of the Revolution.

21. Fond of the snappy phrase, Alva thus concludes one essay: "Hagamos las leyes para el pueblo y no queramos hacer pueblo para las leyes" (Let us make laws for the people and not try to make a people for the law) (*El Monitor Republicano*, November 18, 1893).

22. The above sketch of Alva's professional trajectory comes from primary documents examined at the Fondo Reservado of the Biblioteca Nacional (Mexico City). Hale (1989, 113–15, 238) makes the only significant mention of Alva that I have been able to find in the historiographical literature. His place in the decade between his two major periods of writing—the early 1880s and 1893—remains a mystery.

23. Alva's understanding of the threat of U.S. encroachment is not unusual here, far from it. But his refusal to indulge in the "competing conquerors" rhetoric that framed the Indian as an enemy common to Mexican and American civilization efforts is unique. In the piece he makes only an offhand reference to "los salvajes," focusing his attention on the "colonistas abusistas," by which he means Texan occupiers of Mexican lands. For the dominant tone of the day, we can note that, by contrast, a month earlier the same periodical had published an outlandishly alarmist (and unsigned) essay on "Los enemigos de la civilización," accusing the Indians of being a "plaga funesta" waging a "guerra de exterminación" (*El Monitor Republicano*, February 18, 1881). And, on the same day that Alva's essay appeared (March 10, 1881), *El Siglo Diez y Nueve* published a piece on Chiapas called "Guerra de castas," in which it was predicted that the rumors of indigenous rebellion put the "raza blanca" in danger and that no fewer than 750,000 lives were at stake.

24. The definitive source on this history is Hale (1989; see 21, 55, 88, 92–108, 120 et passim).

25. To wit, Stabb (1959, 418–19) lists the titles of the editorials that appear in *La Libertad* from 1878 through 1879: "Los agitadores de los indios," "La guerra social," "El comunismo en Morelos," and "El plan socialista de Querétaro."

26. I deal with this debate in the next chapter. See also Powell (1968, 23–24).

27. To be clear, this is not to say that he appropriates the rhetoric of socialism *as* socialism, which he later calls "insensato" and the "mal del siglo" (*El Monitor Republicano*, June 6 1893).

28. Alva's protoindigenist terms will not be fully met until well after the Revolution and resonate most harmoniously with Gregorio López y Fuentes's 1935 *El indio*.

29. Alva's essays appear in thirteen editions of *La Libertad* during the summer of 1882, running from June 7 to July 20.

30. For example, Ernest Renan, in his famous discourse "What Is a Nation?" (1882)—delivered, incidentally, in the same year as Alva's essays—goes as far as to reject the "natural" relation between race and nation (8). See chapter 4.

31. During the nineteenth century, this "heterogeneity" was usually thought in terms of the relations among indios, *criollos* ("white" Mexicans), mestizos, and, less frequently, new immigrants. The presence of Africans and African culture in

Mexico has suffered a historical erasure that is palpable in nineteenth-century writing on topics of the nation's interculturality, a theme that has received growing attention in recent decades. See classic works by Aguirre Beltrán (e.g., 1946) and, for more recent studies, Martínez Montiel (1994), Vinson and Restall (2009), and Bennet (2010).

32. As early as 1849, José María Luis Mora argues for actively encouraged *mestizaje* as a way of quelling social violence (1849, 277). Francisco Pimentel (1864) is the first to make the case in terms of national development, and Vicente Riva Palacio begins to craft state policy around protoeugenic ends through new immigration policies in 1877 (see González Navarro 1960).

33. On the basic outlines of Sierra's vision of the "nación mestiza" as a kind of "utopía de la integración nacional," see Moya López (2003).

34. While the previous citations of Sierra and Riva Palacio are taken from important texts that appear after Alva's essays, their basic thrust can be found throughout the authors' writings. Both were explicitly concerned with the place of the Indian in Mexican society, and both looked optimistically to policies of colonization. Sierra had long been an advocate of colonization; Riva Palacio had promoted the policy as minister of development in the first Díaz regime. See González Navarro (1960); Hale (235).

35. This move, which Neil Larsen calls "re-racialization" (2006), is basic to the Latin Americanist "hybridist" critique of race.

36. I say "ostensibly" here because Alva's production of an abject Indian is itself an effect of the discourse that guides his assumptions. Although vast numbers of indigenous communities were materially and culturally oppressed, so were indigenous communities active social formations that could muster the strength to force the state to negotiate in a number of conflicts. See the collection of essays edited by Leticia Reina and Cuauhtémoc Velasco, *La reindianización de América, siglo XIX* (1997).

37. The dream of engineering a strong population through breeding is captured in the chilling comment at the end of Frías's novel *Tomochic* when the narrator declares that the valiant women and children who survived the massacre at Tomochic will be transferred to the custody of local families, becoming "seedbeds" for a future national race (1893, 146).

38. The idea of biological mestizaje as a means for easing social conflict has a long and stable history in Mexican discourse, running from the nineteenth-century liberals to the current titan of Mexican historiography, Enrique Krauze (1997, 221–22).

39. For a nice collection of primary documents dealing with indigenous and peasant uprisings, see Reina's *Las rebeliones campesinas en México (1819–1906)* (1980). See also John Tutino's *From Insurrection to Revolution in Mexico* (1986).

While it is conventional wisdom that most of these actions took place before 1880, their reputation reverberated throughout the Porfiriato as part of a discourse whose material effects included state violence and massive military deployments such as the conquest of the Yaquis in the early twentieth century.

40. The case of Aguilar is fascinating in itself but would take me too far afield to fully pursue here. Federico Aguilar was a Jesuit priest sent to Mexico by the Colombian state, then under the auspices of a conservative movement remembered today as "La Regeneración." As the governmental decree put it, his task was "un trabajo científico y literario." The commission, approved in 1880 and reprinted in *La Libertad,* continues: "Comisiónase al mismo Dr. Aguilar para que se traslade á las Repúblicas de México y Centro América y haga de ellas un estudio científico que llene los objetos á que se ha aludido, para comunicarlo á la prensa colombiana; en el cual . . . no pierde de vista ventaja ni desventaja de condicion que observar respecto de las nuestras, ni institucion útil que merezen plantearse entre nosotros" (Dr. Aguilar is hereby commissioned in order to relocate to the Republics of Mexico and Central America and make of them a scientific study that fulfills the objectives to which have been alluded, in order to communicate these findings to the Colombian press; in which . . . be omitted neither advantage nor disadvantage of condition observed relative to ours, nor any useful institution that deserves to be established among ours) (*La Libertad,* May 9, 1880). Arriving at Mexico City in 1882, he gave a series of well-attended and semiscandalous sermons at the Templo de la Encarnación (then a convent and church, today the Secrataría de la Educación Pública, one of Mexico's most beautiful state monuments, world famous for its murals by Diego Rivera). His theology was heterodox, an attempt to reconcile scientific discovery (especially geological findings that clashed with the biblical narrative of history) and revelation, and it provoked wild polemics—in which Aguilar happily participated—in the Catholic press. As Aguilar's reports to Colombia made their way back to the Mexican capital, he upset local sensibilities by declaring that Mexico would soon be absorbed into the United States, a delicate (and real) topic of the moment. Alva, for his part, is responding to Aguilar's claim that Mexico's backwardness was due to its vast indigenous population and that U.S.- or Argentine-style extermination was the only hope for progress. Aguilar seems to have left Mexico City on bad terms and then proceeded to create some sort of fracas in Puebla. The *Diario del Hogar* reported that he had been chased out of his formal speaking engagement and was preaching on the street in the barrios (July 22, 1882). When he died five years later, the *Diaro del Hogar* took another shot at his legacy, noting his obvious intelligence and lamenting his social confusion, which the editors attributed to his Jesuit indoctrination (September 21, 1887). Several of his books can still be found in libraries, and Siquisiri (Mexico) republished an 1885 collection of his writings on Mexico, with a useful introduction by Martha Poblett. The 1882 reports that caused

such consternation among the Mexico City intelligentsia are available only in their original publication format, in Bogotá's *El Pasatiempo*.

41. Even ten years later, when the anarchist Frías finds the authentic Mexican in the victims of Porfirian state repression, he is careful to distinguish this fount of authenticity as mestizo, that is, nonindigenous. See *Tomochic* (Frías 1893).

42. The resonance here with Arendt's (1958) famous critique of Marx that turns around the categories of labor, work, and action is provocative and worth noting. Patrick Dove (2006) offers a brief but suggestive analysis of the relations between Agamben's "bare life" and Marx's "living labor." Cf. Brennan (2006).

43. As Laclau (1971) reminds us, the homology of this formulation—"civilization and barbarism"—provides the basic model of social analysis for Latin American liberals since the early nineteen century, a model that would guide the left toward various theories of developmentalism.

44. Writers from Mariátegui (1928) to Ortiz (1940) to García Canclini (1989) have made a convention of the next logical step beyond Alva, which is to explore the ways in which traditional practices "persist" within and even give shape to an uneven, transcultural, hybrid, or heterogeneous Latin American modernity.

45. See Schwarz's essay "Nationalism by Elimination" in *Misplaced Ideas* (1992) and also Larsen (2001, 80).

46. My invocation of "biopolitics" is informed by Giorgio Agamben's (1995) revision of Michel Foucault's (1976) idea. Both Foucault (e.g., 252–58) and Agamben (e.g., 130–32) understand the science of race, its articulation to nation, and its management by the state as central to the work of biopolitics.

47. Melgarejo's specific context of analysis here is the nineteenth-century jurist Andrés Bello. However, the model of "political language" that she sketches is relevant to a general consideration of nineteenth-century Latin America.

48. We must make of the Indian a consumer, citizen, and free man.

49. See the important lectures delivered by Subcomandante Marcos in 2007.

50. See Reina's (1980) collection of documents around the 1868 rebellion of Julio López for one dramatic example. See also Anaya (1997) and Falcón (2002).

2. Altamirano's Burden

The chapter epigraphs read as follows in the originals:

"Si el preopinante dice: 'es una palabra hueca la salud pública,' para mí no es. Estoy convencido de que la revolución sucumbirá en el carril constitucional. El moderantismo se obstina en que el Congreso se limite a servir de comitiva fúnebre a las víctimas de la reacción. Mi regla será siempre: 'La salud del pueblo es la suprema ley'" (Altamirano).

"El quietismo que reina abajo, cuando la arbitrariedad impera arriba, no es la paz, es la guerra en estado latente" (Alva).

1. Alva's beef with Lerdo revolves around his claim that, rather than relent to the orderly transition that a liberal democratic republic demands, the great democrat Lerdo succumbed to hubris: "reunir en su persona todo el poder, toda la autoridad, y toda la ciencia" (consolidating in his person all power, all authority, and all knowledge) (November 23). He continues: "de haberse creido invulnerable como Aquiles é infalible como Dios" (having believed himself to be invulnerable like Achilles and infallible like God), Lerdo opened the door to the antidemocratic strongman "haciéndose, por su orgullo y sus errores, el autor de su propia ruina y el obrero de su propio derrumbe" (making himself, through his pride and his errors, the author of his own ruin and the agent of his own destruction) (ibid.).

2. Tutino calls this social dynamic agrarian "compression" (1986, 277), referring to the capitalist penetration of peasant lands and the ensuing unrest stemming from the redirection of flows of profits.

3. Ignacio Ramírez was one of the great voices of unabashed liberalism during the mid-nineteenth century. Like Altamirano, he was a man of many talents who helped shape Mexico's intellectual culture of the subsequent decades. He was largely responsible for establishing the scholarship that led Altamirano to Toluca. On his relationship with Altamirano, along with a general history of the Instituto, see Nicole Girón's excellent book *Ignacio Manuel Altamirano en Toluca* (1993).

4. Christopher Conway offers a nice bibliography on the institutionalization of the "Cult of Benito Juárez" and its basic tenet, that "Juárez's life vindicated the Indian class and provided an example for all Mexicans to follow" (2006, 38). Conway argues that the "myth of Altamirano the Indian was quite similar" in its didactic thrust (ibid.). For a gripping dramatization of the Cult of Juárez, see Emilio "El Indio" Fernández's 1948 film *Río Escondido,* starring a ferocious María Félix.

5. I have not been able to confirm any data regarding the Afro-descended population in Tixtla, but there certainly is one, whether culturally recognized or not. And although I have never seen reference to any African lineage in Altamirano's ancestors, the possibility cannot be discounted, given the little that we know about his family history and the relative proximity of Tixtla to the Costa Chica, a center of Afro-Mexican culture.

6. The biographical canon on Altamirano includes three major contemporary works: Chávez Guerrero (1985), Fuentes Díaz (1986), and Girón (1993).

7. A number of Spaniards play pivotal roles in Altamirano's youth. Besides his family history, when he was around nineteen a wealthy Spaniard named Luis Rovalo became Altamirano's "protector" during his residency in Cuautla. When Rovalo died in 1858, Altamirano continued to receive financial assistance from the family, now by way of Rovalo's son, Agustín (Sol 2000, 70). In his discourse *La educación popular* (1870), he declares, "He debido mi instrucción primaria a la beneficiencia de mi pueblo, y la instrucción secundaria a la beneficiencia del gobierno liberal y a la de un digno y noble español a quien no puedo recordar sin la más tierna

gratitud" (I have owed my primary education to the beneficence of my pueblo, and the secondary education to the beneficence of the liberal government and that of a dignified and noble Spaniard, whom I cannot remember with anything less than the most tender gratitude) (*Obras completas*, 1:211).

8. Altamirano's impact on the cultural politics of modern Mexico cannot be overstated. He was a massively influential critic of literature, theater, and art; was at the center of several publications on literature and politics; and hosted salons attended by a wide swath of Mexico's young writers and intellectuals. The cultural agenda of literary nationalism set forth in his short-lived review, *El Renacimiento* (1869), would stand as Mexico's most influential at least until the creative ferment surrounding the Ateneo de la Juventud of the Revolutionary period. See *Obras completas*, 143:9–21. The list of contributors to Altamirano's farewell party includes, among others, Ángel de Campo, Guillermo Prieto, Porfirio Parra, Manuel Gutiérrez Nájera, and Justo Sierra. See Tola de Habich (1984).

9. It is also worth noting that there is no mention of Altamirano's alleged monolingualism or illiteracy in Girón's (1993) more thorough account of his arrival at Toluca.

10. See Reina (1980, 85–122) on the various stages of these interrelated rural rebellions.

11. Conway (2006, 34–39) dwells on the "indio feo" discourse at length.

12. Girón (1993, 57–61) casts ample doubt on this widely repeated account. Her reasoning is that Altamirano himself never directly confirmed the anecdote (it comes down to us through his acquaintances) and that it would be completely out of character for the Instituto's director. Drawing on archival correspondence, she hypothesizes that what may have been a rocky start to Altamirano's studies at the Instituto likely had to do with insufficient funds for tuition provided by his sponsoring municipality.

13. Thus the cultural expression of and meditation on race relations emerges in a very different form in the two countries. Classic works of the complexities of American race relations—Faulkner's *Light in August* (1932), Wright's *Native Son* (1940)—have no equivalent in Mexico, just as a mainstream manifesto on the virtues of race-mixing, such as Vasconcelos's *La raza cósmica* (1925), has no equivalent in the United States (the "melting-pot thesis" of early New York pluralism does not really capture the racial politics and spirit of the cosmic race thesis).

14. Catalina Sierra and Cristina Barros (1998) have brought together a dramatic collection of images of Altamirano, from portraits to lampoons.

15. Altamirano makes this case in a number of places, most explicitly in an 1882 article "Generalización del idoma castellano" (*Obras completas*, 15:200–210; see also Palazón Mayoral and Galván Gaytán 1997, 110–12). Justo Sierra puts it more bluntly around the same time: "Enseñarlos [los idiomas indígenas] a los maestros de los indios, tiene para nosotros el objeto capital de destruirlos, de enseñar a todos el

idioma castellano y de suprimir así esa barrera formidable opuesta á la unificacion del pueblo mexicano" (To teach indigenous languages to the teachers of the Indians has for us the ultimate objective of destroying them, of teaching to all the Castilian language and of thus suppressing this formidable barrier opposed to the unification of the Mexican pueblo) (1885, 2). It is worth pointing out that much of this debate over language education places indigenous Mexicans in the middle of a fight between competing colonial projects, the local "Hispanic" one versus the threat of imperialist intervention from the north. Sierra finishes his thought: "Porque es este uno de los objetos de la multiplicacion de las escuelas, son centros de contacto del indígena con el mundo moderno, son en consecuencia, centros de civilizacion. Y esto, si nosotros no nos apresuramos á hacerlo, otros lo harán, aunque en distinto idioma; y el águila del nopal, símbolo de union de la vieja raza azteca, será olvidado por el indígena, cuya mirada convierta el maestro á las constelaciones boreales" (Because this is one of the objectives of the expansion of the schools, which are centers of contact between the indigenous and the modern world, and are, consequently, centers of civilization. And this, if we do not hurry to do it, will be done by others, although in a different language; and the eagle of the cactus, the symbol of union for the old Aztec race, will be forgotten by the indigenous, whose gaze the teacher will direct to the northern constellations) (ibid.).

16. When Altamirano's identity finally does come up in the debate, it is only in passing and to make a point about his lack of ethnic identity. His opponent, Francisco Cosmes, in order to throw into doubt Justo Sierra's (Altamirano's ally in the debate) understanding of the "problema del indio," noted: "Es que tú no sabes, compañero mio, lo que es esta raza indígena. En materia de indios, no conoces mas que á Altamirano, que tiene mucho de ateniense" (It's that you don't know, my friend, what this indigenous race really is. In terms of Indians, you only know Altamirano, who's pretty Athenian) (1883, 1).

17. On the whole, the piece is not as tendentious as it sounds from this excerpt. Palazón and Galván, clearly well grounded in the complexities and contradictions of theories of the nation, appreciate the ambivalence of liberalism. They see liberalism as an ideology that can promote a strong state that by definition will be a despot for some and yet, through its commitment to the freedoms of individual rights, contains within itself its own theory of protest against state excess. In turn, while condemning Altamirano for his position on indigenous cultures, they praise him as a tireless architect of what they call "defensive nationalism" (1997, 113) against U.S. interventionism.

18. Both passages are almost universally cited in contemporary studies that deal with Altamirano's handling of race. Many have read the features ascribed to the protagonist of *Clemencia* as fulfilling certain stereotypes of indigenous ethnicity: "moreno, pero tampoco de ese moreno agradable de los españoles, ni de ese moreno oscuro de los mestizos, sino de ese color pálido y enfermizo que revela o una enfermedad crónica

o costumbres desordenadas . . . ojos pardos y regulares, nariz un poco aguileña, bigote pequeño y negro, cabellos lacios, oscuros y cortos, manos flacas y trémulas . . . laborioso, reservado, frío, este joven tenía un aspecto repugnante, y en efecto era antipático para todo el mundo" (dark, but neither of that agreeable complexion of the Spanish, nor of that rich brown of the mestizos, but rather of that pale and sickly color that reveals either a chronic sickness or disordered habits . . . eyes brownish and regular, nose a little aquiline, mustache slight and black, hair straight, dark and short, hands thin and tremulous . . . laborious, reserved, cold, this young man had a repugnant aspect, and in effect was unpleasant for everybody) (*Obras completas*, 3:164). The description of Nicolás, the hero of *El Zarco*, moves to the opposite extreme in that the indigenous character is no longer sickly but now has his beauty and enlightenment presented as an indigenous exception: "Era un joven trigueño, con el tipo indígena bien marcado, pero de cuerpo alto y esbelto, de formas hercúleas, bien proporcionado. . . . Se conocía que era un indio, pero no un indio abjecto y servil, sino un hombre culto ennoblecido por el trabajo" (He was a swarthy young man, with a well-marked indigenous type, but with a body tall and svelte, of herculean shape, well proportioned. . . . It was known that he was an Indian, but not an abject and servile Indian, rather an educated man ennobled by work) (1901, 125).

19. The following lines demonstrate the hidden radicalism (which, let us recall, is always a kind of purism) of Altamirano's project, as interpreted by Monsiváis: "Para la burguesía naciente y creciente del siglo XIX, las apariencias no son velos sino guías hacia el auténtico Yo de quien lleva los trajes, tan indeciblemente significativos. . . . En la República Restaurada o en el porfiriato, Altamirano ve crecer el amor por las apariencias, y el culto por personalidades casi siempre falsas y pomposas, y desde sus novelas resiste a tan desdichada convicción. Su actitud corresponde a una idea de sí mismo (la vanidad de su fealdad) y a su férreo y desesperanzado pensamiento democrático" (For the nascent and growing bourgeoisie of the nineteenth century, appearances are not veils but rather guides to the authentic ego of the wearer of the clothes, so unspeakably significant. . . . In the Restored Republic or the Porfiriato, Altamirano sees the love of appearances growing, along with the cult of personalities almost always false or pompous, and from his novels he resists such unfortunate conviction. His attitude corresponds to an idea of himself (the vanity in his ugliness) and to his fiercely and hopelessly democratic thought) (1999, 14).

20. Manuel Sol does a nice job of situating the novel in his wonderful critical edition of *El Zarco*, which is the version that I handle throughout this chapter. Taking the narrative voice as the voice of the author, he surmises that the first chapters of *El Zarco* were written in 1874, based on a reference in the book's opening lines to 1854 and its subsequent indication that twenty years have since passed (Altamirano 1901, 29).

21. It can be noted, too, that Altamirano does not necessarily see indigenous villages as "vulgar." In his *costumbrista* scenes of indigenous village life, harshly

critical language tends to revolve around poverty, implicating larger questions of national political economy, rather than around indigenous customs as such. Some of his portraits of rural indigenous life are frankly laudatory. See Segre (2000), Wright-Rios (2004), and Conway (2006) for interpretation of these moments in Altamirano's work.

22. Xochimancas, the narrator reports, was an ancient site for the cult of Coatlicue, the Aztec goddess of flowers who took serpent form. Xochimancas is then described as having fallen into ruin, inhabited only by reptiles. Later the place will be occupied by, in Escalante's reading, "la versión humana de los reptiles" (1997, 202), the bandits. By way of the metonymic reptile, the bandits become Indianized. But as usual, ample ambivalence remains. Coatlicue, as Escalante mentions, would be tranculturated into the icon of Mexican Catholicism, the Virgin of Guadalupe. And Altamirano's position on Guadalupe as the center of Mexican national identity ranges from ringing endorsement (see "La fiesta de Guadalupe" in *Obras completas,* vol. 5) to high skepticism; see Wright-Rios 2004 (esp. 57–58) for a good treatment of Altamirano on the Virgin of Guadalupe.

23. Escalante (1997) conflates the narrative voice with the historical author. This is traditional practice when reading Altamirano, in that his major novels are also transparent political commentaries wherein the narrative voice conforms to his journalistic writings on the topics of the day.

24. Escalante's exact wording is "su etnia" (1997, 200). *Etnia* does not translate precisely as "ethnicity" (which would be *etnicidad*), and one could make a case for translating it as "race." But it comes closest to describing a group of people who are ethnically circumscribed by a common identity; the referent of *etnia* is the people, not a quality encapsulated by the people (e.g., their ethnicity or race).

25. In another essay on public education from the same year, Altamirano describes the indigenous communities that have received state-sponsored education, writing: "Los indígenas de allí están muy lejos de parecerse a los desgraciados y abyectos indígenas del centro del país, analfabéticos y miserables" (The indigenous from there resemble nothing of the disgraceful and abject indigenous of the center of the country, illiterate and miserable) (*Obras completas,* 15:232).

26. The documents collected in Reina's *Las rebeliones campesinas* (1980) are especially illustrative in this regard. Although rebellion was widespread throughout the nineteenth century, it would not become nationally articulate until the very end of the century.

27. The verse does not translate well; it means something like "I am an Indian, the ugliest of all."

28. Altamirano is often read as a kind of elitist, but scholars have found a palpably progressive strain in his work. Introducing his historical writings, Moisés Ochoa Campos concludes that Altamirano "se convierte en el primer historiador mexicano moderno, imbuido de sentido social y que concibe la lucha de clases como motor

de la historia" (becomes the first modern Mexican historian, imbued with a social sense and conceiving class struggle as the motor of history) (*Obras completas*, 2:9). Palazón and Galván indicate how his populist strain weathered the decades, from an 1859 speech that distinguished him from "los liberales ortodoxos porque nunca renegó de su 'condición de pueblo'" (the orthodox liberals because he never denied being a "man of the people") to an 1880s essay in which he denounced the condition of the "'desheredados de la suerte' que habitaban los suburbios de la ciudad de México, invitando a las 'autoridades indolentes' a que visitaran ese 'círculo negro' que vivía bajo la represión policiaca" ("those disinherited by fate" who inhabited the suburbs of Mexico City, inviting the "indolent authorities" to visit this "black circle" that lived under police repression) (1997, 98).

29. On Altamirano's personal familiarity with Morelos, the region where the action of *El Zarco* takes place, see Girón (1997).

30. I could amass citations, but the canonical reading on this point is Sommer (1991).

31. *El Zarco* was first published in Barcelona. The original editor, Santiago Ballescá, justifies the long delay between the delivery and the publication of the manuscript by explaining that the copyist lost part of the original, which went unrecovered until much later (Ballescá 1901). Manuel Sol maintains that the text that we know as *El Zarco* descends from the Barcelona edition and was transformed at the editorial stage. He explains that it was probably modified by a second copyist who "introdujo algunas modificaciones con el propósito de adecuarlo a lo que él consideraba 'correcto' y que, en la mayoría de los casos, correspondían a algunas normas del español de España y, en general, a las reglas y acepciones de la *Gramática y Diccionario de la Real Academia Española*. Normas y criterios que no eran ciertamente de Altamirano" (introduced some modifications with the purpose of adjusting it to what he considered "correct" and that, in the majority of cases, corresponded to some norms of the Spanish from Spain and, in general, to the rules and usages of the *Gramática y Diccionario de la Real Academia Española*. Norms and criteria that certainly were not those of Altamirano) (2000, 17). For example, *embellecido* is replaced by *ennoblecido*, which would have a "'connotación nobiliara' totalmente ausente en un mexicano de espíritu liberal como Altamirano" (ibid.). Passages that could possibly offend a Spanish audience—for example, implicating Spanish mercenaries in the introduction of kidnapping practices in Mexico—were also removed or transformed (ibid.).

32. Being well armed is a minor obsession of Altamirano, cited favorably no less than thirteen times in the novel (cf. 1901, 118, 126, 203, 209, 254, 297, 306, 311, 315, 320, 324, 330). There is a historical immediacy behind the curiosity: arms were preferred booty on the part of both soldiers and bandits, villages often found themselves disarmed, and, then as now, the state institutions of security—the military and police—could not always count on a firepower advantage over bandit gangs. This theme is explicitly staged in *El Zarco* (203).

33. For extensive analysis of the theme of corruption in *El Zarco*, including the historical basis of the accusations Altamirano leveled in the novel, see Rivas Velázquez (1992), Sol (2000), and Robinson (2003).

34. Citing the historical work of Paul Vanderwood, Sol (2000, 51) explains that this was an actual title associated with semiformal security forces governed by local prefects and state authorities and thus distinct from the professional, federally supported military.

35. On the relations between spaces and figures of "exception," such as the bandit and the sovereign, see Agamben (1995).

36. Sol's bibliography (2005, 55) on this topic is indispensable. He traces the appearance of Martín Sánchez from Pablo Robles's *Los plateados de Tierra Caliente* (1891) to Lamberto Popoca Palacios's flamboyantly titled *Historia—de—El bandalismo* [sic]—*en el—Estado de Morelos ¡Ayer como ahora! ¡1860! ¡Plateados! ¡1911! ¡Zapatistas!* (1912) and finally to Enrique Juventino Pineda's *Morelos legendario* (1936).

37. José Luis Martínez calls Robles's book a kind of historical companion to *El Zarco*, one that drew directly from Altamirano's novel (1986, 8, 14), but his own account undermines this thesis. *Los plateados de Tierra Caliente* was published in 1891. The only known publicity around *El Zarco* before its 1901 release was Altamirano's presentation of the first thirteen chapters in, as Altamirano himself explains in a handwritten note on the manuscript, "las sesiones públicas y privadas del Liceo Hidalgo, en 1886" (Martínez 1986, 13–14). And these first chapters do not include the story of Martín Sánchez.

38. Again, this research would have been quite arduous without the previous work of Sol, who offers an entire bibliography on Altamirano's journalistic and editorial writings on banditry (2000, 55). See also Rivas Velázquez (1992).

39. It is important to remember that "bandit," of course, was a rhetorical weapon wielded by the state (much as "terrorist" is today). Social formations of all kinds, especially peasant communities that actively asserted their constitutional rights, had a way of finding themselves suddenly inscribed by the category "bandit" even if they did not literally participate in the practices (robbery, extortion, kidnapping) usually associated with banditry. One fascinating example of this process can be witnessed by tracing the transformations in state rhetoric over time as it confronted the Julio López uprising of 1868–69. See Reina (1980) for reprints of the relevant documents around the López case.

40. Sol notes that villages could expect to be pillaged by liberal forces rescuing them from conservatives or bandits (2000, 51), a fact of life converted into a scene of *El Zarco* in the form of a complaint from Yautepec's prefect: "Pasó primero Márquez con los *reaccionarios* y quitó todas las armas y los caballos que pudo encontrar.... Pasó después el general González Ortega con las tropas liberales y mandó recoger todas esas armas y todos esos caballos que habían de quedar, de manera que nos

dejó con los brazos cruzados" (First came Márquez with the *reactionaries* and he confiscated all of the arms and horses that he could find. . . . Then came the general González Ortega with his liberal troops and he ordered that those remaining arms and horses be seized, such that we were left empty handed) (1901, 203). Sol cites Francisco López Cámara's sociological study of Reforma-era Mexico, noting that the bandit gangs were populated by, among others, "soldados y oficiales del ejército regular que desertaban después de cada guerra civil" (2000, 53). Citing Miguel Galindo y Galindo, Sol notes the well-known fact that *plateados* fought "en las filas del ejército liberal" (60). Finally, Vanderwood concludes that bandit mercenaries did not work "for pay in the usual sense. They were instead allowed to plunder as they went. Pillage sustained and rewarded them" (2000, 6). This was an especially serious problem during the Juárez years: "However much the participants [in the civil wars] lamented the necessity of employing known bandits as combatants, they did it just the same, especially the beleaguered Liberals under President Benito Juárez" (ibid.).

41. When Juárez says, "Bueno," he is responding most immediately to Martín Sánchez's revelation of the corrupt insider within the state apparatus. He follows by indicating that this official will be removed and then asks, "¿Qué más desea usted?" (324). It is interesting, and I think important, that Juárez never explicitly says, "Yes, you may commit extrajuridical executions." The sovereign must simply let it happen.

42. "Public health," of course, sounds funny today and would be more adequately translated "public safety" or "public security." But the conflation of the safety of the social body with its very survival—its "salud," literally "health"—is important, especially historically, with roots in the Comité de Salut Public created in the wake of the French Revolution, and therefore I leave it literal.

43. Without treading any undiscovered ground around the interpretation of the function of Martín Sánchez in *El Zarco*, Sol (2000, 64–67) treats Escalante's critique directly by asking that we be more understanding of the historical conditions in which Altamirano produced his text. He ultimately points out that what Escalante perceives as despotism was in fact a constitutionally authorized maneuver.

44. The context, in fact, is an election season, the intense 1880 debate around who would succeed Porifirio Díaz. The suspension in question, vigorously defended by Altamirano, revolves around the failure to contain bandit gangs in the margins of Mexico City, the neighborhoods and railroads around San Ángel and Barranca del Muerto (*Obras completas*, 19:11–22).

45. Anybody who would have read a little ways into the future would have shuddered.

46. The pretext for the proposed suspension is laid out in the previous essay, "Ineficaz jurado popular" (*Obras completas*, 19:11–14), a strongly worded condemnation of the acquittal of the members of a group accused of robbery and murder on a local train.

47. In defending "life," what he recites here is nothing less than the central Enlightenment gesture of sovereignty, a fundamentally biopolitical gesture, one that Michel Foucault captures in the slogan "make live and let die" (1976). Altamirano would be happy to let the bandit die. But he does not call for the people to take his life. He calls for him to be brought to justice within the constitutional order.

48. In "Ladrones y asesinos" Altamirano is responding in part to a specific debate over the ineffective institutions of criminal justice that were at work throughout rural Mexico. One aspect of this conversation revolved around the advantages of the semiformalization of "Lynch laws," basically paramilitarism, versus the so-called *estado primitivo* in which "cada uno se haga justica por su propia mano" (*Obras completas*, 19:15). Attacking a common line in favor of the Ley Linch in prominent newspapers such as *La Libertad*, *La Industria Nacional*, and *La Tribuna*, which saw in these turns to popular justice "el único recurso a que tiene que apelar el pueblo para hacerse justicia" (ibid.), he wrote: "Antes que apelar a la *ley Linch* y al *estado primitivo*, es decir, a la desesperación, hay que echar mano de un recurso conocido, prescrito por las leyes, obligatorio para la administración, cuando las leyes comunes no bastan para dar seguridad al pueblo" (Before appealing to the *Lynch law* and the *primitive state*, that is, to desperation, we must move toward a known recourse, prescribed by the law, obligatory for our administration, when the common laws do not suffice to give security to the pueblo) (19, emphasis in original). This, of course, is the suspension of constitutional guarantees. The law provides for its own exception.

49. 1: Y mucha conciencia, Señor Sánchez. 2: Usted lleva facultades extraordinarias, pero siempre con la condición de que debe usted obrar con justicia. 3: La justicia ante todo. 4: Sólo la necesidad puede obligarnos a usar estas facultades. 5: Que traen tan grande responsabilidad. 6: Pero yo sé a quién se los doy. 7: No haga usted que me arrepienta.

50. In real life, Juárez was equally preoccupied with this arrangement. Vanderwood unearths this citation of Juárez's unease with bandit recruits in the struggle against French intervention: "I regret the excesses of [the bandit paramilitary forces]... but it is necessary to tolerate them, or else they will abandon us, and I have made our allies [the Americans] understand that such guerrillas operate in order to take all sorts of supplies from the enemy" (1998, 57).

51. Sierra's famously racialized historical template is from the 1885 outline for his *Evolución política*: "Pudo decir verdad el orador que en el cuerpo legislativo francés, en tiempo del Imperio, pintaba a los indígenas adorando y bendiciendo al joven austríaco de mirada azul y flotante barba rubia, como un nuevo Quetzalcóatl; pero en el vericueto de la próxima montaña, espiaba, con el rifle listo, el guerrillero: éste era el mestizo; para éste, Maximiliano nunca fue una divinidad, sino el enemigo" (The orator could truthfully say that in the French legislative body, in the time of the Empire, was painted the indigenous, worshipping and blessing the

young Austrian with his blue-eyed gaze and flowing blond beard, like a new Quet-zalcóatl; but in the redoubt of the next mountain spied, with rifle at the ready, the warrior: this was the mestizo; for him, Maximiliano was never a divinity; he was the enemy) (1885, 316).

3. Misplaced Revolution

The chapter epigraph reads as follows in the original:

> "Las revoluciones son caníbales, al final se alimentan de los revolucionarios" (Garro).

1. It would be impossible for me to improve on Esther Allen's eloquent translation of Castellanos's subtle prose, so throughout this chapter I defer to her. In moments of translation ambiguity, I will intercalate Castellanos's original word choice. Regarding pagination, all English citations refer to Allen's translation; any page numbers not accompanied by a direct quoted translation refer to the Spanish version.

2. Menchú writes: "Sigo ocultando lo que yo considero que nadie sabe, ni siquiera un antropólogo, ni un intelectual, por más que tenga muchos libros, no saben distinguir todos nuestros secretos" (I keep hiding what I think nobody knows, not even an anthropologist, not an intellectual, even if you have many books, they do not tell all our secrets) (Burgos and Menchú 1982, 271); on the silence of the subaltern in Latin American literary and cultural studies, see Acosta (2010).

3. *Guerra de castas,* or *caste war,* is a term used in Mexico to describe rural violence that is easily racialized, in other words, made intelligible through reduction to a typically misleading binary struggle between Indians and non-Indians. It is most often, although not exclusively, associated with uprisings in southern Mexico. The so-called Caste War of Yucatán, remembered in the English-speaking world through Nelson Reed's classic study (1964; revised edition 2001) of that mid-nineteenth-century conflict, is the most common point of reference. The term implies a certain historical trajectory, usually back to the nineteenth century or prior; for example, it would be strange to refer to the current conflict between the Mexican state and the Ejército Zapatista de Liberación Nacional as a caste war.

4. For an efficient review and analysis of the Chamula rebellion, including primary documents, see Reina (1980, 45–60). For a more aggressively critical appraisal of how the rebellion has been historically interpreted, see Rus (1983).

5. This is why three generations of novels of the Mexican Revolution so obsessively thematize agrarian reform and its limits.

6. At least part of Foucault's conceptual weakness around the idea of race can be explained by the fact that mobilizing "race," in this context, is an attempt to provoke. By the end of the lectures it becomes increasingly clear that his heterodoxical genealogy of racism is invoked as a critique of the twentieth-century Left and its

failure to thoroughly grapple with the rise of biologism and to critically recognize its own commitment to it (1976, 261–63), often clothed in the language of class struggle and economism (13–15).

7. Here is his definition in full: "Although this discourse [race war] speaks of races, and although the term 'race' appears at a very early stage, it is quite obvious that the word 'race' itself is not pinned to a stable biological meaning. And yet the word is not completely free-floating. Ultimately, it designates a certain historico-political divide. It is no doubt wide, but it is relatively stable. One might say—and this discourse does say—that two races exist whenever one writes the history of two groups which do not, at least to begin with, have the same language or, in many cases, the same religion. The two groups form a unity and a single polity only as a result of wars, invasions, victories, and defeats, or in other words, acts of violence. And finally, we can say that two races exist when there are two groups which, although they coexist, have not become mixed because of the differences, dissymmetries, and barriers created by privileges, customs and rights, the distribution of wealth, or the way in which power is exercised" (Foucault 1976, 77). The empiricist commitment to the objective fact of these "two groups" is striking and owes much to Renan (1882) (as we will see in chapter 4).

8. On the origins of the Lerdo law of land privatization and the limits of its ambiguous application against the ejido, see Tutino (1986, 263, 271, 312–13), Hale (1989), Ducey (1997), Knowlton (1997), Boyer (2003, 70), and Craib (2004, 56).

9. Thinking about the history of the ejido form as a neat process of degradation (during nineteenth-century liberal hegemony) and restoration (after the Revolution) provides a useful summary, but it is also somewhat mystifying. The two historic moments mark an important political distinction around the ejido. The ejido of the nineteenth century represented a conservative position insofar as it staked a claim to a traditional understanding of the commons rooted in Spanish colonial law; its discourse was fundamentally defensive in nature. The ejido of postrevolutionary Mexico after 1917 represented a progressive position insofar as it was an instrument in land reform and was explicitly linked to land redistribution and the reinstitutionalization of collective land tenure; its discourse was fundamentally offensive in nature. In both historical cases, country people—the *campesinaje*—expressed a heterogeneous range of attitudes toward the ejido form and its relation to state policy. For an excellent history that takes the diversity of rural Mexicans into account, see Boyer (2003). The classic text on the history of land reform and *agrarismo* in Mexico is Silva Herzog (1959).

10. See the work of Fischer and Brown (1996), whose conclusions on race relations in highland Guatemala pertain equally to highland Chiapas. Racial naming is complicated in Chiapas, a fact reflected in Castellanos's prose. Although a thorough problematization in ethnographic terms would take me too far afield, here is a quick

primer in terms of Castellanos's writing: The indigenous communities can go by the generic term *indio*, but are more commonly identified by their specific Maya language group—Tzotzil, Tzeltal, and so on. They are also sometimes called Chamulas, indicating indigenous peoples from in and around San Juan Chamula, an important village—for both market and religious reasons—just outside of San Cristóbal de las Casas, the old colonial center of highland Chiapas. Nonindigenous characters go by three names. *Ladino* is a racialized cultural category used in lower Meso-America to signify nonindigenous people (and therefore it is a broader and even more fluid category than *mestizo*). *Coleto* refers to the dwellers of San Cristóbal de las Casas and carries an aristocratic tinge. To complicate things further, San Cristóbal, in Castellanos's prose, takes its old colonial name of Ciudad Real or its indigenous name of Jobel. Finally, *caxlán* is the indigenous name for people identified with European descent, speakers of *castellano* (Spanish); it implies a certain authority.

11. It is worth noting that although the neo-Zapatista fight around indigenous rights puts Chiapas on the map internationally, on the national scene an equally pressing issue is the ongoing feud between Catholic and Protestant indigenous communities and their respective political affiliations. Castellanos thematizes this dynamic in the short story "Arthur Smith salva su alma" (1960a), and it is a conflict that still erupts with some regularity.

12. See her essay "El hombre del destino" (1970).

13. See *Cartas a Ricardo* (1996); for an excellent compilation of Castellanos's later reflections on her government work in Chiapas, see Navarrete Cáceres (2007).

14. In a letter to Ricardo Guerra, she writes: "Fuimos al Museo del Hombre y yo quería llorar toda feliz y triste porque en una de sus vitrinas de arte precolombino había lanzas y vestidos de las lacandones y chamulas y retratos de sus chozas. Fíjese, ya no era siquiera México cuyo recuerdo me es más o menos soportable. Sino Chiapas, como quien dice la mera entraña de uno" (We went to the Musée de l'Homme, and I wanted to cry, all happy and sad, because in one of the display cabinets on pre-Columbian art, there were spears and costumes of the Lacandones and the Chamulas, as well as sketches of their huts. Listen, this wasn't even Mexico City, a more or less tolerable memory. This was Chiapas, as they say, one's heart and soul) (1996, 97). Not insignificantly, this description is part of a longer passage on Paris as a center of world culture, from Leonardo, Rembrandt, the Impressionists, and Picasso to the Guimet and its collection of Asian art.

15. See *Leyendas de Guatemala* (1930), *Hombres de maíz* (1949), and "Foreword" (1975).

16. There is clear geographical continuity between the highlands of Chiapas and Guatemala, and they share a pre-Columbian history of Maya civilization. Modern Chiapas was annexed from Guatemala by Mexico in stages during the nineteenth century. On Castellanos's familiarity with Guatemalan and Chiapaneco writers, which was significant, see Navarrete Cáceres (2007, 35–36).

17. For more elaborate development of the relations between Asturias's Mayanist writings and the nation-state, see Lund and Wainwright (2008 and an undated ms.); cf. Morales (2000).

18. The INI was inaugurated by the Mexican government in 1948; the Tzeltal-Tzotzil branch in Chiapas was its first regional coordinating center (centro coordinador), established in 1951. Hewitt de Alcántara's study (1984) is still a classic summary of the theoretical basis and practical history of the INI and its centros, and it includes an ample bibliography. For a more detailed account that places the INI within a larger institutional trajectory, see the fifteen volumes that constitute *La antropología en México* (Mora 1987), a panoramic history of national anthropology published by the Instituto Nacional de Antropología e Historia. For a good critical review of Castellanos's relationship with the INI, see O'Connell (1995); for a more descriptive review, including the republication of many enlightening documents written by Castellanos herself (letters, essays, and stories), see Navarrete (2007). In 2003 the INI was dismantled and replaced, with much fanfare, by the Comisión Nacional para el Desarrollo de los Pueblos Indígenas, representing the formal end of the state's sponsorship of the integrationist-acculturalist approach to indigenous affairs and the formal institutionalization of a multiculturalist paradigm.

19. The collective talents of this generation cannot be overestimated. Gastón García Cantú was one of the century's great social historians. Alfonso Caso was the first director of the INI and a prominent indigenista, both political and scholarly (as an archaeologist). Gonzalo Aguirre Beltrán was a leading ethnohistorian and scholar of Mexican race relations for half a century. Julio de la Fuente is famous for his collaborations with Bronislaw Malinowski on the market cultures of Oaxaca, and his theoretical insights helped to transform the practice of state-sponsored indigenismo that would lead to the establishment of the INI and its centros. See Hewitt de Alcántrara (1984) and Téllez Ortega (1987).

20. See Navarrete (2007) for this history, including the reprinting of most of Castellanos's puppet plays. The titles give a clear indication of the content: "Petul y Xun juegan a la Lotería"; "La Bandera"; "Benito Juárez"; "Petul y el diablo extranjero"; "Petul, promotor sanitario"; "Petul en la campaña antialcohólica"; "Gallinero de Xun"; "Los pollos de Xun"; "Lázaro Cárdenas."

21. See Castellanos's own reflections on this time from a set of 1960 essays, reprinted in Navarrete (2007, 115–25), and also her published "Cartas a Elías Nandino" (1956) from 1956–57.

22. This transformation in acculturative techniques did not always move in a softer direction. Some early Revolutionary mandates prohibited the use of the traditional white garb of the indigenous peasantry in towns; modern pants and hygiene practices were made obligatory; and postrevolutionary Mexico was a practitioner of a standard ethnocidal policy widely associated with the transformation of settler colonialism to modern nationalism: the Ley de Instrucción Rudimentaria made

it illegal to use indigenous languages in rural schools (see Rivermar Pérez 1987, 120–21).

23. See Aguirre Beltrán's *El proceso de la aculturación* (1957, esp. 164–84) and De la Fuente's *Relaciones interétnicas* (1965), which includes his theoretical work dating back to the 1940s.

24. For a systematic account of the Centro Tzeltal-Tzotzil's theory and practice, see Villa Rojas (1962). The essay is included in *Los Centros Coordinadores* (1962), an extraordinary volume published by the INI that reviews each of nearly all of the regional centers.

25. The Museo Nacional functioned as a kind of "base institucional de la antropología durante el Porfiriato" (Suárez Cortés 1987, 25). For a succinct history of national anthropology, see Lomnitz (2001). Lomnitz also suggests that the field of anthropology itself emerges out of Edward Burnett Tylor's travels to Mexico, published as *Anahuac* (1861) (2001, 235).

26. Largely forgotten, Belmar made significant contributions to the study of indigenous languages. Politically, his work was important for promoting the idea that Nahua, Zapotec, and various Maya languages were fully evolved in their expressive capacity and capable of high abstraction (science and literature) on a par with European languages (Suárez Cortes 1987, 62). He refuted Francisco Pimentel's influential classification of native Mexican languages (Rivermar Pérez 1987, 116).

27. The conference was held at the Museo Nacional. *El Imparcial*, a Mexico City newspaper, offered three days' coverage of the event, and it is their report that I cite here. The language of the conference was stilted, with ample references to racial "regeneration," the "retrograde" state of indigenous communities, their "moral weakness," and so on. In contrast, the conference itself seems to have been something of a circus, in the best sense. Between effusive expressions of gratitude to men in high places and thematically dissonant performances of European chamber music (Tchaikovsky, performed by the Orquesta Beethoven), there was serious debate about national versus local education, comments on the responsibility of the dominant culture for the impoverishment of indigenous cultures, homages to indigenous soldiers and statesmen (including one from Díaz), and a denunciation of doctrines of racial superiority ("Abraham Castellanos . . . dijo que sólo los pseudo-filósofos asentaban que las razas blancas eran superiores á las negras") (*El Imparcial*, 1910c, 4]). One participant, Francisco Salazar, called out a powdered Díaz, reminding everyone of the president's Mixteca heritage. Channeling Alva, Esteban Castellanos, in a "rapto de entusiasmo por los indios," closed the conference on a polemical note by linking the Indian to the production of an authentic national culture: denouncing a perceived lack of first-order poets (no Mexican Darío) and painters (only imitators), he said it is "preciso educar á los indios para que estos formaran nuestro arte nacional y salvaran á la Patria" (*El Imparcial*, 1910d, 13). The last paragraph of *El Imparcial*'s reports notes that a small group of Indians was in attendance, although

apparently without a speaking role. It is unclear from the language if they were obligated to be there: "El señor [illeg.] hizo asistir al Congreso á varios indígenas traídos
de los pueblos vecinos" ("Se clausura el Congreso Indianista," 13).

28. See Brading (1988) for more on Gamio and what he calls "official" indigenism and Swarthout (2004, 95–104) on Gamio and what she calls "scientific"
indigenism.

29. For a review of Boas's career and his wider impact on anthropology as a field,
see Herskovits (1953) and Stocking (1974, 1981). The intellectual relationship
between Boas and Gamio was, of course, mutually beneficial, a fact unacknowl-
edged by Stocking; see Castañeda (2003). Castañeda's critique of the deification of
Boas within the dominant historiography of North American anthropology is an
important engagement with that tradition. And although he questions the usefulness of calling Gamio a "Boasian," it is beyond dispute that, as Castañeda himself
puts it, "Gamio's anthropology . . . did emerge in part from a few basic ideas about
culture and cultural relativism taken from Boas" (256). "Basic," here, should be
understood as transformative, not elementary.

30. We saw undeveloped versions of this attitude in Luis Alva, Justo Sierra, and
Ignacio Altamirano; José López Portillo's *La raza indígena* (1904) is premised on the
idea that culture, not race, denotes human difference. This does not prevent it from
becoming a strikingly racist tract on indigenous cultures.

31. It is no exaggeration to say that in Gamio's Mexico, everything was about the
nation. The calls for cosmopolitanism of even a prominent universalist like Alfonso
Reyes are still grounded in a national concern: Mexico (the nation) should see itself
as a participant in world culture; only thus can it realize its nationness.

32. Boas (1911a) did more local work as well, such as his famous studies on the
descendants of immigrants in New York City. But he would tie the implications of
his research not so much to the national question as to his larger concern with the
morphability of human types in relation to contexts.

33. Lomnitz (2001) argues that this disarticulation between two kinds of anthropology rests "on epistemological conditions that run deeper than mere patriotic rejec-
tion or language barriers" (258). Casteñeda (2003) finishes the thought: "Whereas
Boas fought to professionalize anthropology in the university as a science separate
from the state and the politics of nationhood, Gamio created an anthropology that
was directly tied to the state as the scientific agency and means of both 'good government' and nation-building. . . . These contrasting visions of the discipline can be
characterized as 'university anthropology' and 'governmental anthropology'" (243).

34. Among Gamio's empirical studies is his fieldwork at Teotihuacán (1922),
widely celebrated for its creative and rigorous merging of archaeological and ethnological methods.

35. A 1922 document authored by David Siquieros under the auspices of the
Syndicate of Technical Workers, Painters and Sculptors and signed by a group of

prominent artists of the Revolution states: "The noble work of our race, down to its most insignificant spiritual and physical expressions, is native (and essentially Indian) in origin" (in Harrison and Wood 1992, 406). Luis Villoro will bring this idea to its culmination with his existentialist meditation on Mexican identity, *Los grandes momentos del indigenismo* (1950).

36. On this point, Gamio's debt to Molina Enríquez (1909), while uncited, is significant.

37. *Guardias blancas,* or *white guards,* is a term that has, since the late Revolutionary period, extended throughout Latin America to denote paramilitary forces mobilized specifically to destabilize or undo land reform efforts. The etymology of the term has been linked to resistance to the land reform program of the Russian Revolution. In at least one instance in Mexico the *guardias blancas* were compared to the Ku Klux Klan; see Craib (2004, 227–30).

38. Joanna O'Connell concurs, drawing on historical accounts of Chiapaneco race relations to conclude that "the two ethnic communities are not two separate worlds" (1995, 136). Cf. Navarrete Cáceres (2007, 42–43). Sommers interprets Castellanos's thematization of this interdependency as a sly critique of the fashion for integrationist discourse that guided Indian policy during the INI years (1978, 87).

39. Leonardo confesses to Julia Acevedo, his lover, that events leading up to the attack on the Indians were fabricated. When a couple of the town's night watchmen turn up dead, the Indians are blamed for the murder, but it was actually a case of friendly fire between the jittery guards. Leonardo: "Pero no los mataron los indios. Eso lo inventamos nosotros" (Castellanos 1962b, 334). Rus's (1983) critical reading of the historiography around the Chamula uprising of the 1860s lends historical weight to this turn in the novel. After a careful presentation of the archival material, he concludes: "The Indian movement of 1867–69, when it *was* their movement, appears to have been a peaceful one. What they sought was to be left alone to farm their fields, conduct their markets, and worship their saints as they themselves chose. That they could not do these things—that they were finally slaughtered for trying—is not so much evidence of passivity and submissiveness on their part as of the inhumanity of those who regarded them, not as people, but as objects, 'resources,' to be fought over and controlled" (159–60). Although there is more than just a hint of the romantic in Rus's wording here, his political outline is impeccable when read against the historical archive on the uprising.

40. This is a strange point of critique given that, as Sommers (1978) knows, "pessimism" is a hallmark of Latin American prose fiction writ large. See Castellanos (1975a).

41. This theme comes up in the essay "Herlinda se va" (1973), a moving reflection on female solidarity within the context of social class inequality. Castellanos writes: "Así que María se fue a trabajar con Gertrudis Duby, quien no salía de su asombro (y así me lo dijo con reproche) de que después de tantos años de

convivencia y no le hubiera enseñado a María ni a leer bien ni a escribir. Yo andaba de Quetzalcóatl por montes y collados mientras junto a mí alguien se consumía de ignorancia. Me avergonzé" (Thus María left to work with Gertrudis Duby, who never lost her shock [and so she told me, with reproach] that after so many years of living with me, I never taught María how to read well or to write. I was running around over hill and dale, thinking myself some sort of Quetzalcóatl, while right next to me somebody was consumed by ignorance. I was ashamed) (264).

42. Although it is a topic that would take me too far afield to develop here, it should be noted that Castellanos was adamant in her resistance to being associated with literary indigenismo. As she bluntly put it to Emmanuel Carballo: "Si me atengo a lo que he leído dentro de esta corriente [el indigenismo], que por otra parte no me interesa, mis novelas y cuentos no encajan en ella" (If I consider what I have read in this trend [indigenism], which by the way doesn't interest me, my novels and stories don't fit into it) (Carballo 1965, 422). Her only significant essay on the topic that I know of, "Teoría y práctica del indigenismo" (1964b), deals exclusively with the state-sponsored indigenism of the INI and has nothing to do with artistic creation. She is scrupulous in avoiding the term in her literary criticism. She calls indigenist Bruno Traven, author of the monumental *Rebelión de los colgados* (1936), "un escritor mediocre" (1960a, 112) whose prose lacked a human dimension. At the same time, she cautiously endorses Eraclio Zepeda's *Benzulul* (1960a), although notably not as a work of indigenism but as a contribution to Chiapaneco regionalism and the continued relevance of the Mexican realist tradition. Nevertheless, literary history is stubborn in placing Castellanos within this genealogy that she apparently disavowed. As a way of distinguishing the literary sophistication of her writing from an earlier and more stilted thematization of the Indian, she is usually named as one of the protagonists—alongside Asturias and Arguedas—in a midcentury turn to neoindigenismo. But the affiliation is arbitrary and stands solely on the fact that indigenous characters play a significant role in her most prominent novels. By this standard, Castellanos could just as well be placed within a number of other thematic subgenres, such as the *novela de la tierra* or the *novela de la Revolución Mexicana*. But nobody would think to place her peers—Juan Rulfo, Carlos Fuentes, Elena Garro, José Revueltas, and Juan José Arreola—with whom she shares a general commitment to existentially inflected high modernism, in any of these categories.

43. The remark is not exactly an exception. In the same interview, she compares the indigenous "mentality" to that of the infant: "Este mundo infantil es muy semejante al mundo de los indígenas, en el cual se sitúa la acción de la novela *[Balún-Canán]*. (Las mentalidades de la niña y de los indígenas poseen en común varios rasgos que las aproximan)" (This infantile world is very similar to the world of the indigenous, in which the action of the novel *[Balún-Canán]* is situated. [The mentalities of the little girl and the indigenous possess various features in common that bring them together]) (Carballo 1965, 419). In a letter to Gastón García Cantú

while she was working with the INI in Chiapas, she reports that the "parajes indígenas" that she frequently visits are populated by "una masa enorme de gente escan-
dalosamente pobre, radicalmente ignorante" (in Navarrete Cáceres 2007, 22).

44. Tarica's chapter on Castellanos in *The Inner Life of Mestizo Nationalism*
(2008) takes this line of criticism the furthest and is also a source of bibliography
on the topic.

45. O'Connell argues that "Castellanos' literary work joins that current of *indigenista* debate that was in the minority at the 1940 Pátzcuaro Congress [the first
major international conference on Indian policy], where socialists promoted radical
changes in Mexican society itself while the majority promoted changing 'Indians'
instead" (1995, 77). She therefore, along with Sommers (1978), reads Castellanos
as a precursor to the ethnocide critique that would rise up against INI policies in
the 1960s, most notably through the work of Bonfil Batalla. Whether Castellanos
gets that far is debatable, but the interesting point is the departure from the INI
boilerplate in her complex literary output when it is placed alongside her published
comments on the work of the INI. The latter are mostly straightforward and favorable expressions of mainline institutional indigenism and its conceptual paradigm
established by Gamio, Aguirre Beltrán, de la Fuente, and Caso, among others.

46. It is important to emphasize Tarica's assessment that, following from basic
INI theory, the "entire regional culture" and its transformation is very much at stake
for Castellanos. While Castellanos's group was in Tuxtla and San Cristobal, part of
their mission involved the work of provoking an ideological shift among dominant
sectors of Chiapaneco society. So while puppet plays were being produced for the
Indians, cultural magazines, which were published for the nonindigenous urban
classes, tried to reframe the Indian problem around rights, citizenship, and development and through the positive terms of a productive transculturation. Written
in Spanish, these publications attempted to embody biculturalism by gestures such
as carrying Tzotzil titles. One was called *Winik*—in Tzotzil, significantly, "hombre"
(man)—and another was a bilingual (Tzeltal-Spanish) publication called *Sk'oplal
te Mejikolum/La palabra de México*, again significant for its appellation of Tzeltal
(Mejikolum) as a participant in the nation (Mexico). Literacy rates among Tzeltal
and Tzotzil speakers were extremely low, so the publication's bilingualism itself
was an ideological tool, placing two socially unequal languages together, on the
same page. See Navarrete Cáceres (2007, 33–34). Later Castellanos reflects: "[El
INI] modifica la conciencia que el indio y el blanco tienen de sí mismos y de su rela-
ción. . . . Ya ni la palabra indio va cargada forzosamente de desprecio ni la palabra
ladino de esa ambigüedad que oscila entre le elogio y el insulto. El Centro instaura
una posibilidad. De cada uno de nosotros depende que esa posibilidad se realice"
([The INI] modifies the consciousness that the Indian and the white man have of
themselves and their relation. . . . No longer does the word Indian carry such force-
ful contempt nor does the word Ladino have that ambiguity that oscillates between

praise and insult. The Center initiates a possibility. That this possibility be realized depends on each of us) (1964, 294).

47. A similar scene unfolds in one of Castellanos's best-known testimonial essays regarding her work with the puppet theater in Chiapas, "Incidente en Yalentay" (1963).

48. Throughout Castellanos's fiction, the critique of the expectation of gratitude is a powerful, and regularly staged, trope. The idea of the "ungrateful Indian" is regularly expressed by her Ladino protagonists. This is clearly a problem that Castellanos wrestled with in her everyday life. In "Herlinda se va," she speaks of her guilt-ridden realization of the perversity that governed her relationship with her childhood servant and vows "pedir perdón a quien había yo ofendido" and "no aprovechar mi posición de privilegio para humillar a otro" (to ask forgiveness of the one that I had offended [and] not take advantage of my position of privilege in order to humiliate another) (1973, 262). The result: "¿Entre una María rebosante de gratitud y una Rosario cargada de escrúpulo moral se estableció una amistad respetuosa? No. Entre una María desconcertada y una Rosario enerme ya no hubo contacto posible" (Between a María overflowing with gratitude and a Rosario charged with moral scrupulousness, was a respectful friendship established? No. Between a disconcerted María and a defenseless Rosario contact was no longer possible) (262–63).

49. The standard biographical origins of this idea are efficiently expressed by Gerardo Estrada in his prologue to *Rosario Castellanos: Homenaje nacional* (1995): "La joven Rosario, marginada por su condición de mujer, se identificó en su opresión con los indígenas" (3). See O'Connell (1995) for a healthy antidote to the extrapolation of this biographical claim to Castellanos's literature.

50. The ambivalence of their belonging adds another layer of complexity: the narrator is constantly overlooked in favor of her brother, and Nana is attacked and wounded by the Indians for her employment as a domestic servant with the ranch family (Castellanos 1957, 15–16).

51. For an extensive analysis along these lines, see Strobel (2010).

52. The historical tapestry of *Oficio de tinieblas* is infinitely rich, and another theme at play here is the fact that the conflict plays out with the counterrevolutionary uprising of the Cristero rebellion still fresh in everybody's minds. The assault against church privilege that arose out of the Revolution was resisted with particular stubbornness in conservative rural areas such as Chiapas. It is thus a subtle irony that the women are rounded up for the crime of worship.

53. On the 1712 rebellion, see Viqueira (1994). The 1867 rebellion is the historical referent that Castellanos is restaging here; see Rus (1983). The reference to 1917 must be an allusion to the ratification of the new revolutionary Constitution and its Article 27, which requires the breakup of large estates and protections for the ejido form of communal land ownership.

54. It is highly unlikely that there is any intention on the part of Castellanos to draw association between Cárdenas and her literary creation. She was an ardent *cardenista* and credited the president with effectively saving her from a life of dreary village aristocracy. But within the context of the novel, Cárdenas is a ghostly figure, always just barely discernible behind the land reform gone wrong in Chiapas. Any invocation of his presence in the text (as the "president" or the "ajwalil") signals a politics of progressive redistribution and public welfare, in short, a general affirmation of the life of the citizen that Foucault will call "biopolitics." With Leonardo Cifuentes's assumption of state functions in the local scene of Ciudad Real, we see the dark side of biopolitics, the politics with power over life that affirms necessary death in the form of state racism. Although we tend to remember Foucault's biopolitical turn at its most chilling—the discourse of letting die—philosophers and historians have more recently emphasized the ambivalence of biopolitics, on the one hand an affirmation of life but on the other hand a calculation of death. See Esposito (2008) and Campbell (2011). With race war as the condition of the history of Chiapas, we can perhaps read *Oficio de tinieblas* as a problematization of race itself, as the single coin that reads Cárdenas on one side, Cifuentes on the other.

55. The title of the document is extraordinary, and it opens up a wormhole in the text that immediately transports the narrative back four centuries. "Ordenanzas militares" are the formal rules governing the practices, procedures, and responsibilities (including limits and restrictions) of armed forces. They are an important development in the professionalization and modernization of formal militaries. The late medieval Spain of the Reyes Católicos, mesmerized by an ever-expanding juridical discourse, is crucial in the history of this codification of military service, and their codes were rewritten as distinctly "national" ordenanzas in the postindependence era of Latin America. Ordenanzas militares break two ways: negatively, they restrict the actions of military forces and in this sense attempt to preserve power in the hands of the sovereign; positively, they authorize and legitimize the possession and means of violent force vis-à-vis that same sovereign and, by extension, society at large. The first significant ordenanzas issued in Meso-America emanated from none other than the conquistador himself, Hernán Cortés. Regarding the *Ordenanzas militares dadas por Hernando Cortés in Tlaxcallan* (1520), Anthony Pagden explains: The ordenanzas that Cortés reads aloud and then recounts in his third letter are "intended to persuade the emperor that in attempting to take Tenochtitlan by force, he is acting both in the best interests of the Crown and in accordance with the law. The Mexica, he argues, are not free citizens but rebellious vassals and must be punished as such" (in Cortés 1971, 482). In short, Cortés uses the ordenanzas as one of his many claims to *jus ad bellum* in his attack on Aztec civilization. Through them, his army is transformed from a rogue paramilitary force into a legitimate military defending the rights of the king. In *Oficio de tinieblas*, as Leonardo presents his

actions to the local governor, the exact same logic is invoked in order to formalize the paramilitarization of society: patriotic citizens are defending national treasure (equated with their lands) from the mob, the rabble that has taken up violence and placed itself outside of the nation and its laws. The state, bewildered, acquiesces, swallows this version of events, and sees its discourse recolonized by the old, expert colonizers.

56. For the rebels themselves, total genocide: death to them and their families, destruction of their villages, salt in their fields (1962b, 341). For the rest, deportation and forced colonization (ibid.). Race returns home as Alva's old strategy for state-sponsored integration is now invoked at the law of a radical segregation.

57. This is O'Connell's reading: "The implication is that their struggle will be advanced only when they have access to and understanding of the means used to dominate them, when they can read all of the signs" (1995, 169), a point that she shares with Sommers (1978). But it falls flat when we consider the Coletos. Like all parties involved (themselves, the Tzotzils, the revolutionary state), they have only partial understanding, at best, of "the signs" at play in this struggle, and yet they are able to maintain a certain level of domination over the region. Perhaps it simply comes down to the means and volition to use violent force.

4. Elena Garro and the Failure of Alliance

"Es natural que ahora cuelguen ellos si antes colgaron ustedes" (Garro 1963, 104).

1. The historical context in question is known as the Cristero rebellion, generally understood as a conservative and popular reaction against the postrevolutionary state's restrictions on the church. Its moment of highest intensity ran from roughly 1926 through 1929. Jean Meyer's three-volume history *La Cristiada* (1973) still stands as the most thorough treatment of the uprising.

2. What Nicolás actually says is quoted in the unnumbered note above.

3. In reality she was something of a heterodoxical anticommunist, understanding land reform and redistribution as the only way that Mexico would escape the same kind of communist influence that, in the wake of the Cuban Revolution, was stronger in the global south than in the fully industrialized north. She understood this position as true to the Revolutionary Constitution and referred to herself as an "agrarista guadalupana." In a 1965 interview with Carlos Landeros, she goes on to offer this cogent summary of her political outlook: "Ahora, ser colonia de nosotros mismos es una ofensa que nos infligimos y que nos reduce a seres indignos" (Now, being colonized by ourselves is an offense that we inflict on ourselves and that reduces us to unworthy beings) (interview in Landeros 1965, 63–65).

4. The most thorough, if not critical, attempt at an account of Garro's activism and polemics around 1968 can be found in her official biography; see Lopátegui (2002).

5. Here is how she responds to Elena Poniatowska's doubts around her fashion choices for a meeting with peasant activists: "No soy una hipócrita. Que me vean, que me conzcan tal y como soy. No tengo nada que esconder a diferencia de otros sepulcros blanqueados, escritores que se fingen indigenistas y en el fondo son racistas. Juegan un doble juego porque se fingen salvadores de los indios pero están muy contentos de ser blancos y rubios. ¡Qué gran asco me dan! Si soy dueño de un abrigo de pieles me lo pongo en el juzgado, donde sea y cuando sea. No lo voy a esconder" (I'm not a hypocrite. I hope they do see me and know me as I am. I have nothing to hide, unlike other whitened tombs, writers that pretend to be indigenists, but are racists on the inside. They play a double game because they pretend to be the saviors of the Indians, but they're actually very content to be white and blonde. They disgust me! If I own a fur coat I'll wear it to trial, wherever and whenever. I'm not going to hide it) (in Poniatowska 1999, 12). This is from Poniatowska's recollection, but reading it against Garro's many interviews, it sounds about right.

6. http://www.maryferrell.org/wiki/index.[h[/Elena_Garro_de_Paz_ Allegation (accessed November 9, 2011).

7. Mara García reports that between 1996 and 2001, no fewer than eighteen doctoral dissertations on her work were approved (2009, 13).

8. Another, much smaller, round of correspondence, the Gabriela Mora Collection of Elena Garro, was opened in 2008.

9. This comes through quite clearly in the roll call of prominent eulogies to Garro collected in García's 2009 volume. Carlos Monsiváis calls her a "mezcla de genialidad y locura" (in García 2009, 216). Margo Glantz describes her as "un personaje ejemplar por su antisolemnidad, su odio a las instituciones, su capacidad crítica, su locura, su gran talento" (in García 2009, 213).

10. A first draft of *Recuerdos* was composed before Garro developed her activism around land reform, as early as the late 1940s, while she was in Europe, but much of that manuscript was destroyed; the final, revised version was published in 1963. The Jaramillista movement holds an important place in a larger trajectory of agrarian struggles in modern Mexico and its attendant dialectic between land activism and state repression. The assassination of its leader and his family was a national scandal, and the movement is often credited with helping to consolidate the 1960s activism that would culminate in the student protests of 1968. Tanalís Padilla offers this cogent summary of the movement and its context: "Under the leadership of Rubén Jaramillo, campesinos fought for better crop prices, credit, and land reform. The struggle of the Jaramillistas, as the participants became known, lasted from 1942 until Jaramillo's assassination in 1962. . . . Influenced by the legacy of Emiliano Zapata's agrarianism, the hope created by Lázaro Cárdenas's (1934–40) populism, the disillusionment brought about by subsequent administrators, and the renewed expectations for radical change [eventually] inspired by the Cuban Revolu-

tion, the Jaramillistas are emblematic of campesino resistance during this period. As post-Cardenista administrations abandoned a commitment to the countryside, they quelled Jaramillista petitions with violence" (2007, 255). See also Padilla's book-length study of the movement, *Rural Resistance in the Land of Zapata* (2008).

11. Garro was impressed by the Montiel Baronas and based her short story "El arbol" (1964a) on aspects of Antonia's life.

12. On the surrealist elements of Garro's work, see Stoll (1999) and León Vega (2006).

13. On Malintzin, see note 23.

14. The translation that I cite here is by Martin Thom and appears in Homi Bhabha's edited volume *Nation and Narration* (1990b).

15. Although Arendt's potential relevance for postcolonial thought has long been acknowledged, its sustained exploration is overdue, especially given that Renan already occupies a slot in that critical canon. For some opening moves in this direction, see Grosse (2006), Swift (2009, 78 et passim), and Lee (2011).

16. Nevertheless, Renan is a dicey figure on whom to base any postcolonial critique of the nation-form, with an ethnocentric tendency that Edward Said features prominently in his *Orientalism* (1979).

17. The critical action of his rhetoric, of course, does not free Renan from any "racism," which, even though he could be charmingly self-reflective about such matters, is well known. See Said (1979, 148).

18. Kant makes this case in "Of the Different Human Races" (1777), which is often read as the first systematic interpretation of race as a scientific concept.

19. Indeed, historically race emerges alongside and within the rise of the nation-state. See Goldberg (2002).

20. Gobineau writes: "By the mere fact of its wants and powers increasing, [a tribe] inevitably finds itself in contact with other similar associations, and by war or peaceful measures succeeds in incorporating them with itself" (1851, 61). This "step," he goes on to argue, is one that "every tribe must take if it is to rank one day as a nation" (ibid.).

21. It is via this logic that Renan can still stand as something of an imperialist, as Said makes clear, while simultaneously offering a critique of expansion by attacking the foundations of the race–nation couplet. In this he is explicitly with Hegel, who notes, in his *Philosophy of Right* (1820): "The civilised nation is conscious that the rights of barbarians are unequal to its own and treats their autonomy as only a formality" (§351). Wardman is thus mistaken when he implies that the essay is a correction of Renan's earlier "ideas on racial inequality" (1964, 162).

22. The gesture at work here again recalls Neil Larsen's "re-racialization" (2006). In developing the idea, Larsen is working through the specific scene of Gilberto Freyre's *Casa-grande e senzala* (1933), but it is a historical-materialist insight

that could likely be expanded to most Latin American thought on the race–nation problem. Indeed, Renan was a big hit in Latin America, but not, ironically, for the possible destabilization of the idea of race that can be teased out of his hybridization of the nation. Rather, he was invoked time and again—by Rodó, Vasconcelos, and others—for trumping the problem of national race-mixing with his ideas of the nation as a spiritual project or common soul.

23. La Malinche, or Malintzin, is the well-known translator who accompanies Hernán Cortés and figures prominently in Bernal Díaz's and Gómara's accounts of the invasion and conquest of New Spain. Alternatively read as villain and hero, she is the subject of innumerable creative works and critical essays, my favorite of which is Jean Franco's 1999 effort, "La Malinche: From Gift to Social Contract," which reads La Malinche in the context of a critique of the "mediating woman." See Margo Glantz's essay "Las hijas de la Malinche" (1991) and Messinger Cypess (1991) for sustained readings of Garro's novel as an allegorical reference to la Malinche.

24. Louis Agassiz, a nineteenth-century paleontologist and naturalist, was a prominent advocate of "polygenesis" (human genealogy as traceable to separate geneses as opposed to a single family of mankind) and an influential critic of "race-mixing." Samuel George Morton was a famous anthropologist and phrenologist of the same era and held that the human races could be divided into permanent levels of civilizational advancement. Although both were hostile to the idea of evolution, Francis Galton, cousin to Charles Darwin, made the first systematic case for eugenics, an evolutionary theory of social engineering that took on many of the racially hierarchical assumptions of the polygenesists.

25. Compare, for example, the famous opening chapters of Octavio Paz's *El laberinto de la soledad* (1950).

26. See Sierra 1885, 299, 301); Molina Enríquez (1909, 138); Gamio (1916, 117–18); Vasconcelos (1925).

27. Although aesthetically this passage brings to mind similar experiments in hyper-editorialization that mark the other great *cristero* novel, José Revueltas's *El luto humano* (1943), in terms of content it is rich beyond adequate comment here. Two points require brief mention. First, along with other cues in the novel (such as the Moncada siblings' sarcasm in the face of the motivations for the rebellion), it clearly distances Garro from the banal reading of the novel as a "defense" of the reactionary politics and popular Catholicism associated with the *cristero* uprising, thereby at the same time mitigating the "heroism" of Ixtepec's leading families' participation in it. Second, it at once recites Garro's interest in the marginal figures of the Revolution (e.g., Ángeles) and recenters the Indians as a fount of more adequate (than the bourgeoisie) historical memory.

28. Homi Bhabha is well known for his readings of the psychoanalytic subtleties of this conflict between "colonizer and colonized" (here master and servant, nation-

alizer and nationalized), and any number of his essays from the mid-1980s, reproduced in *The Location of Culture* (1994), can shed light on the interclass and interrace dynamics at play in Ixtepec. On the passage that follows this note, see his "Sly Civility," especially for its citation and reading of Freud's theory of "the paranoid" (93).

29. Earlier in the novel, it is noted that Inés is being courted by the sergeant, precisely following the soldiers' declared need for an informant ("soplón") (Garro 1963, 187); as the conspiracy is falling apart, at one point Rosas demands that somebody bring her to him, and two soldiers later claim that somebody squealed. So although there is circumstantial suggestion, the reader never witnesses a scene of betrayal involving Inés. And then, beyond innocence and guilt, there is the more involved problem of betrayal itself; see Franco (1999).

30. By *alliance* I mean the (real or potential) articulation of disparate social-political formations in pursuit of a common goal (e.g., defending the church against the state in Ixtepec, which ostensibly brought together rich and poor [Garro 1963, 158]). In contemporary Marxist thought, alliance is usually placed in tension against "solidarity," with the former understood as a temporary means to an end and the latter as at once means and end, a necessary condition for real revolution. Alliance and its efficacy have emerged as important topics of debate over the last couple of decades, especially in the context of the so-called new social movements and, today more than ever, regarding the *alter-mundista* movements centered around the World Social Forum, Occupy Wall Street, and others.

31. Two classic texts can lead us to suggestive readings on the power of this scene. On the idea of violence as the essence of human action, see Walter Benjamin's "Critique of Violence" (1921). On the idea of speech and its relation to the political, see Hannah Arendt's *The Human Condition* (1958).

32. Kaminsky throws doubt on the idea that Isabel was in love at all, attributing such readings to the "residual authority" that guides our reception of antipatriarchal narratives: "Isabel's relationship with Rosas . . . had to do with neither love nor self-sacrifice but rather was a complex matter of destruction and self-destruction" (1993a, 94; see also 1993b, 105–7). For other interpretations of Isabel's motivations, see Duncan (1992), León (2000), and Gladhart (2005).

33. A suggestive reading of this point might involve thinking it through Giorgio Agamben's studies of the idea of sovereign power in Western thought. See especially his critique of Carl Schmitt's theory of sovereignty as "the place of extreme decision" via Walter Benjamin's reconstruction of the baroque sovereign as one who cannot decide (1995, 54 et passim).

34. The town's hysterical invocations of Zapata, who wavers between popular hero and rapacious marauder in Ixtepec's recollections, charges the desire for the revolutionary justice of Abacuc with a certain irony.

35. On the politics of the figure of Gregoria, see Kaminsky (1993b).

36. It is tempting, on this point, to read Garro's critique of political inaction against Octavio Paz's reception of her 1950s-era public outspokenness, which could be described, most generously, as nervous. See Garro's interview with Melgar (in Melgar and Mora 2002, esp. 245).

Bibliography

Acosta, Abraham. 2010. "Contingencies of Silence: Subalternity, the *EZLN*, and the Accounting of Speech in Latin America." *Journal of Latin American Cultural Studies* 19, no. 2: 203–23.

Agamben, Giorgio. 1995 [1998]. *Homo Sacer: Sovereign Power and Bare Life.* Trans. Daniel Heller-Roazen. Stanford, Calif.: Stanford University Press.

———. 2005. *State of Exception.* Trans. Kevin Attell. Chicago: University of Chicago Press.

Aguilar, Federico Cornelio. 1895 [1995]. *Último año de residencia en México.* Mexico, D.F.: Siguisiví.

Aguirre Beltrán, Gonzalo. 1946. *La población negra de México, 1519–1810: Estudio etno-histórico.* Mexico City: Ediciones Fuente Cultural.

———. 1957 [1992]. *El proceso de aculturación y el cambio socio-cultural en México.* Mexico City: Instituto Nacional Indigenista.

Altamirano, Ignacio. 1871 [2001]. *La navidad en las montañas.* Mexico, D.F.: Porrúa.

———. 1901 [2000]. *El Zarco: Episodios de la vida mexicana en 1861–1863.* Ed. Manuel Sol. Veracruz: Clásicos Mexicanos, Universidad Veracruzana.

———. 1986–2001. *Obras completas.* Vols. 1–24. Ed. Nicole Girón. Mexico City: Secretaría de Educación Pública.

Alva, Luis. 1881. "Economías." *El Monitor Republicano,* February 24.

———. 1882. "La colonización extranjera y la raza indígena." *La Libertad.* 13 vols., June 7–July 20.

———. 1893. "Boletin del 'Monitor.'" *El Monitor Republicano.* Multiple volumes, May 23–November 23.

Anaya Pérez, Marco Antonio. 1997. *Rebelión y revolución en Chalco-Amecameca, Estado de México, 1821–1921.* 2 vols. Mexico City: Instituto Nacional de Estudios Históricos de la Revolución Mexicana.

Anderson, Benedict. 1991. *Imagined Communities.* London: Verso.

Arendt, Hannah. 1951. *The Burden of our Time.* London: Secker and Warburg.

———. 1958. *The Human Condition.* Chicago: University of Chicago Press.

Asturias, Miguel Angel. 1930. *Leyendas de Guatemala.* Ed. Alejandro Lanoël. Madrid: Cátedra, 1995.

———. 1949. *Hombres de maíz.* Ed. Gerald Martin. Nanterre: ALLCA, 1996.

———. 1975. "Foreword." In *Maya,* by Pierre Ivanoff, 6–10. New York: Madison Square Press.

Azuela, Mariano. 1915 [1992]. *Los de abajo.* Madrid: Cátedra.

Balibar, Etienne, and Immanuel Wallerstein. 1991. *Race, Nation, Class: Ambiguous Identities.* London: Verso.

Ballescá, Santiago. 1901. "Nota del editor." In *El Zarco (Episodios de la vida mexicana en 1861–63),* by Ignacio Manuel Altamirano. Barcelona: Establecimiento editorial de J. Ballescá y Ca., Sucesor.

Barreda, Gabino. 1867 [1941]. "Oración cívica." *Estudios.* Mexico City: UNAM.

Basave Benítez, Agustín. 1992. *México mestizo: Análisis del nacionalismo mexicano en torno a la mestizofilia de Andrés Molina Enríquez.* Mexico City: Fondo de Cultura Económica.

Benjamin, Walter. 1921 [1997]. "Critique of Violence." Trans. Edmond Jephcott. In *Selected Writings,* vol. 1, *1913–1926,* 236–52. Cambridge, Mass.: Belknap Press of Harvard University Press.

Bennett, Herman. 2010. *Colonial Blackness: A History of Afro-Mexico.* Bloomington: Indiana University Press.

Beucker, Verónica. 2002. "Encuentro con Elena Garro." In *Elena Garro: Lectura múltiple de una personalidad compleja,* ed. Lucía Melgar and Gabriela Mora, 37–53. Puebla: Benemérita Universidad Autónoma de Puebla.

———. 1990a. "DissemiNation: Time, Narrative, and the Margins of the Modern Nation." In *Nation and Narration,* ed. Homi Bhabha, 291–322. London: Routledge.

Bhabha, Homi, ed. 1990. *Nation and Narration.* London: Routledge.

———. 1994. *The Location of Culture.* London: Routledge.

Boas, Franz. 1894 [1974]. "Human Faculty as Determined by Race." In *The Shaping of American Anthropology, 1883–1911: A Franz Boas Reader,* ed. George Stocking, 221–42. New York: Basic Books.

———. 1911a [1969]. "Instability of Human Types." In *Papers on Inter-racial Problems,* ed. G. Spiller, 99–103. New York: Arno Press.

———. 1911b [1938]. *The Mind of Primitive Man.* New York: MacMillan.

Bonfil Batalla, Guillermo. 1987 [2001]. *México profundo: Una civilización negada.* Mexico, D.F.: CONACULTA.

Boschetto, Sandra. 1989. "Romancing the Stone in Elena Garro's *Los recuerdos del porvenir." Journal of the Midwest Modern Language Association* 22, no. 2: 1–11.

Boyer, Christopher. 2003. *Becoming Campesinos: Politics, Identity, and Agrarian Struggle in Postrevolutionary Michoacán, 1920–1935.* Stanford, Calif.: Stanford University Press.

Brading, David. 1988. "Manuel Gamio and Official Indigenismo in Mexico." *Bulletin of Latin American Research* 7, no. 1: 75–89.

Brennan, Timothy. 2006. *Wars of Position: The Cultural Politics of Left and Right*. New York: Columbia University Press.

Burgos, Elizabeth, and Rigoberta Menchú. 1982 [1998]. *Me llamo Rigoberta Menchú y así me nació la conciencia*. Mexico, D.F.: Siglo Veintiuno.

Campbell, Timothy. 2011. *Improper Life: Technology and Biopolitics from Heidegger to Agamben*. Minneapolis: University of Minnesota Press.

Carballo, Emmanuel. 1965. *Diecinueve protagonistas de la literatura mexicana del siglo XX*. Mexico City: Empresa.

Caso, Alfonso. 1955 [1971]. "Los fines de la acción indigenista en México." In *La comunidad indígena*, 137–45. Mexico City: Secretaría de Educación Pública.

———. 1958. *Indigenismo*. Mexico City: Instituto Nacional Indigenista.

———. 1962. "Los ideales de la acción indigenista." In *Los Centros Coordinadores: Edición conmemorativa en ocasión del XXXV Congreso Internacional de Americanistas*, 7–13. Mexico City: Instituto Nacional Indigenista.

Castañeda, Quetzil. 2003. "Stocking's Historiography of Influence: The 'Story of Boas,' Gamio, and Redfield at the Cross-road to Light." *Critique of Anthropology* 23, no. 3: 235–63.

Castellanos, Rosario 1956 [2003]. "Cartas a Elías Nandino." In *Mujer de palabras: Artículos rescatados de Rosario Castellanos*, vol. 1, ed. Andrea Reyes, 61–67. Mexico City: CONACULTA.

———. 1957 [2007]. *Balún-Canán*. Mexico City: Fondo de Cultura Económica.

———. 1960a. "Arthur Smith salva su alma." In *Ciudad Real*, by Castellanos, 165–219.

———. 1960b [2003]. "Benzulul, un nuevo nombre en la tradición del realismo mexicano: Eraclio Zepeda, con su libro de cuentos." In *Mujer de palabras: Artículos rescatados de Rosario Castellanos*, vol. 1, ed. Andrea Reyes, 110–14. Mexico City: CONACULTA.

———. 1960c [2008]. *Ciudad Real*. Mexico City: Punto de Lectura.

———. 1960d. "El don rechazado." In *Ciudad Real*, by Castellanos, 151–64.

———. 1960e [1998]. "El idioma en San Cristóbal de las Casas." In *Obras II: Poesía, teatro, y ensayo*, ed. Eduardo Mejía, 533–37. Mexico City: Fondo de Cultura Económica.

———. 1960f. "La rueda del hambriento." In *Ciudad Real*, by Castellanos, 111–50. Mexico City: Punto de Lectura.

———. 1960g [2003]. "Teatro Petul." In *Mujer de palabras: Artículos rescatados de Rosario Castellanos*, vol. 1, ed. Andrea Reyes, 85–103. Mexico City: CONACULTA.

———. 1962a [1998]. *The Book of Lamentations*. Trans. Esther Allen. New York: Penguin.

———. 1962b [1998]. *Oficio de tinieblas*. New York: Penguin.

———. 1963 [2003]. "Incidente en Yalentay." In *Mujer de palabras: Artículos rescatados de Rosario Castellanos*, vol. 1, ed. Andrea Reyes, 203–6. Mexico City: CONACULTA.

———. 1964 [2003]. "Teoría y práctica del indigenismo." In *Mujer de palabras: Artículos rescatados de Rosario Castellanos*, vol. 1, ed. Andrea Reyes, 291–94. Mexico City: CONACULTA.

———. 1965 [2003]. "Teatro Petul." In *Mujer de palabras: Artículos rescatados de Rosario Castellanos*, vol. 1, ed. Andrea Reyes, 299–304. Mexico City: CONACULTA.

———. 1970 [1974]. "El hombre del destino." In *El uso de la palabra*, 204–8. Mexico City: Ediciones de Excelsior.

———. 1973 [1974]. "Herlinda se va." In *El uso de la palabra*, 261–64. Mexico City: Ediciones de Excelsior.

———. 1975a [1998]. "El pesimismo latinoamericano." In *Obras II: Poesía, teatro, y ensayo*, ed. Eduardo Mejía, 871–74. Mexico City: Fondo de Cultura Económica.

———. 1975b [1998]. "José María Arguedas y la problemática indigenista." In *Obras II: Poesía, teatro, y ensayo*, ed. Eduardo Mejía, 860–64. Mexico City: Fondo de Cultura Económica.

———. 1996. *Cartas a Ricardo*. Mexico City: Consejo Nacional para la Cultura y las Artes.

Chadbourne, Richard. 1968. *Ernest Renan*. New York: Twayne.

Chávez Guerrero, Herminio. 1985. *Ignacio Manuel Altamirano*. Chilpancingo: Instituto Guerrerense de la Cultura.

Christ, Ronald. 2007. "Translator's Note." In *El Zarco, the Blue-Eyed Bandit: Episodes of Mexican Life between 1861–1863*, by Ignacio Manuel Altamirano, trans. Ronald Christ, 37–43. Santa Fe, N.M.: Lumen.

Conway, Christopher. 2000. "Lecturas: Ventanas de la seducción en *El Zarco*." *Revista de Crítica Literaria Latinoamericana* 26, no. 52: 91–106.

———. 2006. "Ignacio Altamirano and the Contradictions of Autobiographical Indianism." *Latin American Literary Review* 34, no. 67: 34–49.

———. 2007. "Native Republican: Ignacio Manuel Altamirano and *El Zarco, the Blue-Eyed Bandit*." Introduction to *El Zarco, the Blue-Eyed Bandit: Episodes of Mexican Life between 1861–1863*, by Ignacio Manuel Altamirano, trans. Ronald Christ, 7–35. Santa Fe, N.M.: Lumen.

Cope, R. Douglas. 1994. *The Limits of Racial Domination: Plebeian Society in Colonial Mexico City, 1660–1720*. Madison: University of Wisconsin Press.

Cortés, Hernán. 1971. *Letters from México*. Trans. and ed. Anthony Pagden. New York: Orion.

Cosío Villegas, Daniel. 1955–76. *Historia de México*. Mexico, D.F.: Editorial Hermes.

Cosmes, Francisco. 1883. "Cartas de Junius." *La Libertad*. Multiple volumes, January 30–March 14.

Craib, Raymond. 2004. *Cartographic Mexico: A History of State Fixations and Fugitive Landscapes.* Durham, N.C.: Duke University Press.

Cruz, Jacqueline. 1994. "La moral y la identidad mexicana vistas a través de los personajes femeninos de *El Zarco.*" *Explicación de Textos Literarios* 22, no. 1: 73–86.

Dabove, Juan Pablo. 2007. *Nightmares of the Lettered City: Banditry and Literature in Latin America, 1816–1929.* Pittsburgh: University of Pittsburgh Press.

De la Fuente, Julio. 1965. *Relaciones interétnicas.* Mexico City: Instituto Nacional Indigenista.

Dove, Patrick. 2006. "Living Labour, History, and the Signifier: Bare Life and Sovereignty in Diamela Eltit's *Mano de obra.*" *Journal of Latin American Cultural Studies* 15, no. 1: 77–91.

Ducey, Michael. 1997. "Liberal Theory and Peasant Practice: Land and Power in Northern Veracruz, Mexico, 1826–1900." In *Liberals, the Church, and Indian Peasants: Corporate Lands and the Challenge of Reform in Nineteenth-Century Spanish America*, ed. Robert Jackson, 65–94. Albuquerque: University of New Mexico Press.

Duncan, Cynthia. 1985. "'La culpa es de los tlaxcaltecas: A re-evalution of Mexico's past through myth." *Crítica Hispánica* 7, no. 2: 105–120.

———. 1992. "Time and Memory as Structural Unifiers in Elena Garro's *Los recuerdos del porvenir.*"*Journal of Interdisciplinary Literary Studies* 4, nos. 1–2: 31–54.

Escalante, Evodio. 1997. "Lectura ideológica de dos novelas de Altamirano." In *Homenaje a Ignacio Altamirano (1834–1893)*, ed. Manuel Sol y Alejandro Higashi, 189–203. Veracruz: Instituto de Investigaciones Lingüístico-Literarias Universidad Veracruzana.

Esposito, Roberto. 2008. *Bíos: Biopolitics and Philosophy.* Trans. Timothy Campbell. Minneapolis: University of Minnesota Press.

Estrada, Gerardo. 1995. "Prologue." In *Rosario Castellanos: Homenaje Nacional*, 3. Mexico City: Consejo Nacional para la Cultural y las Artes.

Falcón, Romana. 2002. *México descalzo: Estrategias de sobrevivencia frente a la modernidad liberal.* Mexico City: Plaza and Janés.

Favre, Henri. 1998. *El indigenismo.* Mexico City: Fondo de Cultura Económica.

Fernández, Emilio. 1948. *Río Escondido.* Film.

Fischer, Edward, and R. Mckenna Brown, eds. 1996. *Maya Cultural Activism in Guatemala.* Austin: University of Texas Press.

Foucault, Michel. 1976 [2003]. *"Society Must Be Defended": Lectures at the College de France, 1975–1976.* Trans. David Macey. New York: Picador.

———. 1978 [2008]. *The Birth of Biopolitics: Lectures at the College de France, 1978–1979.* Trans. Graham Burchell. New York: Palgrave Macmillan.

Franco, Jean. 1989. *Plotting Women: Gender and Representation in Mexico.* New York: Columbia University Press.

———. 1999. "La Malinche: From Gift to Sexual Contract." In *Critical Passions:*

Selected Essays, ed. Mary Louise Pratt and Kathleen Newman, 66–82. Durham, N.C.: Duke University Press.

Freyre, Gilberto. 1933 [1992]. *Casa-grande e senzala.* Rio de Janeiro: Editora Record.

Frías, Heriberto. 1893 [1989]. *Tomochic.* Mexico City: Porrúa.

Fuentes Díaz, Vicente. 1986. *Ignacio Manuel Altamirano: Triunfo y viacrucis de un escritor liberal.* Mexico, D.F.: Gobierno del Estado de Gue.

Gamio, Manuel. 1916 [1992]. *Forjando patria: Pro-nacionalismo.* Mexico, D.F.: Porrúa.

———. 1922. *La población del valle di Teotihuacán.* Mexico, D.F.: Talleres Graficos.

García, Mara. 2009. "Prólogo." In *Elena Garro: Un recuerdo sólido,* ed. Mara García, 11–24. Veracruz: Universidad Veracruzana.

García Canclini, Néstor. 1989 [1992]. *Culturas híbridas: Estrategias para entrar y salir de la modernidad.* Buenos Aires: Sudamericana.

Garro, Elena. 1963 [2001]. *Los recuerdos del porvenir.* Mexico, D.F.: Joaquín Moritz.

———. 1964a. "El arbol." In *La semana de colores.* Veracruz: Universidad Veracruzana.

———. 1964b. "La culpa es de los tlaxcaltecas." In *La semana de colores.* Veracruz: Universidad Veracruzana.

———. 1964c. *La semana de colores.* Veracruz: Universidad Veracruzana.

Gates Jr., Henry Louis, and Kwame Anthony Appiah, eds. 1986. *"Race," Writing, and Difference.* Chicago: Chicago University Press.

Girón, Nicole. 1993. *Ignacio Manuel Altamirano en Toluca.* Toluca de Lerdo: Instito Mexiquense de Cultura.

———. 1997. "Altamirano en Cuautla." In *Homenaje a Ignacio Manuel Altamirano (1834–1893),* ed. Manuel Sol and Alejandro Higachi, 21–48. Veracruz: Instituto de Investigaciones Lingüístico-Literarias Universidad Veracruzana.

Gladhart, Amalia. 2005. "Present Absence: Memory and Narrative in *Los recuerdos del porvenir.*" *Hispanic Review* 73 (Winter): 91–111.

Glantz, Margo. 1991. "Las hijas de la Malinche." In *Literatura mexicana hoy: Del 68 al ocaso de la revolución,* 121–29. Frankfurt: Verfuert Verlag.

Gobineau, Arthur de. 1851 [1970] "Essay on the Inequality of the Human Races." In *Gobineau: Selected Political Writings,* ed. Michael Biddiss, 37–176. London: Jonathon Cape.

Goldberg, David Theo. 2002. *The Racial State.* Malden: Blackwell.

González Navarro, Moisés. 1960. *La colonización en México, 1877–1910.* Mexico City: Estampillas y Valores.

Grosse, Pascal. 2006. "From Colonialism to National Socialism to Postcolonialism: Hannah Arendt's *The Origins of Totalitarianism.*" *Postcolonial Studies* 9, no. 1: 35–52.

Hale, Charles. 1968. *Mexican Liberalism in the Age of Mora, 1821–1853.* New Haven, Conn.: Yale University Press.

———. 1989. *The Transformation of Liberalism in Late Nineteenth-Century Mexico.* Princeton, N.J.: Princeton University Press.

Harrison, Charles, and Paul Wood. 1992. *Art in Theory: 1900–1990.* London: Blackwell.

Harss, Luis, and Barbara Dohmann. 1967. *Into the Mainstream: Conversations with Latin American Writers.* New York: Harper and Row.

Hegel, Georg Wilhelm Friedrich. 1820 [1967]. *Hegel's Philosophy of Right.* Trans. T. M. Knox. London: Oxford University Press.

———. 1830 [2007]. *Hegel's Philosophy of Mind: Being Part Three of the "Encyclopaedia of the Philosophical Sciences."* Trans. W. Wallace and A. V. Miller. Oxford, U.K.: Clarendon.

———. 1835 [1956]. *Philosophy of History.* Trans. J. Sibree. New York: Dover.

Herskovits, Melville. 1953. *Franz Boas: The Science of Man in the Making.* New York: Scribner.

Hewitt de Alcántara, Cynthia. 1984. *Anthropological Perspectives on Rural Mexico.* London: Routledge.

El Imparcial. 1910a. "¿Puede el Indio Civilizarse?" March 24.

———. 1910b. "Anoche fue inaugurado un notable congreso." Vol. 29, no. 6,056. October 31.

———. 1910c. "La primera sesión del Congreso de Indianistas." Vol. 29, no. 6,057. November 1.

———. 1910d. "Se clausura el Congreso Indianista." Vol. 29, no. 6,062. November 6.

———. 1910e. "El Congreso Indianista obtiene un triunfo." Vol. 29, 6,085. November 29.

Inclán, Luis Gonzaga. 1865 [1946]. *Astucia, el jefe de lost Hermanos de la Hoja o los Charros Contrabandistas de la Rama.* Mexico, D.F.: Porrúa.

Kaminsky, Amy. 1993a. *Reading the Body Politic: Feminist Criticism and Latin American Women Writers.* Minneapolis: University of Minnesota Press.

———. 1993b. "Residual Authority and Gendered Resistance." In *Critical Theory, Cultural Politics, and Latin American Narrative,* ed. Steven Bell, Albert LeMay, and Leonard Orr, 103–21. Notre Dame, Ind.: University of Notre Dame Press.

Kant, Immanuel. 1777 [2000]. "Of the Different Human Races." In *The Idea of Race,* ed. Robert Bernasconi and Tommy Lott, 8–22. Indianapolis: Hackett.

Katz, Friedrich. 1991. "The Liberal Republic and the Porfiriato, 1867–1910." In *Mexico since Independence,* ed. Leslie Bethell, 49–125. Cambridge: Cambridge University Press.

Katzew, Ilona. 2004. *Casta Painting: Images of Race in Eighteenth-Century Mexico.* New Haven, Conn.: Yale University Press.

Knight, Alan. 1990. "Racism, Revolution, and *Indigenismo:* Mexico, 1910–1940." In *The Idea of Race in Latin America, 1870–1940,* ed. Richard Graham, 71–114. Austin: University of Texas Press.

Knowlton, Robert. 1997. "Dealing in Real Estate in Mid-Nineteenth-Century Jalisco: The Guadalajara Region." In *Liberals, the Church, and Indian Peasants: Corporate Lands and the Challenge of Reform in Nineteenth-Century Spanish America*, ed. Robert Jackson, 13–36. Albuquerque: University of New Mexico Press.

Krauze, Enrique. 1997. *Mexico, Biography of Power: A History of Modern Mexico, 1810–1896*. Trans. Hank Heifetz. New York: HarperCollins.

Laclau, Ernesto. 1971. "Feudalism and Capitalism in Latin America." *New Left Review* 67 (May–June): 19–38.

Landeros, Carlos. 2007. *Yo, Elena Garro*. Mexico City: Lumen.

Larsen, Neil. 2001. *Determinations: Essays on Theory, Narrative, and Nation in the Americas*. London: Verso.

———. 2006. "O 'híbrido' como fetiche: 'Raça', ideologia, e narrativa em *Casa-grande e senzala*." In *Gilberto Freyre e os estudos latino-americanos*, ed. Joshua Lund and Malcolm McNee, 379–94. Pittsburgh: IILI.

Lee, Christopher. 2011. "Locating Hannah Arendt within Postcolonial Thought: A Prospectus." *College Literature* 38, no. 1: 95–114.

León, Margarita. 2000. "Las voces femeninas en el umbral de la conciencia: Las heroínas en la obra de Elena Garro." *La Palabra y el Hombre* 113: 127–133.

León Vega, Margarita. 2006. "La realidad está en otra parte: El surrealismo en la obra de Elena Garro." In *Elena Garro: Recuerdo y porvenir de una escritura*, ed. Luzelena Gutiérrez de Velasco y Gloria Prado, 25–41. Toluca: Tecnológica de Monterrey.

Lewis, Laura. 2003. *Hall of Mirrors: Power, Witchcraft, and Caste in Colonial Mexico*. Durham, N.C.: Duke University Press.

Lizardi, José Joaquín Fernández del. 1816, 1831 [1992]. *El Periquillo Sarniento*, ed. Carmen Ruíz Barrionuevo. Madrid: Cátedra.

Lomnitz, Claudio. 2001. *Deep Mexico, Silent Mexico: An Anthropology of Nationalism*. Minneapolis: University of Minnesota Press.

Lopátegui, Patricia Rosas. 2002. *Testimonios sobre Elena Garro*. Monterrey: Ediciones Castillo.

López Alvarez, Luis. 1974. *Conversaciones con Miguel Angel Asturias*. Madrid: EMESA.

López y Fuentes, Gregorio. 1935 [1972]. *El indio*. Mexico City: Porrúa.

López Portillo y Rojas, José. 1904. *La raza indígena: Breves reflexiones*. Mexico, D.F.: Viamonte.

Lund, Joshua. 2006. *The Impure Imagination: Toward a Critical Hybridity in Latin American Writing*. Minneapolis: University of Minnesota Press.

Lund, Joshua, and Joel Wainwright. 2008. "Miguel Angel Asturias and the Aporia of Postcolonial Geography." *Interventions: International Journal of Postcolonial Studies* 10, no. 2: 141–57.

———— n.d. "Vous êtes maya: The Problem of Asturias's Early Work."

Marcos, Subcomandante Insurgente. 2007. "Ni el centro, ni la periferia." Lecture delivered at the Primer Coloquio Internacional in Memoriam Andrés Aubry, Chiapas, December 2007. http://enlacezapatista.ezln.org.mx. Accessed January 2008.

Mariátegui, José Carlos. 1928 [1952]. *Siete ensayos de interpretación de la realidad peruana.* Lima: Amauta.

Martínez, José Luis. 1986. "Altamirano novelista." In *Obras completas,* vol. 3, *Novelas y cuentos 1,* by Ignacio Manuel Altamirano, ed. José Luis Martínez, 7–20. Mexico City: Secretaría de Educación Pública.

Martínez, María Elena. 2008. *Genealogical Fictions: Limpieza de Sangre, Religion, and Gender in Colonial Mexico.* Palo Alto, Calif.: Stanford University Press.

Martínez Montiel, Luz María, coord. 1994. *Presencia africana en México.* Mexico City: Consejo Nacional para la Cultura y las Artes.

Marx, Karl 1852 [1977]. "The Future Results of British Rule in India." In *Selected Writings,* ed. David McLellan, 332–37. Oxford: Oxford University Press.

————. 1867 [1961]. *Capital: A Critique of Political Economy,* vol. 1. Trans. Samuel Moore and Edward Aveling. New York: International Publishers.

May, Herbert, and Bruce Metzger, eds. 1973. *The New Oxford Annotated Bible with Apocrypha: Revised Standard Version.* New York: Oxford University Press.

Melgar, Lucía, and Gabriela Mora. 2002. *Elena Garro: Lectura múltiple de una personalidad compleja.* Puebla: Benemérita Universidad Autónoma de Puebla.

Melgarejo, María del Pilar. 2006. "El discurso de la lengua nacional en Freyre y Bello." In *Gilberto Freyre e os estudos latino-americanos,* ed. Joshua Lund and Malcolm McNee, 181–202. Pittsburgh: Instituto Internacional de Literatura Iberoamericana.

Messinger Cypess, Sandra. 1991. *La Malinche in Mexican Literature: From History to Myth.* Austin: University of Texas Press.

Meyer, Jean. 1973. *La Cristiada.* 3 vols. Mexico, D.F.: Siglo Veintiuno.

Molina Enríquez, Andrés. 1909 [1978]. *Los grandes problemas nacionales.* Mexico, D.F.: Era.

Monsiváis, Carlos. 1999. "*El Zarco:* Los falsos y los verdaderos héroes románticos." In *El Zarco,* by Ignacio M. Altamirano, 9–23. Mexico, D.F.: Editorial Océano.

Montes Garcés, Elizabeth. 2007. "Redefining Identities in Elena Garro's 'La culpa es de los tlaxcaltecas.'" In *Relocating Identities in Latin American Cultures,* ed. Elizabeth Montes Garcés, 117–32. Calgary, Canada: University of Calgary Press.

Mora, Carlos García, coord. 1987. *La antropología en México: Panorama histórico.* 15 vols. Mexico City: Instituo Nacional de Antropología e Historia.

Mora, José María Luis. 1849 [1994]. "Carta dirigida al Gobierno de México, Londres, julio 31 de 1849." In *Obras completas,* vol. 7, *Obra diplomática,* 275–78. Mexico City: Instituto Mora/CONACULTA.

Morales, Mario Roberto. 2000. "Miguel Ángel Asturias: La estética y la política de la interculturalidad." In *Cuentos y leyendas: Edición crítica*, by Miguel Ángel Asturias, ed. Mario Roberto Morales, 553–607. Paris: Colección Archivos.

Mörner, Magnus. 1967. *Race Mixture in the History of Latin America*. Boston: Little, Brown.

Moya López, Laura Angélica. 2003. *La nación como organismo: México, su evolución social, 1900–1902*. Mexico City: Porrúa.

Navarrete Cáceres, Carlos. 2007. *Rosario Castellanos: Su presencia en la antropología mexicana*. Mexico City: UNAM.

Ochoa Campos, Moisés. 1986. "Prólogo." In *Obras completas*, vol. 2, *Obras históricas*, by Ignacio Manuel Altamirano, ed. Moisés Ochoa Campos, 9–15. Mexico City: Secretaría de Educación Pública.

O'Connell, Joanna. 1995. *Prospero's Daughter: The Prose of Rosario Castellanos*. Austin: University of Texas Press.

Ortiz, Fernando. 1940 [1995]. *Cuban Counterpoint: Tobacco and Sugar.* Trans. Harriet de Onís. Durham, N.C.: Duke University Press.

Ortiz Vidales, Salvador. 1949. *Los bandidos en la literatura mexicana*. Mexico: Tehutle.

Padilla, Tanalís. 2007. "From Agraristas de Guerrilleros: The Jaramillista Movement in Morelos." *Hispanic American Historical Review* 87, no. 2: 255–92.

———. 2008. *Rural Resistance in the Land of Zapata: The Jaramillista Movement and the Myth of the Pax Priísta, 1940–1962*. Durham, N.C.: Duke University Press.

Palazón Mayoral, María Rosa, and Columba Galván Gaytán. 1997. "El centro contra las periferias (El nacionalismo defensivo de Altamirano)." In *Homenaje a Ignacio Manuel Altamirano (1834–1893)*, ed. Manuel Sol and Alejandro Higashi, 97–114. Veracruz: Universidad Veracruzana.

Payno, Manuel. 1889 [2000]. *Los bandidos de Río Frio*, ed. Manuel Sol. Mexico, D.F.: CONACULTA.

Paz, Octavio. 1950 [1961]. *El laberinto de la soledad.* Trans. by Lysander Kemp as *The Labyrinth of Solitude: Life and Thought in Mexico.* New York: Grove Press.

Paz Garro, Elena. 2003. *Memorias*. Mexico City: Oceano.

Pimentel, Francisco. 1864. *Memoria sobre las causas que han originado la situación actual de la raza indígena de México, y medios de remediarla*. Mexico City: Andrade y Escalante.

Pineda, Enrique Juventino. 1936. *Morelos legendario*. Cuernavaca: Ediciones Bernal Díaz.

Poblett, Martha. 1995. "Prólogo." In *Último año de residencia en México*, by Federico Cornelio Aguilar. Mexico, D.F.: Siguisiví.

Poniatowska, Elena. 1999. "Elena Garro y sus tormentas." In *Baúl de recuerdos. Homenaje a Elena Garro*, ed. Mara García and Robert Anderson, 5–15. Tlaxcala: Universidad Autónoma de Tlaxcala.

Popoca Palacios, Lamberto. 1912. *Historia del bandalismo en el Estado de More-los: ¡Ayer como ahora! ¡1860! ¡Plateados! ¡1911! ¡Zapatistas!* Puebla: Tipografía Guadalupana.

Portal, Martha. 1980. *Proceso narrativo de la Revolución Mexicana.* Madrid: Espasa.

Powell, T. G. 1968. "Mexican Intellectuals and the Indian Question, 1876–1911." *Hispanic American Historical Review* 48, no. 1: 19–36.

Ramírez, Ignacio. 1872 [1960]. "Los habitantes primitivos del continente ameri-cano: Discurso leído en la Sociedad de Geografía y Estadística." In *Obras de Ignacio Ramírez,* vol. 1, 199–211. Mexico City: Editora Nacional.

Ramírez, Luis Enrique. 2000. *La ingobernable: Encuentros y desencuentrso con Elena Garro.* Mexico City: Hoja Casa Editorial.

Reed, Nelson. 1964 [2001]. *The Caste War of Yucatán.* Stanford, Calif.: Stanford Uni-versity Press.

Reina, Leticia. 1980 [1988]. *Las rebeliones campesinas en México (1819–1906).* Mexico City: Siglo Veintiuno.

Reina, Leticia, and Cuauhtémoc Velasco. 1997. *La reindianización de América, siglo XIX.* Coord. Leticia Reina. Mexico City: Siglo Veintiuno.

———, eds. 1997. "Introducción." In *La reindianización de América, siglo XIX,* coord. Leticia Reina, 15–25. Mexico City: Siglo Veintiuno.

Renan, Ernest. 1882 [1990]. "What Is a Nation?" In *Nation and Narration,* ed. Homi Bhabha, 8–22. London: Routledge.

Restall, Matthew, ed. 2005. *Beyond Black and Red: African–Native Relations in Colo-nial Latin America.* Albuquerque: University of New Mexico Press.

Revueltas, José. 1943. *El luto humano.* Mexico, D.F.: Era.

Riva Palacio, Vicente. 1889. *México a través de los siglos,* vol. 2. Mexico City.

Rivas Velázquez, Alejandro. 1992. "Altamirano y su nueva visión de la novela en *El Zarco.*" In *Reflexiones lingüísticas y literarias,* vol. 2, *Literatura,* ed. Rafael Olea Franco and James Valender, 169–86. Mexico City: El Colegio de México.

Rivermar Pérez, Leticia. 1987. "En el marasmo de una rebelión cataclísmica (1911–1920)." In *La antropología en México: Panorama histórico,* vol. 2, *Los hecho y los dichos (1880–1986),* coord. Carlos García Mora, 89–132. Mexico City: Instituo Nacional de Antropología e Historia.

Robinson, Amy. 2003. "Imagining Mexican Bandits: The Literary Construction of Late Nineteenth-Century Criminality." Paper presented at the Latin American Studies Association meeting, Dallas, Texas, March 27–29.

Robles, Pablo. 1891 [1982]. *Los plateados de Tierra Caliente: Episodios de la Guerra de Tres Años en el estado de Morelos; Cuento semi-histórico.* La Matraca, Mexico.

Rosenblatt, Helena. 2004. "Why Constant? A Critical Overview of the Constant Revival." *Modern Intellectual History* 1:439–53.

———, ed. 2009. *The Cambridge Companion to Constant.* Cambridge: Cambridge University Press.

Ruiz, José Salvador. 2005. "El laberinto de la aculturación: Ciudadanía y nación mestiza en *El Zarco* de Ignacio Manuel Altamirano." *Revista de Crítica Literaria Latinoamericana*, September 1, 27–35.

Rus, Jan. 1983. "Whose Caste War? Indians, Ladinos, and the 'Caste War' of 1869." In *Spaniards and Indians in Southeastern Mesoamerica: Essays on the History of Ethnic Relations*, ed. Murdo MacLeod and Robert Wasserstrom, 127–68. Lincoln: University of Nebraska Press.

Said, Edward. 1979. *Orientalism*. New York: Vintage.

Sánchez Prado, Ignacio. 2009. *Naciones intelectuales: Las fundaciones de la modernidad literaria mexicana (1917–1959)*. West Lafayette, Ind.: Purdue University Press.

Sayles, John. 1998. *Men with Guns*. Film.

Schmidt, Friedhelm. 1999. "Amor y nación en las novelas de Ignacio Manuel Altamirano." *Literatura Mexicana* 10, nos. 1–2: 99–117.

Schwarz, Roberto. 1992. *Misplaced Ideas: Essays on Brazilian Culture*. London: Verso.

Segre, Erica. 2000. "An Italicised Ethnicity: Memory and Renascence in the Literary Writings of Ignacio Manuel Altamirano." *Forum for Modern Language Studies* 36, no. 3: 266–78.

Sierra, Catalina, and Cristina Barros. 1998. *Ignacio Manuel Altamirano: Iconografía*. Mexico, D.F.: Fondo de Cultura Econonómia.

Sierra, Justo. 1885 [1960]. *Apuntes para un libro: México social y político*. Mexico City: Secretaría de Hacienda y Crédito Público.

———. 1900–1902. *México: Su evolución social*. Barcelona: Ballescá.

El Siglo Diez y Nueve. 1881. "Guerra de castas." March 10.

Silva Herzog, Jesús. 1959 [1964]. *El agrarismo mexicano y la reforma agraria: Exposición y crítica*. Mexico City: Fondo de Cultura Económica.

Sol, Manuel. 2000. "Introducción." In *El Zarco*, by Ignacio Manuel Altamirano, ed. Manuel Sol, 13–90. Veracruz: Instituto de Investigaciones Lingüístico-Literarias Universidad Veracruzana.

Sommer, Doris. 1991. *Foundational Fictions: The National Romances of Latin America*. Berkeley: University of California Press.

Sommers, Joseph. 1978. "Forma e ideología en 'Oficio de tinieblas' de Rosario Castellanos." *Revista de Crítica Literaria Latinoamericana* 4, nos. 7–8: 73–91.

Sosa, Francisco. 1901. "Prólogo." In *El Zarco (Episodios de la vida mexicana en 1861–63)*, by Ignacio Manuel Altamirano. Barcelona: Establecimiento editorial de J. Ballescá y Ca., Sucesor.

Stabb, Martin. 1959. "Indigenism and Racism in Mexican Thought, 1857–1911." *Journal of Inter-American Studies* 1, no. 4: 405–23.

Stocking, George, ed. 1974. *The Shaping of American Anthropology, 1883–1911: A Franz Boas Reader*. New York: Basic Books.

Stoll, Anita. 1999. "Elena Garro y el surrealismo." In *Baúl de recuerdos: Homenaje a Elena Garro,* ed. Mara García and Robert Anderson, 111–22. Tlaxcala: Universidad Autónoma de Tlaxcala.

Strobel, Leah. 2010. *Can Silence Speak? Reading the Marginalized Woman in Three Novels of Female Development.* Pittsburgh: University of Pittsburgh.

Suárez Cortés, Blanca Estela. 1987. "Las interpretaciones positivas del pasado y el presente (1880–1910)." In *La antropología en México: Panorama histórico,* vol. 2, *Los hecho y los dichos (1880–1986),* coord. Carlos García Mora,13–88. Mexico City: INAH.

Swarthout, Kelley. 2004. *"Assimilating the Primitive": Parallel Dialogues on Racial Miscegenation in Revolutionary Mexico.* New York: Peter Lang.

Swift, Simon. 2009. *Hannah Arendt.* London: Routledge.

Tarica, Estelle. 2008. *The Inner Life of Mestizo Nationalism.* Minneapolis: University of Minnesota Press.

Téllez Ortega, Javier. 1987. "'La época de oro' (1940–1964)." In *La antropología en México: Panorama histórico,* vol. 2, *Los hecho y los dichos (1880–1986),* coord. Carlos García Mora, 289–338. Mexico City: INAH.

Tola de Habich, Fernando, ed. 1984. *Homenaje a I. M. Altamirano (1834–1893).* Mexico, D.F.: Premià.

Traven, Bruno. 1936 [1952]. *Rebelión de los colgados.* Trans. as *The Rebellion of the Hanged.* New York: Knopf.

Tutino, John. 1986. *From Insurrection to Revolution in Mexico: Social Bases of Agrarian Violence, 1750–1940.* Princeton, N.J.: Princeton University Press.

Vanderwood, Paul. 1992. *Disorder and Progress: Bandits, Police, and Mexican Development.* Wilmington, Del.: Scholarly References.

———. 1998. *The Power of God against the Guns of Government: Religious Upheaval in Mexico at the Turn of the Nineteenth Century.* Stanford, Calif.: Stanford University Press.

Vasconcelos, José. 1925 [1979]. *The Cosmic Race/La raza cósmica.* Baltimore, Md.: Johns Hopkins University Press.

Villa Rojas, Alfonso. 1962. "El Centro Coordinador Tzeltal-Tzotzil." In *Los Centros Coordinadores: Edición conmemorativa en ocasión del XXXV Congreso Internacional de Americanista,* 51–68. Mexico City: Instituto Nacional Indigenista.

Villoro, Luis. 1950. *Los grandes momentos del indigenismo en México.* Mexico City: El Colegio de México.

Vinson, Ben, and Matthew Restall, eds. 2009. *Black Mexico: Race and Society from Colonial to Modern Times.* Albuquerque: University of New Mexico Press.

Viqueira, Juan Pedro. 1994. *María de la Candelaria, india natural de Cancuc.* Mexico City: Fondo de Cultura Económica.

Wardman, H. W. 1964. *Ernest Renan: A Critical Biography.* London: Athlone.

Weber, David. 2005. *Bárbaros: Spaniards and Their Savages in the Age of Enlighten-ment.* New Haven, Conn.: Yale University Press.

Wolf, Eric. 1982. *Europe and the People without History.* Berkeley: University of Cali-fornia Press.

Wright-Rios, Edward. 2004. "Indian Saints and Nation-States: Ignacio Manuel Altamirano's Landscapes and Legends." *Mexican Studies / Estudios Mexicanos* 20, no. 1: 47–68.

Index

abandonment: of Indian by the law, Alva on, 19–20, 22, 24, 25; regeneration and, 23–24

acculturation/assimilation: acculturative techniques, 169n22; Gamio's program of aggressive, 91–92; as goal for *raza indígena* in nation-state articulation, 83, 84; through indigenous education, 91, 102

Acosta, Abraham, 166n2

Africans and African culture in Mexico, xi, 153n31, 157n4

Agamben, Giorgio, 19, 67, 156n42, 156n46, 163n35, 181n33

Agassiz, Louis, 130, 180n24

agrarian "compression": Tutino on, 157n2

agrarian reform *(reforma agraria)*, 166n5; Alva on, 29–30; Castellanos's relocation to Mexico City due to, 78; crushing potential radicalization of, in Garro's *Los recuerdos del porvenir*, 113–14, 134; ejido as instrument in postrevolutionary, 167n9; *guardias blancas* (white guards) and resistance to, 96, 172n37; of 1930s, conflation of race war with, 73; translating stake in land to stake in nation, 96

agricultural colonies, Alva's proposed mixed, 21, 24, 25

Aguilar, Federico Cornelio, 18, 155n40

Aguirre Beltrán, Gonzalo, xi, 82, 83, 84, 154n31, 169n19, 170n23

Allen, Esther, 166n1

alliance: failure of, Garro on, 131–43; use of term, 181n30

Altamirano, Don Francisco (godfather), 35–36

Altamirano, Francisco (father), 35

Altamirano, Ignacio Homobono Serapio "Manuel," xvi, xviii, xix, 13, 16, 29, 33–69, 93, 149n6, 161n23, 161n28; biography, conventional narrative of, 33–34, 36, 157n4–6; *costumbrista* sketches of, 41–42, 160n21; critics' expectation to transcend historical context, 48, 49–50; death of, 53; debate on obligatory education (1883), 48, 161n25; defusing race by displacing it with character, 44; diplomatic post of, 53; education of, 34, 36, 38, 42, 157n3, 157n7, 158n9, 158n12; Escalante's critique of, 44–47, 54, 61–62, 63, 64, 161n22–24, 164n43; family history of, 34–40; hidden radicalism of, 44, 160n19;

197

Altamirano, Ignacio Homobono Serapio
"Manuel," *(continued)*, impact on
cultural politics of modern Mexico,
36, 158n8; indigenous identity/
Indianness, 35, 37–38, 42, 157n4,
159n16; as *letrado*, 50; on Lynch
law, 66–67, 165n48; Palazón and
Galván's critique of, 34, 42–44, 48,
158n15, 159n17, 162n28;
pedagogical intent of writings of, 53;
political writings about bandits, 58;
problem of cultural difference, 76;
race in literary analyses of, 40–51,
159n18; race in literary analyses
of, affirmative position, 41–42, 50;
race in literary analyses of, negative
position, 42–51; on suspension of
constitutional individual guarantees, 63–67, 165n48. *See also Zarco:
Episodios de la vida mexicana en
1861–1863, El* (Altamirano)
"Altamirano y su nueva visión de la
novela en *El Zarco*" (Rivas
Velázquez), 61
alter-mundista movement, 181n30
Alva, Luis, xvi, xvii–xviii, 2–27, 84,
153n21–23, 153n28–30, 154n36;
abandonment as key term for,
23–24; on abandonment of Indian
by the law, 19–20, 22, 24, 25; on
agrarian reform, 29–30; Altamirano's relation to, 48, 50;
barbarism defined by, 11–12;
colonization essays, 12–20, 76,
154n34; critique of Pax Porfiriana
and *ley fuga*, 30–33, 152n18; death
of, 7–8; on de-Indianization, 23–26,
27, 40; Gamio's position on Indian
problem compared to, 92, 93;
Indianization, 14–20, 23; law of
progress for, 151n16; on Lerdo, 32,

157n1; liberal critique of racism
demonstrated by, 2, 11, 14, 20, 21,
26–27; opposition to Científicos,
8–9; political controversies written
about by, 9–10; problem of cultural
difference, 76; publication projects,
7, 152n17; on regeneration of
Indian, 23–24; response to Aguilar,
18, 155n40; on threat of U.S.
encroachment, 12, 153n23;
understanding of race, 10–12, 16;
work on newspapers, 6, 7
Alva, Ramón L., 8
American race relations, 38, 39,
158n13
Anahuac (Tylor), 170n25
Anaya Pérez, Marco Antonio, 156n50
Anderson, Benedict, 121, 126
Angeles, Felipe, 132
anthropology, 82–86; Boas and
progressive revolution in, 86,
87–88; disarticulation between
two kinds of, 171n33; as modern
science in Mexico, 86–97, 170n25;
nineteenth-century institutionalization of, 85; purpose of, for Gamio,
94; race from anthropological
perspective, 123; role in nation-
building, xix
antropología en México, La (Mora), 169
Appiah, Kwame Anthony, 147n3
"Arbol, El" (Garro), 179n10
Arendt, Hannah, 120–21, 149n7,
156n42, 179n15, 181n31
Arguedas, José María, 79, 173n42
Arreola, Juan José, 173n42
"Arthur Smith salva su alma" (Castellanos), 168n11
assimilation. *See* acculturation/
assimilation
Astucia (Inclán), 149n6

Tzeltal-Tzotzil in, 82–84, 169n18, 170n24; Mexican annexation from Guatemala, 168n16; race relations in, 167n10; as race war, 104, 176n54

Chilapa: revolution of (1840s), 37

Christ, Ronald, 36, 37

Científicos (intellectual clique), 8–9

citizenship, racially neutral, xviii, 44

ciudad and *campo*: national relation between, 119

Ciudad Real (Castellanos), 81, 112

class: failure of alliance in Garro's *Los recuerdos del porvenir* and, 131–43

Clemencia (Altamirano), 43, 44, 52, 159n18

Coatlicue: cult of, 161n22

Coletos, 177n57; in Castellanos's *Oficio de tinieblas*, 99, 100, 107, 108, 110; Castellanos's use of term, 168n10

Colombia: Aguilar's commission to Mexico from, 155n40

colonial relations of power, 105–6, 109

"Colonización extranjera y la raza indígena, La" (Foreign colonization and the indigenous race) (Alva), 12, 14

colonization, Mexico's 1880s project of, 2, 4–27, 149n7–8, 150n8, 159n15; Alva's colonization essays, 12–20, 76, 154n34; foreign immigrants and, 4, 14, 15, 17, 19, 21, 24, 150n8; González Navarro's definition of politics of colonization, 149n8; Indian as colonizing participant, Alva on inclusion of, 17–20, 154n36; meaning of colonization, 4; *el problema del indio* and, 4–6, 150n10

Columbus, Christopher, 11

Comisión Nacional para el Desarrollo de los Pueblos Indígenas, 169n18

Comte, Auguste, 7, 151n16

consent: conversion of foundational violence into, 142; national forgetting transferred to, 127, 139–40

Constant, Benjamin, 6, 152n16

Constituent Assembly of 1856–57, 149n5

constitutionalists in Porfiriato Mexico, 6, 8. *See also* Alva, Luis

Constitution of 1857, 2, 149n5; Article 7, 1890s revision of, 7; "extraordinary faculties" and authorization of *ley fuga,* 31, 32; rights granted in, 19–20; suspension of individual guarantees, 63–67, 165n48; tension between individual guarantees and capitalist mode of production, 32–33, 76–77

consumer, transformation of Indian into an active, 22, 24, 25

contextualist position on race, Alva's, 10–11, 16

contextualist solution to Indian problem, 91–92

contextualist terms of culture, 87, 90–91

Conway, Christopher, 34, 37, 41, 42, 54, 64, 157n4, 158n11, 161n21

Cope, R. Douglas, 147n1

corrido (music), 56

corruption in *El Zarco:* theme of, 55–56, 61, 62, 163n33, 164n41

Cortés, Hernán, 176n55; Malinche myth and, 130, 136–37, 180n23; La Noche Triste (Night of Sorrows) and, 118

Cosío Villegas, Daniel, 152n20

Cosmes, Francisco, 13, 32, 159n16

214   *Index*

Joshua Lund is associate professor of Spanish at the University of Pittsburgh. He is the author of *The Impure Imagination* (Minnesota, 2006) and coeditor of *Gilberto Freyre e os estudos latino-americanos*.